Melodrama

I *THE COLLEEN BAWN*

EILY O'CONNOR : Save me. Don't kill me. Don't, Danny. I'll—do anything, only let
me live. *A shot rings out, and he falls from the rock* (Adelphi Theatre, 1860)

MELODRAMA

PLOTS THAT THRILLED

by

M. WILLSON DISHER

Illustrated from the
Raymond Mander and Joe Mitchenson
Theatre Collection

ROCKLIFF
SALISBURY SQUARE · LONDON

Made and printed in Great Britain by Richard Clay and Company, Ltd.,
Bungay, Suffolk

CONTENTS

6216

(Throughout the book, the titles of plays are printed in italics, the titles of novels in Roman type.)

ILLUSTRATIONS

Thanks are due to Mr. Bert Hammond of the Prince's Theatre for generous assistance

vii

LINE ILLUSTRATIONS

Introduction

1850 to 1950 onwards

SHAKESPEARE'S audiences liked blood, Restoration wits preferred sex, eighteenth-century exquisites favoured sentiment and Victorians demanded morals. Midway through the nineteenth century the theatres of London, Paris, and New York were overwhelmingly devoted to the display of virtue in conflict with vice. Authors depicted the struggle in novels and artists in pictures; it was the dominant theme of the age.

Our shelves can soon be burdened with masses of badly printed " penny plays " belonging to the period. To read them all untiringly may not be difficult once they have become an acquired taste, but to discover some sort of order into which these manifestations of the zest for righteousness may naturally fall, seems impossible and very nearly is. We foresee at the start an objection that drama has in all ages represented the conflict between good and evil, and we must agree that it may well be so; but in melodrama, where these are called virtue and vice, there is a difference. They are more sharply defined and of less magnitude than elemental forces; they do not get out of control, and in the end, happy or unhappy, sin is not only published—as it always has been in the tragic masterpieces of the world—but punished in such a manner that a cosmic partiality for the virginal is powerfully made known. You will not find that in Shakespeare.

With this as a basis for enquiry an attempt may be made to trace the progress of the idea. Earlier in the century a solid conviction had been established that Virtue Triumphant was the law of science and of nature, and while Dickens wrote his novels secure in this faith, a multitude of hacks, whose scribblings bear a strong family likeness to his, exploited it just as conscientiously, though without his genius. It must not be forgotten that stage versions of his works, hastily adapted by the " resident playwright " at many a theatre, were as much the mainstay of the Victorian stage as Shakespeare's works were of the Jacobean. Long after the half-way line of the nineteenth century had been passed there were still dramatizations of Dickens, and still the same insistence on the triumphs of virtue.

xiii

What, then, was new in melodrama as the twentieth century approached? Strictly speaking, the answer might be, "Nothing", since essentials remained unchanged; but there was a continual outcry over scenic superficialities, and these are well worthy of our concern in spite of, or because of, their insensibility to the absurd—always one of melodrama's hallmarks. Realism, which altered nothing, was supposed to alter everything. In the vain hope of achieving truth to life, scenes were constructed to reproduce on the one hand calamities reported in the newspapers, and on the other the small, insignificant details of ordinary homes. Realism had yet another meaning. When uttered in a tone of horror it stood for the encroachment into fiction of such scandalous subjects as bigamy and infidelity or worse—straight from courts of law, in modern dress.

These were judged to be immoral in their tendency, and something had to be done to counterbalance them. Hence the ever-increasing stress laid on the sense of guilt, the argument being that if sinners in plays were sufficiently conscience-stricken their influence over audiences would be good or, at least, not quite so bad. Here is the clue to the maze of dramatic literature which reflects the divergent beliefs that set everybody at loggerheads while the old century was giving birth to the new. Neither Ibsen nor Irving can be left out of our reckoning: both were involved in the sense of guilt, though one saw in it a sign of grace and the other a proof of damnation. And when Ibsen had won the day, so that virtue could no longer be regarded as a sure means of profit, since he had so clearly demonstrated it to be its own painful reward, the day not only of melodrama but also of melodramatic thinking might reasonably have been said to be over. But it was not. First it took on a new lease of life in the theatre, and then started a fresh existence in films, talking-films, radio, television and three-dimensional films with other mechanized metamorphoses to follow.

Such lively survivals of the spirit which has been my study, means that this book cannot be regarded in a purely antiquarian light. People still weigh existence in terms of praise and blame, and still believe, despite all the evidence to the contrary accumulated during two world wars, that heroes prosper while villains die miserably. Perhaps it is possible to prefer this in modern entertainments to beer and skittles, perhaps not, but we need not be deluded by it now we know whence it comes and what it is worth. In Victorian settings it had a charm altogether lacking in ours. After the feeble displays of half-hearted wickedness that we are treated to by living authors who aspire to be moralists, playgoers might like to be reminded what genuine melodramas were like when vice and virtue were cherished not as the luxuries they seem to be now, but as necessities.

1 Magdalens

Jane Shore

BODIES roped to railway lines, heroes in cellars where tide-water is rising, circular saws or steam-hammers threatening the lives of helpless victims, early Christians about to be thrown to the lions, sinking ships, cars over precipices, earthquakes, volcanoes, tempest, fire and flood—spectacles such as these are expected by audiences that await the rising of the curtain on melodrama. Yet it still functions when deprived of scenic excitement. How little it needs such " special attractions " as real water, real animals or real machinery, has been demonstrated over and over again. Its essence was once supposed to be the contrast of innocence in poverty with vice amid wealth, but while many hundreds of plays support this theory, many dozens do not. Virtue triumphant is the theme of some and crime exultant of others, from which it has been argued that all characters in a world peopled by heroes, heroines, villains, over-wrought parents and loyal servants must be either black or white. Otherwise how could right do battle against wrong? That is reckoning without the sense of guilt which contains the struggle within one breast.

There never has been a more popular protagonist than the erring woman who is chaste in soul though guilty in deed. "The Magdalen" is her oldest name. She got it in a manner which brings discredit on everybody but herself, for only our inherent love of scandal-mongering can identify the woman in Luke's Gospel who wept for her sins with Mary called Magdalen out of whom went seven devils. It is too late to vindicate her. Magdalens are penitents, and maudlin are the tears we shed over them.

The one who has caused more such floods than any other is as well known in fact as in fiction. Jane Shore, the mistress of Edward IV, did penance outside St. Paul's in 1483, and was represented in plays for centuries after. It remained for a German author to bring upon the stage a Magdalen who was both wife and mother. *Misanthropy And Repentance*, by Kotzebue, won world-wide fame, and under the title of *The Stranger* was constantly acted in England throughout the nineteenth century. The sorrows of its heroine, Mrs. Haller, on returning to the home she formerly deserted, may be gathered from, " My tears flow; my heart bleeds. Already had I apparently overcome my chagrin; already had I at last assumed that easy gaiety once so natural to me, when the sight of this child in an instant overpowered me. When the countess called him William—Oh she knew not that she plunged a poniard in my very heart." With or without William she has been reappearing in some form or other in plays or novels ever since, but these are types merely of tear-compelling penitence. By the time of the Regency the unfortunate wore her sense of guilt with a difference. In *The Miller And His Men* we find her—named Ravinia to indicate her depths of despair—swearing revenge. In the highly explosive finale she takes a torch to the powder-magazine of her betrayer's band of banditti and blows them sky-high. Though she may look to us somewhat like the female villains known as vampires she is honest at heart.

Victorian audiences ought to have grown accustomed to these particular brands of virtue. Yet they could still be shocked by the sinner that repenteth; it was proved when Dumas *fils* invited the world to accept a prostitute for heroine in *La Dame Aux Camélias*. Such a shriek of protest arose from outraged feelings that we are puzzled to observe, during that self-same year of 1852, the welcome given at the Haymarket to a drama which likewise had a harlot heroine.

Its authors were two young barristers, crowned with honours from the older Universities, who soon pushed their way through the many old lags of playwrights. One was Tom Taylor, assistant secretary to the Board of Health, and the other Charles Reade, Vice-President of Magdalen College, Oxford. Their *Masks And Faces* depicted Peg Woffington, the eighteenth-century actress who was as brazen a bad hat as ever capered before the footlights, in the guise of a " fallen creature with a touching sense of her own degradation ".

Yet another kind of Magdalen appeared in 1851 when " Uncle Tom's Cabin " was running as a serial. For all the talk about Uncle Tom himself and Little Eva, the most significant character is Miss Cassy, more cruelly dishonoured than any woman in an English story. " In her eye was a deep settled night of anguish ", added new meaning to the sense of guilt.

Uncle Tom's Cabin (Olympic, 1852)

2   Sensation Dramas

The Colleen Bawn

HOW Mrs. Beecher Stowe came to think in terms of the theatre cannot be explained : she conceived " Uncle Tom's Cabin " with an eye for picturesque suspense which destined it for triumphs when adapted to the stage.   Her affinity with the footlights was uncanny ; that she imagined " situations " in that way is made clear by a pair of curious coincidences.   While she was writing about Eliza's escape across the thawing river, a playwright in Paris named Dennery thought of a mother's courage when leaping from floe to floe, for the melodrama to be known as *The Sea Of Ice* ; and while the pen in America set down how another fugitive swung from a tree that grew in a ravine, Charles Kean at the Princess's in London constructed a " practicable " setting in which the hero of Sheridan's *Pizarro* swung from a tree after the same fashion.

These facts are so queer that they read ironically, but they are set down because of their intrinsic interest and certainly without any intent of directing sarcasm towards the righteousness of Mrs. Stowe.   The purpose of her novel must be set aside if full justice is to be done to the importance of its place in the history of entertainment.   If the spectacular aspects of her fancy are thought of as events in the annals of melodrama, they are seen to possess a surprising significance, for when they were transferred to the stage they began the garish vogue of the Sensation Drama. It is a clear case of cause and effect, for the show-man who " invented " this type of play did so when he tried to exploit her popularity. The influence of Mrs. Stowe, daughter, sister and wife of preachers, upon things purely theatrical was direct.

To understand the success of " Uncle Tom's Cabin " immediately it was published as a novel in 1852, reference must be made not only to the state of slavery but also to the state of fiction. How easily the public had been satisfied up to that precise moment can be judged by examining *Minnigrey; or, The Gypsies Of Epsom*, an insipid drama with a lady-like heroine who is supposed to be of gypsy origin until proved otherwise. This poor stuff aroused enough enthusiasm to cause it to be acted at several London theatres in 1852 before the excitement over Mrs. Stowe's story began so feverishly that one old hack, Edward Fitz-ball, at once wrote three Uncle Toms—for Drury Lane, the Olympic and the Grecian—while rival versions at many other Cockney pleasure haunts included *Uncle Tom And Lucy Neal ; or, Harlequin Liberty And Slavery*, with song, dance, masks, clown and red-hot poker, the White-chapel Pavilion Christmas pantomime of 1852.

Yet, although companies were touring the northern cities of the United States with Uncle Tom in all shapes and sizes, seven years passed without any such representation on Broadway. When he did at last appear there in the December of 1859 his welcome was so well assured that another play on the subject of slavery had been written in order to share in it. This was Dion Boucicault's *The Octoroon ; or, Life In Louisiana*, at the Winter Garden, which told how the papers that would free the heroine are stolen by a scoundrel who is photographed in the act and then, by the light of a burning ship which eventually blows up, stabbed to death by a Redskin in full war-paint. The central idea was taken from *The Creole*, seen in London at the Lyceum twelve years earlier, and the " sensation " of the exploding ship had been seen in New York a few months before, but the up-to-date use of a camera was original.

This method of borrowing a plot from one source and a scenic device from another, and then adding a newly invented apparatus which would remind an audience of its modern life, deserves to be noted be-cause it was one that Dion Boucicault often employed. He was an Irish actor who had Agnes Robertson, his Scottish bride, for leading lady; with her he had left London because there the wages of success were too low. For six years he had been sailing backwards and for-

II *THE SHAUGHRAUN*
New York, 1874: Dion Boucicault as Conn, Jane
Burke as Moya and John Gilbert as Father Dolan

III *THE LONG STRIKE*
Lyceum, 1866: A shot through the hedge lays
Jack Readley low

IV *THE SHAUGHRAUN*
Drury Lane, 1875: The Wake of Conn the Shaughraun

V and VI *RIP VAN WINKLE*

Adelphi, 1865: Joseph Jefferson as Rip before and after his twenty years' sleep in the mountain

VII *THE THIRST FOR GOLD* (alias *THE SEA OF ICE*)

Adelphi, 1853: Benjamin Webster as villainous Pedro abandons the hero and his family on an ice-floe

wards, selling translations, dramatizations and adaptations on both sides of the Atlantic, and still was far from satisfied. Even the fortune he had won at the Winter Garden was not enough. Laying the MS. of *The Octoroon* aside until it should be needed on his next return to London, he set about refurbishing yet another old play that he felt confident of passing off as his own work under the title of *The Colleen Bawn ; or, The Brides Of Garryowen.*

It was based on Gerald Griffin's novel, " The Collegians ", the story of Eily O'Connor, whose faithless husband, having set his heart on marrying a young woman of wealth, causes his colleen to be drowned. Long ago in the 1830s, which was farther back than most playgoers could remember, the hungry tribe of theatrical hacks had avidly seized this sad story with a gallows ending, and set versions of it on most of the boards of Great Britain and America. But the plot lost its police-court squalor when Boucicault added a character to be acted by himself. No sooner had Eily, in his play, been pitched into the waters where they flow into a cave by the shores of a lake, than she was rescued by the gay, lively, impudent poacher, Myles-na-Coppaleen. Thus the needs of both the author and his wife had been well looked after. The strange thing is that when he took the piece to Laura Keene's Theatre for the spring of 1860 it was accepted, though all it had to offer Laura Keene was the vapid part of the wealthy " bride ".

Even on the eve of civil war, New York gave it a whole-hearted welcome. Much was owing to the players and much to the play, but much more to the " sensation ". This occurred when Agnes Robertson, as Eily, first sank beneath, and then rose above, the surface. Excitement was intense because the water, for the first time in stage history, was transparent. Rumour said that this effect, obtained by the use of blue gauze, had been invented by a stage-carpenter. The triumph, nevertheless, was Boucicault's.

His enterprising spirit was now painfully aware that unless he crossed the Atlantic soon he would have no copyright either in a plot that was not his or in a spectacle that belonged to any management in England that might stage it forthwith. No play belonged to its own author until he had established his claim by means of a performance which, to effect copyright, had to be the first in that country. Boucicault returned to London in the summer of 1860. More than one manager in the English provinces had decided to revive *Eily O'Connor* with its new title and stage effects, but by threats and injunctions he fought them off, and by the exercise of blarney he gained the use of the Adelphi from its hard-headed manager, Ben Webster, who had himself presented a version of the play thirty years before and took no pleasure in seeing a young upstart up to such old tricks.   At the Adelphi, on 10 September, 1860, the London vogue of the " Sensation Drama " began.

Canvas waves, and stormy seas with small boys beneath to make the billows angry, had been seen in scores of nautical pieces, but never before had any hero won applause by a death-defying dive into blue gauze, a few yards of which meant more than the finest acting to thousands.   It drew people who had hitherto shunned theatres, inspired Benedict's opera, The Lily Of Killarney, and caused Queen Victoria, who visited the Adelphi three times in one fortnight, to have portraits of the Boucicaults painted for Windsor Castle.

In order to get his threatened drama quickly on to the stage, Boucicault had accepted miserly terms for a " limited number of nights ", which was still the announcement until " re-engagement " took its place on the eighty-fifth.   Webster's point of view is readily understood, for when told that the piece was good he could respond that it always had been.   Clashes between the new star and the cantankerous old despot were thus unavoidable.   Unlike other quarrels which kept Green Rooms amused, this one was paraded before the public so that loafers in the Strand noted on the new playbills each Monday and Thursday how the vendetta was progressing.   News was pasted for their benefit outside the Adelphi as a gratuitous feuilleton which began with innocent words in July about the need of the two stars " to take some rest from their incessant labour " after the 226th night—meaning that Webster wished to show his independence by presenting himself as the star of Lost In London.   Because of a dream that he would die while acting in it, he put on a rustic piece, The Hop Pickers, instead and missed his chance.

Boucicault was " still too exhausted " to act, or so he said, but he made a sudden recovery in September on being conceded terms equal to partnership in management.   The Colleen Bawn was brought back and The Octoroon was at last announced, though even now " accidental occurrences " at rehearsals delayed performances.   On the first night in the November of 1861 the playbills tried to excite interest in it by describing how, during Boucicault's stay in Louisiana, a white man who wanted to marry an octoroon " opened a vein in his arm and introduced into it a few drops of his mistress's blood ", so that he could make oath that he had black blood in his veins.   Next an " episode from Slave history " was quoted to show how a Kentucky planter's lovely daughter came home from Boston at his death, only to be inventoried because of a negro strain she had not suspected; she drowned herself after she had been sold.   Early December playbills became more and more eloquent as it became more and more evident that the piece had failed.   Then

The Octoroon (Adelphi, 1861): The Slave Market

the Adelphi presented *The Colleen Bawn* and *The Octoroon* as a double bill. In response to many letters entreating that the unhappy ending of *The Octoroon* should be modified—or so Boucicault said—the playbills announced a new last act of the drama, " composed by the public and edited by the author ".

Signs of trouble increased in 1862. Agnes Robertson dropped out; her husband, too, was absent occasionally. A new and original drama by him was predicted one week in June, only to be cancelled by another outburst on the playbills which stated that Mr. Dion Boucicault, while claiming to be a partner of Mr. Webster, had " transferred his services and Drama to a rival establishment in the immediate neighbourhood ", which meant Drury Lane for *The Colleen Bawn* with *The Relief Of Lucknow* lined up for the autumn. After airing the quarrel at length, Webster announced " in self-defence " the 331st performance of *The Colleen Bawn* and added, " Shortly will be produced a new and original drama called *Jessie Brown; or, The Relief Of Lucknow* ". But Boucicault had guarded against this long ago : his drama of the Indian Mutiny had been given a copyright performance at Plymouth in 1858. Lacking any sensation scene, it served now merely as a stop-gap until Old Drury's Christmas pantomime went into rehearsal. Then Boucicault had to find some other house. In a letter to *The Times* he offered £5,000 toward providing London with a theatre as well-appointed as the Winter Garden in New York—puff preliminary to a season at Astley's circus, on the south side of Westminster Bridge, which he transformed into the Theatre Royal, Westminster, with stalls separated from the stage by fountains playing in a shrubbery where the sawdust ring had been. *The Trial Of Effie Deans* was billed in the January of 1863. As his success in dealing with managers had not taught him how to be a success as manager himself, he lost all he had and Astley's became Astley's once more.

Losing your all was not then a very serious matter to theatre managers. Webster had to be " saved " at frequent intervals although his enterprise was amazing. Professor Dircks had invented—or so it was generally believed, though his idea is explained in a volume of an earlier date—the optical illusion commemorated in the catch-phrase " all done by mirrors ". It was adapted by Professor Pepper for use in theatres and became known as Pepper's Ghost.[1] The Adelphi playbills in the July of 1863 promised that in between the farce and the burlesque, " At Eight o'clock will be produced, at a vast expense, in consequence of the Extraordinary Machinery and the appliances requisite for the marvellous new Spectral Effects, (which are the property of this theatre only, and duly Registered), a Drama in Three Tableaux, to be called *The Ghost's Bargain*, founded on the popular story of that name, written by Charles Dickens, Esq."

That was outdone when Kate Bateman, at the reopening of the Adelphi for the winter season in the October of 1863, illustrated in *Leah*, " a phasis in the history of Christian nations of which now, happily, the last vestige has disappeared from our own annals, but which on the Continent, and especially in some parts of Germany, subsisted to a very recent period, namely, the persecution and the oppression of the Jewish race ". Gauze waters, burning ships, railway accidents, stone quarries, were all forgotten, and for 210 nights everybody rushed to shudder and weep over a vengeful and brokenhearted Jewess. In *Leah, The Forsaken*, adapted by Augustin Daly from the German, the heroine has a Gentile lover who jilts her. Leah curses him. When befriended by his wife she blesses him instead.

Still drawing from his American bag, Boucicault put on a play at the St. James's and failed. In despair he pulled out a pot-boiler, adapted from the French, about the murder of a man for his wealth, the sufferings of his bereft family in a snowstorm, and the villain's attempt to destroy the man who knows his secret by burning down the tenement where he sleeps. What had been *The Poor Of New York* became *The Poor Of Liverpool* for a try-out at Liverpool, then *The Poor Of Leeds* for

---

[1] Seventy years later this was again announced in London as a novelty. In rivalry with the new talking-films the Holborn Empire presented a programme of " films without the use of a screen "—Pepper's Ghosts.

a try-out at Leeds, and next *The Streets Of London* for a season at the Princess's in the summer of 1864. Thanks to the sensation of a house on fire across the whole breadth of the stage, this restored his fortune. No successor was needed until the following spring, when his thoughts turned to the Ireland of chivalrous conflict between soldiers and rebels while black-hearts betray their kin for gold, land and love. His patriotic urge was not unconnected with the fact that Edmund Falconer, another Irish actor, had just proved such patriotism to be profitable.

The Poor of New York (New York, 1857)

By playing in *The Colleen Bawn*, Falconer had acquired faith in Irish drama. He was born in Dublin in 1814 and went on the stage almost as soon as he could walk. In his twenties he was a leading man at Worcester and at Liverpool. After appearing in a play of his own at Sadler's Wells he became manager of the Lyceum, where he presented his *Peep o' Day; or, Savourneen Deelish* in the November of 1861. It told a tale of the " Peep o' Day " boys, Protestant bands who fought Catholic Defenders at the end of the eighteenth century. Purcell, a middleman's son, incriminates Harry Kavanagh as a " Peep o' Day " boy and has him transported for seven years, lures Kathleen Kavanagh into a mock marriage, and distrains on their old mother for rent before she dies of a broken heart. When he plans to abduct Mary Grace, Harry's betrothed, and marry her by force, he arranges for Kathleen to be murdered in the old quarry. Harry, descending the path from upper flies, grasps a tree-top and swings himself down.

In *Arrah-na-Pogue; or, The Wicklow Wedding*, first played at Dublin in the autumn of 1864, Boucicault provided himself with the part of

Shaun the Post, whose lively wit made him a London favourite at the
Princess's in the March of 1865. Arrah Meelish visits her foster-
brother, Beamish M'Coul, in prison, where he is under sentence of
death for taking part in the rebellion of 1798. While kissing him she
pushes into his mouth the letter (with details of a plan for his liberation)
which gained for her the name of Arrah of the Kiss. When she is
about to be married to Shaun, Beamish waylays Feeney, government
inspector of his confiscated estates, robs him and gives stolen notes to
Arrah. To save her, Shaun declares that he committed the robbery
and is sentenced to death. While breaking out of his prison in Dublin
Castle, he fights Feeney and flings him down to his death in the powerful " sensation scene " of an ivy-clad tower, which sinks (like scarlet-
runners in the pantomime of *Jack And The Beanstalk*) to show Shaun's
climb from the window of his cell to the summit. In Paris *Jean De La
Poste ; ou, Les Noces Irlandaises* ran at the Gaîté for 140 nights.

It was during Boucicault's season at the Princess's that the Fenians
organized their reign of terror. On the afternoon of 13 December,
1865, a cask of gunpowder, fired close to the wall of Clerkenwell Prison
to liberate Irish prisoners, caused nearly a score of deaths and 100 severe
injuries. That night another Irish song was substituted at the Princess's
for " The Wearing o' the Green ". The Prince of Wales was present.
After the performance he went to Boucicault's dressing-room, and
asked casually, sitting on a table and smoking a cigar, " Boucicault, are
you a Fenian? " Dion replied, " No, sir, I am not a Fenian, but I am
an Irishman ".

A drama " from the pen—or desk " of Tom Taylor tried to trade on
antipathies and failed. *The Whiteboy*, at the Olympic the next year,
was a tale of Munster just before the rebellion of '98. It was described
as an elaborate satire upon Ireland and the Irish. The hero was a
drunken idler who called himself a patriot to cover his illicit operations
in the " potheen " trade. The rest of the " bhoys " were " rattling,
roaring " blades, all more or less idle, brutal and venal.

One week's work in which he took no pride, and on a play in which
he had no faith, brought Boucicault a profit of £3,000 and put his name
for a time to *Rip Van Winkle ; or, The Sleep Of Twenty Years*, a masterpiece among melodramas. He did it at the entreaty of Joseph Jefferson,
who had reached London on his way home to America after a world
tour of four or five years. " While the work was in progress I made
an engagement with Benjamin Webster to act the part at his theatre,
the Adelphi ", says Jefferson in all innocence. At the reading both
author and manager were absent. There seemed, he decided, to have
been an old feud between them, " and I presume they did not desire to

meet ". At a dress rehearsal some slight hitch caused Boucicault to launch forth against Webster and the Adelphi with great energy. He denounced the whole establishment, cited the present mistake as typical of the imbecility of the management, and left angrily. Webster, who had been sitting behind the curtains of a private box, set it down in writing that no play of Boucicault should ever be acted in his theatre and left likewise. Jefferson set off by cab in pursuit until he saw the old manager striding up the steps of his home with the very back of his coat in a rage. The housekeeper said her master had just gone upstairs and at that moment a door banged with an angry thud " that echoed through the old house like the ominous thunder that precedes a storm ". Jefferson found Webster pale, his black wig—one of those unmistakable articles with a hard parting on one side and a strong tendency to get away from the back of his head—awry. His grey eyes, wonderfully expressive, " snapped with the reaction of temper ". There was a long, stormy scene, but Jefferson won the right to open the following Monday, 4 September, 1865, and from that day *Rip Van Winkle* revealed its ability to last a life-time.

Its warm sense of humanity holds out interest even more than its astonishing stagecraft, which turns one passage of Washington Irving's prose into a whole act of drama—in particular the monologue in the Catskill Mountains, spoken by Rip to his absent dog, to the trees, to the stranger who gets him to carry a keg, to himself when he sees Hudson's crew : " My, my, I don't like that kind of people at all; No, sir! I don't like any sech kind. I like that old gran'father worse than any of them. How was you, old gentleman? I didn't mean to intrude on you, did I? What? I'll tell you how it was; I met one of your gran'children, I don't know which is the one—they're all so much alike." Twenty years later, when his daughter is being forced into a loveless marriage by her step-father, Rip saves her by pulling out a paper which proves the house to be his—an ending which turns a remarkable work into a conventional play.

During the autumn season of 1866, Boucicault was occupying three theatres and there were rumours of others to follow. The Lyceum had been taken for his *The Long Strike*, which made bubble-and-squeak out of any number of plays by others. What he added was a telegraph office. " Too late ", the heroine is told, but in the midst of her despair the bell of the instrument rings—telegraphic communication with Liverpool has been re-established! This was a great climax, for topical appeal magnified the tinkle into a tocsin. The horse-racing of circus-spectacles inspired Boucicault's drama at the Holborn—built on what had been the post-office stable-yard, part of Jockey's Fields, between

Holborn and Bedford Row—and here *Flying Scud ; or, A Four-Legged Fortune : Showing The Ups And Downs, Crosses, Double Crosses, Events And Vicissitudes Of Life On The Turf* brought to the stage that soon familiar story of attempts to dope the Derby winner, surrounded by " dodgers, dons and diddlers, flunkeys, fools and fiddlers ".

One chance " the busy Dion B " missed. Not he, but his Irish rival, Edmund Falconer, found that even Her Majesty's—the great opera house in the Haymarket—was ready for melodrama. His *Oonagh ; or, The Lovers Of Lisnamora*, blending one of Miss Edgeworth's novels with Carleton's " Fardourougha, the Miser," opened there in the November of 1866. It told the usual story of Ribbonmen in five acts, each with three or four scenes that included a hayfield with real hay-makers. There were thirty-four characters besides supers; it began with an address by the author and lasted five hours; half an hour after midnight, what was left of the audience had some idea that the curtain might at last be about to fall when stage-carpenters pulled the carpet from under the actors' feet. But that majestic building did not long survive. It was gutted by fire in 1867.

Falconer embarked on a tour of the United States only to find that a new standard for sensations had been set by Daly at the Worrell Sisters' Theatre, New York, in 1867, with *Under The Gaslight; or, Life And Love In These Times.* That title was justified the moment the curtain rose on the Courtlands' elegant home : through a window the now could be seen by the light of a street-lamp as Ray, one of New York's " bloods ", visited Laura Courtland, the belle of society. That she is an adopted child, once a little ragged pickpocket, he learns from Pearl Courtland—" pretty but no heart ", as the programme informs us. Social disgrace follows, and Laura earns her own living by colouring photographs until Byke, " whom the law is always reaching for and never touches ", kidnaps her. His claim to be her father is up-held in the Tombs police-court. Ray follows them to Pier 30, North River, where—with Jersey City by starlight for background—Laura is flung into the water; Ray dives after her and holds her until a patrol-boat approaches. Back in the Courtlands' elegant home, she learns that, owing to an interchange of babies in their cradles, she, not Pearl, is the daughter of the house. Rather than allow this disclosure to be made and be the cause of any suffering that would result, Laura leaves at once, trudges to a remote railway station where no more trains will be stopping that night, and accepts the shelter offered her by the signal-man in his store when he goes off duty, though this means that she has to be locked in. Through the barred window she witnesses the pre-parations for a fearful crime : an old servant, Snorkey, who has come in search of her, is lassooed by Byke, who binds him hand and foot, and then lays him on the permanent way out of revenge for the part he has played in disclosing the secret of Laura's birth. This is the sensation:

BYKE (*fastening him to the rails*) I'm going to put you to bed. You won't toss much. In less than ten minutes you'll be sound asleep. There, how do you like it? You'll get down to the Branch before me, will you? You dog me and play the eavesdropper, eh! Now do it, if you can. When you hear the thunder under your head and see the lights dancing in your eyes, and feel the iron wheel a foot from your neck, remember Byke. (*Exit L.*)

LAURA O, Heavens! he will be murdered before my eyes! How can I aid him?

SNORKEY Who's that?

LAURA It is I. Do you not know my voice?

SNORKEY That I do, but I almost thought I was dead and it was an angel's. Where are you?

LAURA In the station.

SNORKEY I can't see you, but I can hear you. Listen to me, miss, for I've only got a few minutes to live.

LAURA (*shaking door*) And I cannot aid you.

SNORKEY Never mind me, miss; I might as well die now, and here, as at any other time. I'm not afraid. I've seen death in almost every shape, and none of them scare me; but, for the sake of those you love, I would live. Do you hear me?

LAURA Yes! Yes!

SNORKEY They are on the way to your cottage—Byke and Judas—to rob and murder.

LAURA (*in agony*) O, I must get out! (*Shakes window-bars*). What shall I do?

SNORKEY Can't you burst the door?

LAURA It is locked fast.

SNORKEY Is there nothing in there? No hammer? no crowbar?

LAURA Nothing (*Faint steam whistle heard in distance*). Oh, Heavens! The train! (*Paralysed for an instant*). The axe!!!

SNORKEY Cut the woodwork! Don't mind the lock, cut round it. How my neck tingles! (*A blow at door is heard*). Courage! (*Another*) Courage! (*The steam whistle heard again—nearer, and rumble of train on track—another blow*). That's a true woman. Courage! (*Noise of locomotive heard, with whistle. A last blow— the door swings open, mutilated, the lock hanging—and Laura appears, axe in hand.*)

Under the Gaslight (New York, 1867)

SNORKEY Here—quick! (*She runs and unfastens him. The locomotive lights glare on scene*). Victory! Saved! Hooray! (*Laura leans exhausted against switch*). And these are the women who ain't to have a vote!
(*As Laura takes his head from the track, the train of cars rushes past with roar and whistle from L. to R.*)

Preparations had to be made at once for a season in London. Knowing the difficulties concerning copyright, which could be secured only by a performance in England, Daly arranged for his play to be seen at Newcastle in the April of 1868. That should have been soon enough to protect his interests; but directly news of *Under The Gaslight* reached the enterprising management of the Britannia, its resident dramatist, Hazlewood, wrote a version of the railroad sensation as part of a diabolical piece of cunning to rob the American of his rewards. Instead of presenting it as his own work or as the work of any living author, he disguised it as part of a melodrama by Charles Selby who had died five years earlier. Accordingly Selby's *London By Night ; or, The Dark Side Of Our Great City*, was made ready for revival. Originally, as performed at the Strand in 1844, it was a mere adaptation, one among many, of *Les Bohémiens De Paris*. Much of the plot, with stirring preliminaries at a railway terminus—Victoria Station this time—was retained, but there was nothing half-hearted about Hazlewood's revision. It came so near to being a new play that a new licence for it had to be obtained from the Lord Chamberlain. (Even minor alterations were supposed to be submitted for censorship, but very seldom were.) In

London by Night (Royal Strand, 1844)

the March of 1868 Selby might well have turned in his grave to discover that his twenty-years-old play contained spectacles uncommonly
like those that were now the talk of both London and New York.
Borrowings from any number of other popular plays could be recognized as the scenes changed from the Adelphi arches to Waterloo
Bridge, from a handsomely furnished saloon in a café-restaurant near
Leicester Square to a tavern concert in the Borough, where the chair-
man hammers vigorously for " order and harmony ", and then to
public tea-gardens in the suburbs. At last the railroad appeared in
" The Brick Fields at Battersea ". A ne'er-do-well named Dognose
locks his daughter in " a lone house ", before he meets his enemies, gets
the worst of it, and is left senseless on the line. Some difference may
be noted, but the heroine's " (in agony) Oh, I must get out " betrays
the plagiarist :

LOUISA (*in the house*) All seems quiet, and yet just now fancy pic-
tured to my mind a struggle of contending men. I hope my father
will soon return—I was very wrong to suffer him to depart alone.
(*Goes to iron grating which forms the door.*) From this spot I can witness his approach. Ah, what is that? My eyes surely cannot
deceive—there is some object lying across the iron road before me
—it can never be a human being in such a dangerous position. I
must warn them. Ah, the gate is locked—how unfortunate. The
train will be down in ten minutes—if the poor creature is not
sleeping, my voice may be heard.
DOGNOSE (*feebly*) Who's that?

LOUISA   Heavens! 'tis my father.

DOGNOSE   Listen to me, and restrain your grief, for I have only five minutes to live.

LOUISA   (*shaking gate*)   Oh, and I cannot aid him.

DOGNOSE   Never mind, you can avenge me.

LOUISA   (*in agony*)   Oh, I must get out (*shakes gate again*).

DOGNOSE   Can't you force out a bar?—I am too weak to move.

LOUISA   Lock and bars alike defy me.

DOGNOSE   Is there nothing in there?—no hammer, no crowbar?

LOUISA   Nothing (*she searches in the apartment. Faint steam whistle in the distance*). Great God! The train! (*Paralysed a moment—resumes her search—shrieks as she discovers an axe*). Heaven has not deserted me—courage—(*strikes gate*)—Courage! (*The steam whistle is heard again nearer, and the rumble of train on the track*). It must give.

> (*Noise of train increases. A last blow—gate flies open and Louisa rushes to Dognose. Just as his head is removed from the track the train passes with a roar and a whistle.*)

This is how the scene was printed in *London By Night*, when published as one of Dick's Standard Plays, headed " First Produced at the Strand Theatre, January 11th, 1844 ", to make stage historians suspect Daly of being an unconscionable liar for claiming it to have been his own original idea. It was some months later, the July of 1868, before *Under The Gaslight* arrived at the Whitechapel Pavilion, and in August Boucicault stole the " sensation " from it, excusing his theft by as brazen a piece of impudence as you will find in the records of forgery and plagiarism. He readily accepted the idea that Selby's old play had the railroad rescue in it. From this he argued that the scene must also have appeared in the French piece Selby had translated. Two thumping falsehoods justified his enterprise in robbing an author who had tried too late to secure the protection of the law.

The playbills of his *After Dark, A Tale Of London Life* at the Princess's described it as the great drama by Dennery and Grange, adapted with their permission—a generous acknowledgment which forestalled any argument that less was owing to Paris than New York. When it came to the climax, fresh novelty was introduced by causing the railway to be the Underground. Instead of station-store or "lone house", Boucicault uses the cellar, in which a hero, captured by villains, pulls down a wall and crawls through the brickwork to drag their victim from the line just before the train puffs out of its tunnel.

By now theatre managers took less interest in pleasing the public than

VIII   Stock Poster (*c.* 1900) for the tour of the English version of Boucicault's *The Poor of New York*

By courtesy of Messrs. Stafford & Co., Ltd.

IX   Stock Poster (*c.* 1900) for the tour of a dramatization of Mrs. Henry Wood's famous novel

By courtesy of Messrs. Stafford & Co

in crossing and double-crossing one another, which might be considered as normal rivalry had they not been engaged in demonstrating the triumphs of virtue. In his everlasting quest of moral precepts Hazlewood picked everybody's brain—paragraphs from Dickens, " leaders " from newspapers, reported sermons, anything that scissors and paste could insert into prompt copies—and not content with these activities on behalf of the Britannia, he appears to have dodged his contractual obligations there by writing *London By Gaslight* for Sadler's Wells under the name of Miss Hazlewood.

What Boucicault could not set before the footlights successfully was the novel, " Foul Play ", which he wrote with Charles Reade. This, adapted by F. G. Maeder for the American stage in 1867, had the sensation scene of a " full-sized ship, 26 feet long ", going down with living souls aboard in full view of the audience. To protect his own interests Boucicault staged *Foul Play* in 1868 at the Holborn, where *For Love*, Tom Robertson's not dissimilar drama of the transport " Birkenhead ", had been seen the year before. Others besides Reade, whose *Scuttled Ship* was staged at the Olympic ten years later, tried their hands at adapting Boucicault's adaptation.

Sensation took another form when he produced *Formosa ; or, The Railroad To Ruin*, with the Boat Race, at Drury Lane in the summer of 1869. It played to crowded houses until the pantomime season, and afterwards went to the Princess's. Critics condemned it as an imitation of *The Flying Scud* and as immoral because the hero saw a side of life that inspired such protests as : " For God's sake, let us leave to the French the exhibition of the sickly splendour and sentiment of the life of the courtesan ". But what had once kept people out of the theatre now drew them in. If Boucicault had persisted in his new course he might well have won the new public. Unhappily, when he was asked by Lord Londesborough to write either a drama or a comedy, he accepted his offer of *carte blanche* for the production but did neither. He played ducks and drakes with the money by mounting *Babil And Bijou*, a " spectacle of enchantment ", at Covent Garden with reckless extravagance. It cost at least £11,000. It failed and Boucicault made a " strange and unaccountable disappearance " to America, before returning to the Gaiety with *The Colleen Bawn* once more.

Other revivals and fresh adaptations followed until he had written a new drama for Drury Lane, *The Shaughraun*. Reading it now leaves the impression of re-reading *Arrah-na-Pogue*, but no such complaint was made in 1875, for it ran for over 100 performances even in that large house before transferring to the Adelphi. The attraction was the author as Conn, the Shaughraun himself, the soul of every fair, the life of every funeral, the first fiddle at every wedding. Here again are honest rebels opposed by honest soldiers; honest colleens opposed by more black-hearted police spies. Here also is a sensational escape, adapted from a French original : " The scene moves—pivots on a point at the back. The Prison moves off and shows the exterior of Tower with Conn clinging to the wall, and Robert creeping through the orifice," and here is the device of a man in a barrel ready with bullet to execute timely justice, none the worse for having done long service in an old drama of Jolly Jack Tars called *My Poll And My Partner Joe.* Boucicault got away with it. He was once more on his feet.

Grief was to throw him down. Willie, his eldest son, was training to be a farmer in Huntingdonshire. "If anything", Dion had said, " should happen to him I should die." On returning to their house after the last night of *The Shaughraun* in 1876, Mrs. Boucicault found her husband with his head in his hands. " I know something's the matter with Willie," she cried. " Where's the carriage? I must go to him at once." Dion started up, and shaking his right hand at her, shouted, " You can't go to him, woman. He is dead." After their loss home became unbearable. There and then Dion set out for America and in a frenzy wished to repudiate his marriage, even to the extent of trying to make his children illegitimate. In the English Courts his wife divorced him instead.

Yet when he returned four years later, in 1880, to play Conn at the Adelphi, the welcome was kindly. In ragged red coat, with his kit slung across his broad back, with brown scratch wig, rouged cheeks and badly worn " tops ", he still looked young. His voice had lost none of its cheeriness, his smile none of its brightness, his wit " none of her thousand cunning tricks of the stage ". The gallery still applauded, but public taste was " not now in the same condition as when stalls, boxes and gallery applauded his Irish dramas to the echo ". Better things were expected of his new play *The O'Dowd.* Its fate was recorded in manifestoes which deceived no one. " In my dramatic pictures of Irish life ", he begins, " you have perceived a desire extending beyond the object of theatrical success." Now his new play sought to remove " the prejudice that we are a thriftless race of good-humoured paupers ". Certain scenes, he said, provoked expressions of displeasure but he declined to alter them. " Rather than lose the favour of any of his audience," the author would amend his error by withdrawing it altogether.

Back at Wallack's he still turned out plays, including *The Omadhaun* —in London another author used this title for another version of the same French play—and the leading part was played by Dion G.

Boucicault, his second son, with whom he went to Australia. Boucicault and his second wife, Louise Thorndyke, came to London in 1886. With fantastic bad taste they appeared in a new play which he called *The Jilt*.

At the time of his death in 1890 several of his plays were always to be found somewhere, either under the titles he gave them with his name attached or in disguise. *The Streets Of London*, the most regularly played of all, was looked upon as anybody's property. *The Shaughraun*, on the other hand, was treated like a classic by younger actors in the touring companies that were replacing the old stock companies because of cheap travel by rail. Later it became evident that he would be remembered by *The Colleen Bawn* alone.

3   The Sins of Society

Black Sheep

"I TAKE my subject in a dream : he takes his in reality. I work with my eyes closed : he works with his eyes open. I shrink from the world at my elbows : he identifies himself with it. I draw : he photographs." So the great Dumas compared himself with his son. By "dream" he meant romance which had begun to wither and was spoken of tenderly; it was now inherently respectable, rather dull. All the excitement was over. Realism, which was denounced on all sides, flourished. The public, like a disobedient child, was doing exactly what it was told not to do by dramatic critics who wrote sermons in the newspapers which they called, with unconscious humour, their "pulpits". More probably the people who went to see the plays characterized as "too" (preceding some colourless adjective or other) were the very people who exercised the contemporary zest for condemnation, but when the modern reader tries to discover what justified those moral outbursts he feels that the cry of murder has been raised over a dead rabbit. Pious wrath against Captain Macheath's misdeeds in *The Beggar's Opera* is the soul of reason compared with exposure of iniquity in the bland, unmeaning story-telling of Tom Taylor. "Whether the scene of Mr. Taylor's comedies or dramas be laid in the Neilgherry Hills, or on a reef in the Red Sea, or in an English borough, the cloven foot of French parentage or suggestion is still distinctly visible," nagged a family newspaper on its many breakfast-tables. "This is bad enough; but it is definitely worse when we find that his dramatic productions show successively a stronger leaven of the radically immoral and shameless cynicism which disfigures the modern French productions. Mr. Taylor has betaken himself to the agreeable task of painting English society as a compact circle of swindlers and demi-reps, which occasionally opens to admit a few fools."

Search for his shamelessly cynical plots finds nothing worse than *Still Waters Run Deep* at the Olympic in 1855. The quiet husband is taken for a fool and the rakish Captain he outwits is a rascal. It is as sentimental as a novelette. With similar innocence, Taylor's *New*

Men And Old Acres at the Haymarket in 1869, upheld the constitution of English society against the new rich. By comparison there was *Black Sheep*, written by Edmund Yates (from his novel) and Palgrave Simpson, for Ben Webster's Olympic season in 1868. This, made in England by English dramatic critics, does show a compact circle of swindlers and demi-reps which opens to admit a few fools. Moreover, unlike anything ever written by Taylor, it takes no unkindly view of sinners. That the criminal and his wife should have been played by Charles James Mathews and his second wife (he married Mrs. Davenport while in America the year following the death of his first wife, Madame Vestris) is proof that they claimed sympathy instead of disapproval for their crimes. What is regarded by Stewart Routh (the part Mathews played) as living by your wits, includes murder. What his devoted Harriet regards as a wife's duty, includes a scheme that will let the noose fall round the neck of the innocent youth who chivalrously trusts her. The purpose is to show how selfless loyalty, thinking no sacrifice of morals too great, can exist in lives of ruthlessly immoral squalor. The play is amoral. Nothing else in all the popular entertainment of the 1860s resembles it.

While realism meant (to his contemporaries) romance in soiled clothes, Yates here denied the whole universe of Blacks and Whites, the whole vision of human nature as a chequered board of vices and virtues. Even when Routh decides to desert his wife for a wealthy American widow, he still speaks, unmelodramatically, like a normal human being, and while the youth is being tried for murder Harriet appears not as a callous monster but as love's martyr—" I think you

Still Waters Run Deep (Olympic, 1855)

ought to know," she says to Stewart as she helps him to cheat the gallows, "I shall live only as long as I know you are still living." No outcry was raised, but an attempt was made to consign this piece of dramatized free-thinking to oblivion. "The Life of Charles James Mathews" (autobiographical) dismisses *Black Sheep* thus, "The next few years were passed in the regular routine of engagements in London and country towns, and offer little or nothing of general interest." Mathews omitted it from the list of plays in his career, and Mrs. Mathews did likewise. Yates and Simpson had denied their faith in the code of virtue triumphant. That was unforgivable even though the public were tiring of it and finding relief from the monotony of melodrama in variants that reflected the changing conditions of life.

Comfort, born of the strong sense of financial security, was creating a new sin and new punishment. The sin was not to know your place in society and the punishment was to lose it. What that meant can be understood by contrasting the squalor out of doors with the warmth within. Dickens did not exaggerate London's murk, nor the utter misery of its homeless. When "Bleak House" came out in monthly numbers between the March of 1852 and the September of 1853 it was dramatized only at unfashionable theatres—except in New York, where Brougham's version immediately appeared at Wallack's with the author and Laura Keene as the Deadlocks. There was at first no such eagerness to play Jo as there had been to play Oliver Twist, and considering how very effective the young "hunted animal" was to be on the stage twenty years later, the reason may be that Dickens' moral was too near home. Half-starved children were still sweeping crossings in all but the main thoroughfares where the new horse-drawn rollers [1] had done them out of a living. Canals of mud rolled slowly over the bulwarks of sweepings, to use Albert Smith's words, as fast as besoms could brush the flood back again.

Where did these poor little urchins come from? The answer, in Sala's "Twice Round the Clock", is dated 1859 and it holds good for another ten, if not twenty, years. St. Giles's was supposed to have been done away with; splendid streets were said to have taken its place. Sala, walking through them from Covent Garden to Bedford Square, saw the gibbering forms of men and women in filthy rags, shock hair beginning just above the eyebrows, gashes filled with yellow fangs for teeth. Children, wolfish by privation, fought and screamed, whim-

---

[1] A query from the publisher makes me realize that this word is obsolete. The "roller" for street-cleaning, still in use in the early hours in some parts of London, is a circular brush to fit half the width of the roadway. It is fixed diagonally so as to roll refuse to the gutter.

pered and crawled, more ragged, dirty and wretched than their elders. Naturally the theatres situated in the slums between Wych Street and Tottenham Street preferred Uncle Tom to Jo. Playgoers in the 1860s would be harrowed by the make-believe death of the crossing-sweeper on the stage, knowing full well that they would see somebody uncommonly like Jo just beyond the lighted portico outside.

The Victorian black-out rigorously shut all that out. Home-life was the greater part of life. Strict obedience was demanded and yielded to the head of the household. The children had to stay young until wedded and then grow suddenly up, which system divided people into the belatedly young and the prematurely aged. Every home, with its ruler who rewarded virtue and punished vice, strove to be a self-contained universe.

The " evening out " was a rare event, though parents were beginning to be scandalized by the " spread " of it. The boom in public amusements, far greater than the boom caused by the first gas-lit street-lamps at the beginning of the century, came from light at night. That ever-ready help in such enquiries, Haydn's " Dictionary of Dates ", reports : " It was said in 1860, that of the gas supply of London a leakage of 9 per cent. took place through the faulty joints of the pipes ". No wonder old playgoers lamented that what they missed in the modern drama was the smell of gas, the characteristic odour of Victorian London—particularly the Surrey side, where it was feloniously " tapped "—though there were many strong local rivals for their nostrils' favour. On the darkest night the Cockney would know where he was by the unmistakable scents of pickle-factories, jam-factories, breweries, soap-works and Thames. Also there was enough soot to be the flour of this atmospheric duff, thus inspissating the gloom which enabled leonine-headed paterfamilias, in all the personal grandeur of his Crimean whiskers and the glow of good fellowship, to keep his womenfolk indoors, to bestow his hospitality regularly upon prospective sons-in-law for solving problems of microcosmic over-population, and to keep the outside world outside. When he went to the theatre he took his family with him. His insistence that the drama must be moral, his outbursts when he thought it was not, sprang from his dread lest anything should offend the ears of the young. Melodrama catered for the family party.

Who would venture out alone? Market-porters lay in wait to cut off stragglers from Covent Garden Opera, and the Olympic was " another nasty place to leave after the performance, except in a cab ". In dimly lighted Drury Lane and Newcastle Street ruffians were always ambushed in stench. Domestic dictatorship had to be endured by all

except spirits so hardy as to be suspected of criminal tendencies themselves. In " Vanity Fair " Becky Sharp shows what happened to them;
she was not content to sit behind drawn curtains and pity the poor
people whose footsteps she could faintly hear outside, not content to
take whatever place might be found for her by well-ordered firesides
amid the encircling smut-laden gloom; she asked too much of life
and therefore doomed herself to mix with " Bohemians, awful
people " on the Continent, according to Thackeray's farewell glimpse
of her. In all shapes and sizes, under all kinds of names, Becky Sharp
henceforth remained the favourite character in fiction of nineteenth-
century England. She had to be heavily disguised so that nobody
should recognize her, but she was always so plainly Society's outlaw
that the wonder is she was regularly regarded as a brand-new fashion.

Naturally there was a companion picture. The social outlaw who
sinned and was doomed to an unhappy ending could always be contrasted with the innocent outlaw who was without offence and therefore on her way to a happy ending. This one comes from Lord
Lytton. " Night and Morning ", the novel he wrote in 1841, espouses
the cause of social rebels. Gawtrey is one because of Fanny, child of
the woman he loved before Lord Lilborne seduced her. Philip Beau-
fort is another because he has been robbed of his rightful heritage by
Lord Lilborne's brother-in-law. Gawtrey is killed by the police.
Fanny, without his protection, is kidnapped, but the scrap of paper she
takes from a secret drawer in order to send a message to Philip, proves
his legitimacy. They marry.

In New York this tale began a brand of stage realism that can be
labelled " The Sins of Society ". Brougham, who dramatized it, was
cherished in America as the most winning proof of the powers of
blarney on the stage. He was born in 1810 in Dublin; he was educated at Trinity College and walked the Peter Street hospital. He first
acted in *Tom And Jerry* in Tottenham Street, went to Covent Garden,
became manager of the Lyceum and left for America, where he took
Lytton's story for his play, *Night And Morning; or, She's Very Like
Her Mother* [1] at Wallack's in 1845 with Lester as the hero and himself as
Gawtrey. Brougham played snakes-and-ladders with fortune, running
theatres under his own name at one time and being glad of " stock "
engagements at others. As a playwright he kept three careers going
more or less concurrently. He constantly adapted Dickens in order to
exhibit his own powers in character, so that his *Dombey And Son* con-

---

[1] Dion Boucicault's *Night And Morning* at the Gaiety in 1872 was an adaptation
of *La Joie Fait Peur* by Madame de Girardin, adapted at the Lyceum in 1854 as
Sunshine Through Clouds.

Captain Cuttle (New York, 1850)

sisted of odd persons floating around Captain Cuttle; he was acclaimed as the nineteenth-century Aristophanes because of the light satire in his burlesques; his third achievement, which consisted of making known what went on in society, was not so handsomely acknowledged, but his output in this category was vast. In his own *Vanity Fair* he played Rawdon Crawley. He adapted *Jane Eyre* for Laura Keene with a background of dowagers who treated the unprotected governess with violent contempt and "bloods" who affronted her with unveiled compliments:

LORD INGRAM She's a magnificent creature, Dent, by Jove! Let's have a close look at her—(*Dent and Ingram walk round Jane with quizzing glasses*)—Bears close inspection too, by Jove!
COLONEL DENT Yes, as close as you can get—those eyes are dangerous, too near.

When the wedding was disturbed by the escape of Rochester's wife and he commanded, "Proceed with the ceremony", bigamy obtained the freedom of the stage. It had been mentioned before without embarrassment, and Charlotte Brontë had not been branded for allowing her heroine to fall in love with a married man. In 1864 Tennyson went further, since the wife of Enoch Arden married again with the first husband still living.

We cannot leave Brougham without mentioning his services to the stage in blowing up ships. His *The Miller Of New Jersey; or, The Prison Hulk*, seen by New York in 1858, was about the miller's daring release of prisoners from the hulk, which then exploded. This climax was still more resounding in his *The Lottery Of Life* at Wallack's in 1867 with himself as the Irish hero. The last scene shows ferry and boathouse. Beyond is a ship made of block tin with transparent portholes, foresails furled, and rigging prepared with turpentine. The ferry puts off. Then the villain soliloquizes, "The drunkenness of an insatiate vengeance fills me with a sense of devilish joy—cries of despair and death are ringing in my ears". He fires the ship too soon, and falls cursing as it explodes and partly sinks by the hull.

The Lottery of Life (New York, 1867)

4

The Woman Novelist

East Lynne

THE Woman Novelist means Mrs. Henry Wood and Miss Braddon in the first flush of best-sellerdom. Respectable people who exacted obedience from their own daughters, wondered what on earth other parents were doing to allow their daughters to put such stuff into print. Fathers then came down leisurely to breakfast, wearers of the velvet smoking-cap in the glorious heyday of the middle classes. The newspaper was propped up before them with marmalade pot and toastrack. It was " the breakfast-table ", not a running-buffet. While servants brushed silk hat and rolled umbrella, clerks in a city office were opening letters, filling ink-wells and dusting the shiny horsehair sofa for the afternoon nap. The telephone was nothing more than the subject of Professor Papper's lecture before the Queen at the Polytechnic and of a musical demonstration at the Queen's Theatre in Long Acre. A mere thousand or two a year enabled a burgher to live like a bashaw. Such a lordly way of beginning the day is now so strange that it has inspired the story of the navvies who comment, as the master is escorted from his door, " 'E don't 'arf come out of the 'ouse, don't 'e? " In the 1860s anyone who was comfortably off did not half come out of the house, and before that momentous event took place, perfect peace, with loved ones far away in the nursery or kitchen, enabled him to read attacks on that old subject the new woman, which could be measured more by the page than by the column. Prosperity's cornucopia became a megaphone for such daily phrases as, " I don't know what the country is coming to ". The type cannot be ignored. As the most opulent playgoer his power over the theatre was unchallenged.

Some of his annoyance was caused by the eldest daughter of Thomas Price, head of one of the leading glove-manufacturing firms in Worcester ; she married Henry Wood, whose interest was shipping. With her first novel, " Danesbury House ", in 1860, she gained a prize of £100 offered by the Scottish Temperance League for the best illustration of the best effects of Temperance. The next year she wrote " East Lynne ", which was by contemporary standards far from temperate, for though Lady Isabel and her Little Willie recall Mrs. Haller and her small William in *The Stranger*, the measure of privacy allotted to each erring wife is altogether different.   When Mrs. Haller appears her sins are past.   In Lady Isabel's story that past is present.   She elopes with Captain Levison when driven frantic by her husband's secret conversations with Barbara Hare, not knowing that these are solely concerned with Richard Hare's efforts to shield himself from a charge of murder.   There is a divorce.   Lady Isabel, betrayed, lets it be thought that she is dead.   Under the name of Madame Vine she returns to her old home disguised as a governess [1] to watch over her son until he dies. After justice has claimed Levison she also dies, because for her there can be no happy ending.

Since dramas of society had become the vogue in New York, it was natural that the first plays of *East Lynne* should be seen there.   From 1856, when Matilda Heron staged *Camille ; or, The Fate Of A Coquette* (her own version of *La Dame Aux Camélias*), leading ladies of America saw themselves in rôles of great suffering.   It was the elegance of *Camille* which told.   Armand Duval receives the camellia from her in a sumptuous apartment, while the Count de Varville is dismissed. After the lovers' brief hour of happiness in their country house, before she sacrifices herself by returning to the Count, they meet again in another splendid house where Armand throws a shower of notes and gold upon her as she falls at his feet.   She dies poorly furnished but still with a birthday present from some dear old duke.   " Other parts she *acted*, this one she lived ", a critic said of Matilda Heron, soon famous for her playing of lost women.   Now came the chance for her rivals. Lucille Western paid Clifton W. Tayleure one hundred dollars for an *East Lynne* which was her starring vehicle for life.   At matinées in the January of 1862, the appeal of the heroine with the cry of, " To be for ever an outcast from society ", was so strong that when put on at the Winter Garden fourteen months later the management signed a contract that bestowed half the gross receipts upon the leading lady.   Rival versions included *Edith ; or, The Earl's Daughter*, by B. Woolff, which Matilda Heron acted at Niblo's in the December of 1862.

The American *East Lynne* which has been printed is an odd mixture. The serious scenes are written by somebody as ill acquainted with the theatre as with actuality.   " Carpenter scenes " where discomfiture of villainy is used as comic relief are written by somebody who knows the theatre only too well.   In the small space before a frontcloth-landscape while the scene for Little Willie's death is being set, Sir Francis Levison

---

[1] Similar ideas occur in *La Gouvernante* (1747), *Norman's Love ; or, Kate Wynsley, the Cottage Girl* (1845), *Jessy Vere ; or, the Return of the Wanderer* (1856).

Camille, or, The Fate of a Coquette, American
version of *La Dame Aux Camélias* (1856)

walks hurriedly about until he encounters Cornelia Carlyle, the steely
sister-in-law whose enmity drove Lady Isabel to despair. The
dialogue runs :

MISS C.   You dare lift your hat to me ? Have you forgotten that I am
     Miss Carlyle ?

LEVISON   It would be a hard matter to forget the face, having once
     seen it.

MISS C.   You contemptible worm, I despise you ! Do you think I am
     to be insulted with impunity ? Out upon you for a bold, bad man.

OFFICER   Francis Levison, I arrest you—you are my prisoner.

LEVISON   Hands off, vermin ! You are too familiar on short acquain-
     tance.

The model of all that is suave in murderers and seducers makes his
exit with, " Goody-day, angelic Miss Carlyle, loveliest of your sex.
I'm sorry this agreeable little comfort was cut so short. I'll come back
and renew it in the morning. Take care of your precious self, and
look out for the naughty, naughty men—ta-ta-ta-ta." To which the
sinister Cornelia, proverbial for venom in the repressed, retorts by
calling after the policeman, " Be sure to get his photograph taken. It
will be an excellent picture for the rogue's gallery "—stock gag for
" dames " in Christmas pantomimes.

   Less appeal to the heart and more to the nerves was made by Miss
Braddon. Her literary career began in 1854 when she went, at the age
of seventeen, with her mother to an old farmhouse near Beverley. Her

" fugitive pieces " about flowers and trees and heroines of history in the
Beverley Recorder were admired by a local printer, who made her the
spirited offer of £10 for a story to be published as Penny Dreadfuls.
In a preface he declared that the pure love which animated the heroine's
breast was of the kind " which makes the youth of England able to
overcome every obstacle, and has been one of the primary causes of
our national greatness ".

Round about the age of twenty-five, the author was publishing three
novels a year. " Lady Audley's Secret ", the last of 1862, and " Aurora
Floyd ", the first of 1863, made one plot serve twice by reversing blacks
and whites. Both novels are dominated by women of decisive
character who are well and bigamously married. Both the genuine
husbands are murdered. But while Lady Audley is a homicidal
maniac, Aurora is a falsely accused innocent; while the husband of one
is inoffensive, the husband of the other is a blackmailer; while the onlooker in one case is merely a witness, the onlooker in the other is the
criminal. Together these companion pictures of the Bad Bigamist and
the Good Bigamist show how to commit the crime and how not to.

Lady Audley, for the sake of wealth and station, takes a second husband, knowing her first husband to be still living, and so as to avoid
the awful consequences she drowns one man and sets fire to Audley
Court in order to burn the other. Aurora Floyd believes herself to be
a widow before she starts her married life with the man she truly loves,
and but for her recklessness in horse-whipping a deformed half-wit for
his brutality to animals, nothing untoward might have occurred. His
vindictive cunning is such that her first husband, who appears and then
accepts a bribe to disappear, is shot in circumstances that cause suspicions
to darken her life. As Aurora has been innocent at heart her happiness
is assured in the end, despite what playbills announced as *The Dark
Deed Done In The Wood*.

Versions of both novels immediately swamped the stage. W. E.
Suter came first in 1863 at the Queen's in Tottenham Street. His
Lady Audley of 21 February was followed by a rival at the St. James's on
28 February; his Aurora of 4 April was preceded in March by rivals at
the Princess's and the Adelphi, with another at the Britannia on 21
April. According to the list of notable productions in John Parker's
" Who's Who in the Theatre " the first stage version of " East Lynne "
to be played in London was *The Marriage Bells ; or, The Cottage On
The Cliff* at the Effingham, Whitechapel, in 1864, and the author was
W. Archer (not to be confused with W. Archer, the critic). The first
to be given without change of title was John Oxenford's version for
Avonia Jones, the Australian tragedienne, at the Surrey in 1866. There

Blow for Blow (Holborn Theatre, 1868)

was a burlesque of the story at the Theatre Royal, Birmingham, in the autumn of 1869. In the January of 1873 a serious version was staged at the Holborn with Mrs. Vezin as Lady Isabel. Another was staged at Nottingham the next year, and another at the Strand in 1878. The craze started in 1879, when the Olympic, the Standard and Astley's all billed *East Lynne*. Lucille Western's American version came to the Standard in 1883. It differed from the English versions in its method of drawing tears; the saddest moment, when Lady Isabel has come back to East Lynne in disguise to watch over her sick child, was arranged like this:

MAD. V. (*rising*) O Heaven! my punishment is more than I can bear. He has gone to bring that woman here that she may mingle her shallow sympathy with his deep grief. Oh if ever retribution came to woman, it has come to me now. I can no longer bear it. I shall lose my senses. O William! in this last, dying hour try to think I am your mother.

WILLIAM Papa has gone for her now.

MAD. V. No, not that woman there, not that woman. (*Throws off cap and spectacles*) Look at me, William. I am your mother! (*Catches him in her arms. He says " Mother " faintly, and falls back dead in her arms.*)

English playwrights were more ruthless. The celebrated line in the most popular of their plays was Lady Isabel's cry, " Dead—and never called me ' Mother' ".

In an attempt to be bracketed with the Woman Novelist, Boucicault wrote *The Two Lives Of Mary Leigh*, which was tried out at Manchester and then billed at the St. James's in the November of 1866 as *Hunted Down ; or, The Two Lives Of Mary Leigh*. It was another drama " turning upon the unsavoury but popular subject of bigamy ". Scudamore, a fearful picture " admirable from its very fearfulness ", was played by Henry Irving, a young provincial actor. To save the situation from sameness, H. J. Byron gave *Blow For Blow* to the Holborn in the September of 1868. A seafaring baronet, happily married for the second time, has the peace of his country home shattered by the sudden appearance of somebody he himself mistakes for his first wife, long given up for dead, until she is revealed as a twin sister.

5

Cup-and-Saucer Comedy

Caste

SINFUL dramas of society did not, in the moralizing fervour that raged midway through the nineteenth century, go unopposed. Others were almost beatifically sinless. In Paris, after six years of the fashion set by Dumas *fils* for the seamy side of life, sheer innocence found a surprising champion. Octave Feuillet,[1] hitherto an active salesman of what English critics called " the staple of French fiction "— meaning sex—unexpectedly wrote a novel as pure as the maiden of bashful fifteen. It was entitled " Le Roman d'un Jeune Homme Pauvre ", and it had a hero, a wrongfully dispossessed heir, who not only burns the Will which would restore to him his estates, but also risks life and limb by leaping from a tower where his presence compromises the honour of a proud beauty locked in with him for the night. Feuillet made a stage version which was acted in Paris in 1858. The next year John Oxenford, dramatic critic of *The Times*, turned it into *Ivy Hall*, which was acted at the Princess's and gained a place in theatrical annals solely because Henry Irving, engaged to make his first London appearance in it, broke his contract because his part was too small. Its American history is also peculiar. Only a few months before *The Romance Of A Poor Young Man* was ready to open at Wallack's, that business of burning a Will for motives of the purest selflessness was introduced into another play : Tom Taylor, then in New York, used the incident to display the virtue of the Yankee hero of his *Our American Cousin* at Laura Keene's in the October of 1858. Taylor included this play among those which were strictly " of my own invention—subjects as well as treatment ". Any number of coincidences of the same sort can be cited to prove that such accidents will happen, and it is fortunate that whether he copied it or reinvented it is of no

---

[1] In 1845, the year in which Octave Feuillet's work began to be published, " feuilleton " meant the reading-matter on the half-leaf or " feuillet " set apart in French newspapers for literary essays. That it now means the kind of light novel that used to be serialized by newspapers is ascribed to the prolific successes he enjoyed in this commodity. Most of our dictionaries have yet to realize that the word, in English usage today, applies solely to fiction.

importance here.   What matters is that this eagerness to present stage
pictures of sinlessness was evident not only in London and Paris but also
in New York.   How Sothern, as a be-whiskered caricature of English
nobility who became world-famous as Lord Dundreary, stole all the
limelight in *Our American Cousin*, both in New York and at the Haymarket, has been handed down as a very familiar story, but by now it
has been forgotten that he made as great a success by nightly burning a
Will when he played Feuillet's young man at the Haymarket in a new
English version called *A Hero Of Romance*, by Dr. Westland Marston,
in 1868.   In his memoir of Sothern, Edgar Pemberton describes how
the dispossessed heir, employed as a steward by the parvenu family of
the haughty young woman he loves, conquered (" off ") the unheard-
of vices of an unmanageable horse, submissively bore the taunts of a
proud and unyielding beauty, rushed for her sake " three steps at a
time " up the steps inside the ruined tower by the light of a pale moon,
and recklessly flung himself from that dizzy height on to a yawning
feather-bed in the unseen depths below.   " Exquisitely dressed in a
perfectly fitting sealskin-trimmed coat, the like of which had never
been seen before (and which no one but the Sothern of those days dare
have worn) ", he burnt the Will as a sacrifice to past love, after which
young men burnt foolscap Wills in candle-flames at penny readings
everywhere.

But this history of Feuillet's lapse into virtue—it deserves to be called
that even though he was merely obeying the *dernier cri*—has gone too
far ahead.   As soon as he disclosed what the public wanted in 1858,
there was a very decided movement in the theatre to supply the
demand, and while vice and lawlessness were still being mirrored in
realism, this other kind of fidelity to life was brought upon the stage by
" naturalism ".   The first to represent the new style was H. T. Craven,
an actor whose highly original ideas on how to set a scene revolution-
ized the art of theatrical " production ".   What is of less importance
nowadays but of far more account when the tone of public morals
comes up for consideration, is that he undoubtedly led the way in
showing how the drama could gratify those critics who demanded
from it " a more healthy tone ".   There had been domestic dramas
before his time.   In these the usual plan was to contrast the heroine's
spotless purity with examples of criminality.   Craven left out murder
and robbery altogether.

Sweet simplicity was his stock-in-trade while demonstrating what
can be done with ordinary everyday furniture on the stage.   If this new
fad deserved the name of naturalism, then Craven was the original
naturalist.   He even went so far as to make costumed characters in

The Romance of a Poor Young Man
(New York, 1859)

historical dramas say what they meant in plain language. When close on thirty years of age he had played Orlando at Drury Lane in 1850. There were then a few plays bearing his name, and in 1853 he wrote *Our Nelly*, a piece of pure Mummerset, for the Surrey, but he was not important enough to be missed at home when he spent some years in Australia. On his return in 1860 his *The Post Boy* was put on at the Strand, a stone's throw from Temple Bar. The moral must be noted. "As a Briton", says Joe to get down the curtain, "I'm proud of our aristocracy, for there we find that noble species—a fine old English Gentleman." At the Strand three years later Craven borrowed the business of burning a Will for reasons of self-sacrifice and called the result *Miriam's Crime*. A rich widow leaves everything to her hired companion, who destroys the Will in order to benefit some scamp of a nephew. The handsomely furnished apartment changes to a neat but humble lodging-house where tables and chairs become a barricade when her enemies hunt for documents unavailingly because the nephew and the companion marry and take everything. Humble maids, outlawed by poverty from the life where they could be admired, were Craven's particular care.

At the Strand in 1864 his *Milky White* achieved naturalism both in the way it was written and the way it was staged. The parlour of Daniel White, dairyman and cow-keeper, unpopularly known as "Milky", is backed by the dairy, a paved and whitewashed chamber with churn, yokes, milk cans. The door has a practicable lock or bolt, and the window-sill real pots. There is a cottage piano; a work-basket with various articles of needlework is on the table; a drugget

D

covers the parlour floor and there is a doormat, upon which the cowboy wipes his feet. In a frenzy of churlishness White drives Annie out of doors and takes to his bed in a bedroom so natural that looking-glass, comb and brush are on the toilet table and " a piece of neat bedroom carpeting on the floor ".

There was no questioning Craven's success while the novelty lasted. In *Meg's Diversion*, at the Royalty in 1866, he told an artless tale which had little more to it than a flirtation which begins in fun and ends in earnest, and yet achieved a run of over 300 performances. This is an event not without importance, for it marks the peak of London's craving for displays of innocence.

His earlier plays at the Strand formed the beginning of triple bills which concluded with farce. The middle, the most popular part, always consisted of the type of burlesque that prompted the joke about actresses who filled not rôles but tights, and in these Marie Wilton was " so stupendously like a boy and unlike a woman that "—or so Dickens said—" it is perfectly free from offence ". While representing all manner of men, including Myles-na-Coppaleen, she aspired to act in comedy; when told to keep to " the merry sauciness of the wicked little boy Cupid ", she felt there was nothing for it but to go into management herself. Meanwhile another " boy " in these burlesques, Fanny Josephs, had come to the same conclusion. Both saw in Craven's comedies the style of the future, and both knew that the time for change was overdue.

The London stage was despotically ruled by old tyrants. Webster was one. Buckstone, who now reigned at the Haymarket as the master of comedy, was another. They were of the theatre theatrical. Up to 1866 they had the power to decide the style of plays, and in that style they were unbeatable—on their own ground old players usually are. Neither the Adelphi nor the Haymarket possessed elegance or comfort and audiences had to sit on hard wooden benches. On the other side of the footlights the furnishings were just as crude; the scenery consisted of backcloths and side-wings with doors and chairs painted on them. Little was thought of illusion, for the acting aimed at make-believe and nothing else; by addressing themselves straight at the public old actors obtained the greatest possible effect. The clothes they wore on the stage proclaimed the exaggerated characters they were supposed to be and bore little relation to what people wore in real life.

This explains why Craven was so successful and why all the young hopefuls of the theatre decided to imitate him. When Fanny Josephs went into management at the Holborn she took his *The Post Boy* with her, though it could not, as a piece already seen, make a stir. When

Marie Wilton went into management she was wiser : as the pet of society she argued that the one thing wrong with Craven's uncommon ideas was that they were "common". Like Madame Vestris one generation earlier, she could be sure that where she went the world of fashion would follow, even into the slums; and in the same way that Vestris had once transformed the Olympic into a *salon* fit for ladies and gentlemen, so Marie Wilton turned the Tottenham Street theatre, then known as a blood-tub, into a drawing-room. Besides carpets and armchairs, private boxes and upholstered stalls in the auditorium, she provided furniture for the stage that would make interiors look like the interiors her patrons, rich or poor, had come from. The company she engaged consisted of players who were capable of ignoring the audience, speaking their lines to one another, and behaving as though acquainted with drawing-rooms. It is worth noting that she did not act fine ladies herself until her husband, Squire Bancroft, had "made a duchess of her".

Fashion had a great deal to do with the triumphs won in Tottenham Street when its theatre, renamed the Prince of Wales's, opened in 1865. Why Craven's share in the "revolution" was so speedily overlooked is because he was not responsible for the sudden promotion of the stage to a higher social sphere. He merely invented naturalism, which was to realism what virtue was to vice; it displayed cups and saucers instead of magnums and glasses, and revolved around marriages instead of adultery. The Bancrofts' contribution was to correct the old antithesis between kind hearts and coronets by picturing society in the way Gilbert chronicles in his lines about hearts true and fair in Belgrave Square. Bad baronets had no place in a "model drawing-room theatre" which had set out to please baronets. That sharp line between innocence in poverty and vice amid wealth could no longer be drawn.

Victorian drama had thus split in two. While Webster went with wealth, wickedness and wine—this alliteration cannot be helped—the new generation saw no evil in rank or riches or quiet behaviour. In essence there was no great difference between the new and the old because both preserved the same unquestioning belief in Virtue Triumphant, but in all inessentials they were at opposite extremes. Floods and oceans as depicted in sensation scenes may be contrasted with a stage-direction in a cup-and-saucer comedy which says, "The umbrellas to be wet". According to the new taste this was as effective as a lake of blue gauze had been to the old.

It had become difficult to define "real". Sometimes it was a term of praise, sometimes of blame. Real cabs or real fire-engines were

despised by the very people who admired real doors—even when they
stuck at awkward moments. The difference concerns size. While
the champions of realism surpassed themselves by exhibiting animals,
vehicles and machines that were better because they were bigger, the
leaders of naturalism who had started with doors, chairs and umbrellas,
won their most resounding triumphs with smaller and smaller things,
down to tongs and spoons on their tea-tables. Here is the secret of the
cup-and-saucer comedies. For at least a dozen years a smooth white
cloth, hanging almost to the floor, a silver urn, a muffin-dish and a
creditable taste in china, reassured audiences at the Prince of Wales's
that this was the theatre for the elect among playgoers. Consequently
tea-tables remained the hallmark of a Bancroft play, however much it
had to change its settings from high life to low. (And if ever it should
be asked why English comedies of succeeding generations should so
often contain prattle of the do-you-take-sugar? order, here is the
reason.)

Tom Robertson was the playwright chiefly associated with the
Bancrofts. For twenty years he had been regularly supplying melodrama to theatres everywhere until he had the good fortune to hit on
the idea of giving an aristocratic flavour to the scenes of sentiment
usually associated with humble life—raising domesticity to the peerage,
it might be called. War in melodramas usually consisted of heroics
for officers and comic relief for men; when Robertson dramatized the
Crimea in *Ours*—played by the Bancrofts at Liverpool in the August of
1866 and in Tottenham Street a month later—his titled characters behaved sometimes in a humorous but never in a high falutin' way.
Mary Wilton herself appeared as a companion, " kept in the room to
save another woman from rising to ring a bell, or hand her the scissors ",
or to play the piano when ordered. The plot was left to Sir Alexander
Shendryn, who will not tell his wife what he does with certain sums of
money, and Lady Shendryn, who thinks the worst: actually her em-
bezzling brother is to blame, and her husband, unlike husbands in real
life, is too chivalrous to speak the truth about his wife's relations.
Robertson is plainly taking advantage of public good-will when he
unravels *Ours*. A sergeant brings news of the Colonel. Lady
Shendryn rises. Mary, the companion, cries, " Hush ". Lady Shendryn says, " You need not speak—I know all! He is dead." When
Sir Alexander enters a minute later she kneels to beg forgiveness. The
play was successful and still more so when revived in 1870. That it
belongs to a drawing-room theatre is apparent in its scene on the eve of
the war when a Russian prince comes to say good-bye to Blanche,
Lady Shendryn's ward:

Ours (Prince of Wales's, 1866): The Hut in the Crimea

PRINCE Should you honour me by favourable consideration of my
demand, in return for the honour of your hand, I offer you rank
and power. On our own lands we hold levees—indeed you will
be queen of the province—of 400,000 serfs—of your devoted
slave—my queen!

BLANCHE (*sits on sofa, L.*) Queen! If I should prove a tyrant?

PRINCE (*standing*) I am a true Russian, and love despotism!

BLANCHE (*smiling*) And could you submit to slavery?

PRINCE At your hands—willingly (*sits on her R.H.*) I assure you
slavery is not a bad thing!

BLANCHE But freedom is a better.

In drama of a more robust type Blanche would have said, " That is
why our countries are fighting ". At Astley's, where the Crimean
War was the subject of a grand military and equestrian spectacle, the
response consisted of several patriotic speeches and a battle, whereas in
Ours the chief event of the siege of Sebastopol was the cooking of a
roly-poly pudding. Another peculiarity of the Bancrofts' performance was the way the heroines behaved while awaiting, in the officers'
mud hovel, the outcome of the battle:

BLANCHE (*in tone of command*) Hi! Ho! Ha! Attention! Form hollow square! Prepare to receive (*prancing over to R.*). Cavalry! (*Blanche charges upon Mary. Mary somewhat frightened retreats to the corner.*)

This was highly popular " business ". Audiences were expected never to grow tired of it. In *Caste* Polly, imitating a soldier on horseback, prances up and down, gallops, imitates bugle, gives point with parasol and nearly spears Hawtree's nose. In *Blow For Blow* Lady Linden " gallops round in imitation of horse in circus, laughing and humming a tune ". Some hint of a hobby-horse was given by the bustle (which did bustle when agitated) or " dress-improver ", so called because it hid that part of the natural shape which was " rude ". To save posterity's confusion we must explain that this refers to the posterior—a later generation disconcertingly transferred offence to the bust.

Caste opened at the Prince of Wales's in the April of 1867. The Marquise de Maur may seem exalted when she says to her son George, " My boy (kissing his forehead), I am sure, will never make a *mésalliance*. He is a D'Alroy, and by his mother's side *Planta-genista*. The source of our life stream is royal," but the Marquise is exceptional. George is human enough to marry Esther, the columbine, daughter of the drunken Eccles, and sister of Polly (Marie Wilton), who is about to marry Sam, honest tradesman in boxed paper-cap. The plot amounts to this : George goes to India and is reported killed in action but returns safe and sound to his wife and baby, whereupon the Marquise, bending over the cradle, says, " My grandson ". How effective it was can be gathered by the line of reasoning it inspired in the critical faculty of Clement Scott when he wrote, " Picture it! A great hulking, handsome, well-bred officer, who becomes a ' great big baby ' again, lisping inarticulate sentences over the infant that he could have crushed to death in his great strong, manly arms." That is the emotional side. The humour kept to jokes that had already proved their worth. Hawtree, moving backwards, bumped against Sam who turned round savagely :

HAWTREE I beg your pardon! (*crossing up stage*). George, will you . . . (*George takes no notice*) will you . . .
GEORGE What?
HAWTREE Go with me?
GEORGE Go? No!
HAWTREE Then Miss Eccles—I mean " my lady ". (*Shaking hands and going ; as he backs away bumps against Sam and business repeated.*)

Esther makes no protest when her father is sent to Jersey, " where spirits are cheap ", with £2 a week in the hope that he will drink himself to death in a year. " I think I could," he says, " I'm sure I'll try ", and Esther plays a sentimental tune on the piano. It is an astonishing reversal of the old stage tradition that the ties between heroine and father were sacred.

6 Detective Stories

The Ticket-of-Leave Man

WERE " the detective police " left out of it, this chronicle would be smoother. Unhappily there is no ignoring them. While slowly fixing their grip on popular imagination, they inspired one or two of the most memorable of melodramas. The inexorable spread of an epidemic which rages yet, must be traced in detail. It started long ago. " The sordid and mechanical occupation of a blood-hunter " is mentioned by Godwin in " Caleb Williams ", and if a very early instance of the deductive method is wanted there is the explanation given by Herodotus of mysterious thefts from what is now technically known as a " sealed room ". There is also Voltaire's Zadig. When asked if he had seen a runaway horse, he answered, " One with a small hoof, a tail three feet and a half long, a bit made of gold and shoes of silver? " He had not seen it but reconstructed it from clues.

No matter how many such facts go to prove that the detective story is of ancient origin, Edgar Allan Poe deserves the credit for shaping it. He was a child of the stage. Two players who came with a company to Boston brought him into the world and soon afterwards died. He was adopted, reared in comfort, and educated at the University of Virginia. Even then he led a wild life until his marriage to his cousin, little more than a child.

The control he was exercising over his turbulent nature expressed itself in fiction which he labelled " semi-scientific " because it was dispassionate. In a civilization hag-ridden by melodrama, the players' child, in between youthful excesses and the final debauch caused by heartbreak over the death of his wife, discovered how to escape from the welter of sentimental emotionalism. Four distinct mechanisms tick round in his tales. " The Murders in the Rue Morgue " is the first murder puzzle. " The Mystery of Marie Roget " is the first example of straightforward crime detection. " The Gold Bug " is the model cryptogram. " The Purloined Letter " sign-posts Secret Service. These were potent to excite public curiosity. Yet so slothful is popular imagination that the effect told only upon generations to come.

CUP AND SAUCER COMEDY

and XI *Caste* (Prince of Wales's, 1867): John Hare as Sam Gerridge, and Marie Wilton (later Mrs. Bancroft) as Polly Eccles

I *Caste* (Prince of Wales's, 1867): Squire Bancroft as Captain Hawtree

XIII *School* (Prince of Wales's, 1869): John Hare as Beau Farintosh

XIV   Henry Neville as Bob Brierley

XV   Miss Raynham as Sam Willoughby and Ly● Foote as May Edwards

THE TICKET-OF-LEAVE MAN (Olympic, 1863)

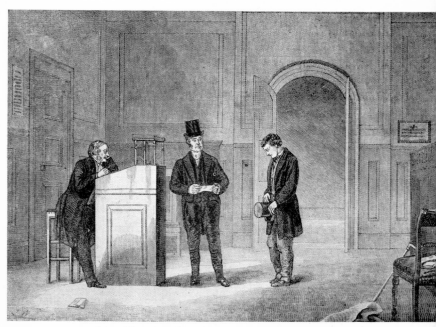

XVI   The returned convict is dismissed from his employment

XVII Olympic, 1871: *The Woman in White*. A new type of villain

XVIII Adelphi, 1867: *No Thoroughfare*. The hero comes back to life

XIX   Mr. and Mrs. Kendal as Dora and Captain Beauclerc

XX   W. H. Kendal and John Clayton as the brothers Beauclerc

DIPLOMACY (Prince of Wales's, 1878)

XXI   Mrs. Bancroft as the Comtesse Zicka, engaged in espionage

While the significance of Poe's " Tales of the Grotesque and Arabesque " had yet to be understood, blundering attempts were being
made to let imagination function in the way he had pointed out. Very
vaguely all mystery-mongers were striving to get away from sexual
morality. Unable though they were to manage without heroines and
villains, they did contrive an unreality where vice meant a desire to
wallow in gore without any ulterior motive. In the previous age
Walpole, Mrs. Radcliffe and " Monk " Lewis had been blindly groping
their way towards the idea which William Dean Howells, the American
novelist, laid down as a new law in his statement that there is something
about murder, " some inherent grace of refinement perhaps ", that
makes its actual representation upon the stage more tolerable than the
most diffident suggestion of adultery. The ideal was realized in the
barn-stormers' stand-by, *Ada The Betrayed*, whose heroine is desired by
the villains purely as one more victim of their sledge-hammer,
butcher's cleaver, assassin's stiletto and arson.

The trouble was, of course, that murder had so often been merely
part of the drama of adultery. Poe changed all that by being " semi-
scientific ". He created the character who has all Hamlet's avidity to
get at the truth without any of Hamlet's feelings in the matter. Of
course the type was not entirely without literary pedigree. There are
Dogberry and Verges, who become sleuths when they eavesdrop.
Next there is the thief-taker, Jonathan Wild, despicable felon who yet
had power to arrest Jack Sheppard in the King's name. Fielding's
novel, the greatest memorial ever raised to a nark, offended Scott because it was a picture of vice, unrelieved by anything of human feeling
and " never, by any accident even, deviating into virtue ". Fielding's
way of seeing things as they were, instead of as they ought to be, would
not do.

When falsely-accused innocence became the most frequently used
plot in all fiction, the Majesty of the Law was respected. Real life
created the scene for playwrights to copy when Corder was arrested for
the murder of Maria Marten in the Red Barn. He had, as Douglas
Jerrold expounded in *Wives By Advertisement ; or, Courting In The
Newspapers* at the Coburg in 1828, found a spinster with money, married her, and lived happily until an officer belonging to Lambeth Street
police-office, London, entered his house. According to this witness's
evidence in court, the prisoner came out of the parlour into the hall in a
hurried manner, said, " Sir, walk into the drawing-room ", submitted
to search, and was taken to the Red Lion at Brentford. Such reports
as the one from which this has been taken were serious rivals of the
Penny Dreadful. The plain-clothes officer belonging to a police-office

was thus a familiar figure to readers before he was known to authors. He had to come and go in reports of fact as ghosts came and went in tales of imagination. The discovery of bodies was made by laymen and the apportioning of blame was the business of coroners upon whom the duty of crime-detection devolved. Since coroners could call upon bystanders to overpower suspects, the police of fiction merged among such background characters as ushers, warders, lawyers and chaplains until news came from abroad concerning " the disreputable calling of a police spy "—another Jonathan Wild.

François Eugène Vidocq,[1] who was born at Arras on 23 July, 1775, and died in Paris past the age of eighty, was the first. He began as a soldier. He was next a thief and as such went to prison. He turned thief-taker and rose so rapidly in his new profession by jugging his old friends, that when a detective force was formed he became the head of it, not so much because of his skill as a sleuth as because of his lack of virtue as a nark. At fifty he retired to run a private detective agency which was closed by the police—temporarily. More important still he wrote his memoirs. These were used by Jerrold at the Surrey in 1829 for *Vidocq, The French Police Spy*. Lord Lytton sketched the portrait of a French police chief, under the name of Favare, in " Night and Morning ", and in Brougham's version, acted at Wallack's Theatre, the type makes his appearance on the stage—unpropitiously. In this play Favare boasts, before putting on mechanic's clothes and a patch over one eye, " Although this fellow has seen me often, I defy him to detect me when I change my outward appearance ". In the coiner's den he is at once unmasked.

There is not so much crime detection here as in *Presumptive Evidence ; or, Murder Will Out* at the Adelphi in 1828. It was based by Buckstone on " Card Drawing ", one of Gerald Griffin's " Tales of the Munster Festivals ", in which a sailor's Trafalgar medal becomes incriminating evidence. His clothes are borrowed by a rogue as a disguise while committing burglary, the medal is left beside the body of the man he murders, and only a last-minute confession saves the sailor's life. There was something so satisfying in the spectacle of villainy's overthrow by remorse that no greater ingenuity was needed, as *The Golden Farmer ; or, The Last Crime* made clear at five of the minor theatres in 1833. Ben Webster, the author, took for his hero a real highwayman who, at his corn-chandler's shop in Thames Street, inspected by day the purses he would cut by night. While varying robbery with a little burglary he is caught red-handed and adjures his assistant, " Oh, if you did but

[1] Since this was written a new biography of Vidocq has appeared in English, written by Philip John Stead.

Vidocq, The French Police Spy
(Surrey Theatre, 1829)

know the heartfelt pleasure of good deeds compared with evil ones,
how soon you'd relinquish your bad courses." When the highwayman is being pursued Webster borrows an episode from Scott that
would reappear in the historical dramas of Dumas and in Wild West
plays about Davy Crockett. When the officers arrive, the wife of the
Golden Farmer tries to close the shutters against them. "Ha!" she
says, "the bar's removed! How to fasten it?—Nothing can save him!
Ha! Thank heaven for the thought!" (Pushes her arm through the
staple).

Hue-and-cry was still the best way authors knew of representing the
approach of doom. Reporters could do better. When the inquest was
held on the body of Maria Marten her step-mother's evidence was, "I
dreamed once before and once after Christmas, that my daughter-in-
law was murdered, and buried in the Red Barn; hearing no tidings of
her, I became so very uneasy that I entreated my husband to make a
search, and he did so." In the "Authentic and Faithful History" of
the crime her statement begins a detective interest that increases as
medical evidence about wounds makes a damning parallel with evidence about weapons in Corder's possession. The popular vogue of
detective stories in England finds some origin here.

The next development in the making of murder-mysteries was the
clue.[1] This can be traced to a French drama, *Une Cause Célèbre*,

[1] False clues, like the handkerchief in *Othello*, were well known; and proofs of
royal birth, like those in *The Winter's Tale*, might be called clues, but though
there was no novelty in the thing itself the use it was put to was different.

The Dumb Man of Manchester (Astley's, 1837)

brought to Astley's in 1837 as Rayner's *The Factory Assassin; or, The Dumb Boy Of Manchester*, with Andrew Ducrow in the title-part—later, because he was middle-aged, it became *The Dumb Man Of Manchester*. Though he delighted his friends with the inelegance of his speech, he thrilled the public with the elegance of his postures, and his sufferings when the poor mute is falsely accused and then found guilty of murder, were heart-rending. But the plot turns on the perspicacity of a lawyer named Palmerston, who has a hunch that the crime at Manchester resembles a crime newly reported from Dieppe, where the victim grasped a locket, snatched from the murderer's neck in the death struggle, containing the portrait of a woman. On his return the lawyer hands the locket to the judge, at the same time producing a witness—a woman who borrowed a tell-tale ladder on the night in question—whereupon the judge exclaims, " What do I see? This woman, this portrait! 'Tis the same person." And her husband is at once found guilty of both murders. That was technically well ahead of its time. In *Susan Hopley ; or, The Vicissitudes Of A Servant Girl*, Dibdin Pitt's domestic drama at the Old Vic in 1841, the heroine reveals that her brother's skeleton is behind the wainscotting, clutching the proof of his innocence in its bony hand, because she has, like Mrs. Marten, dreamed a dream.

Though the word " detect " had long been used in the sense of identifying offenders, little public interest was taken in the process. The Oxford Dictionary traces " detective " no earlier than 1843 when *Chambers's Journal* stated, " Intelligent men had been recently selected to form a body called the ' detective police ' . . . at times the detective policeman attires himself in the dress of ordinary individuals ". Ten years later they left their mark on literature with a full-length portrait in " Bleak House ". They were known as detectives by 1856. " Ferret, a detective ", appeared in the pirated version of *The Dumb Man Of Manchester* (without a line to say) ; fiction and fact were running neck-and-neck, for the amateur detective was making his presence felt in London life. The one who is celebrated in W. S. Gilbert's line, " The keen penetration of Paddington Pollaky ", arrived from the Continent in 1862.

In the May of 1863 the first " great detective " of fiction made his appearance in *The Ticket-of-Leave Man* at the Olympic. His name, " Hawkshaw ", is still proverbial in America, and was so in England until a generation ago. Old actors still " go through the motions " when they utter it. There are three movements : one is for his left hand to remove cap at the word " I ", the second is for his right hand to take off wig while pronouncing, " Hawkshaw ", and the third is for the hand with the cap in it to unfasten false whiskers while he says, " the detective ". The play is so thoroughly English that Tom Taylor can receive the credit for it even though he admitted that he took the story from *Léonard*, founded by Brisbarre and Nuz upon their own story of " Le Retour de Melun " in a series, " Les Drames de la Vie ".

When the Olympic's curtain rose on the Bellevue Tea Gardens two detectives at table were told by Hawkshaw, " Here's Old Moss. Keep an eye on him ". Moss has the beautifullest lot of Bank of England

Susan Hopley, or The Vicissitudes of a Servant Girl (Victoria Theatre, 1841)

flimsies that ever came out of Birmingham. Tiger, his partner, plants them on Bob Brierly, a fuddled Lancashire lad who has just found in May Edwards, a starving street-singer, the girl he wants as his partner for life. Hawkshaw, the cutest in the force, cannot catch the Tiger, but he has the poor innocent Bob sentenced to three years at Portland; all of which is so well arranged that an audience believes not only in the policeman's skill but also in his kindness of heart. On ticket-of-leave Bob becomes a clerk in a bill-broking office, where he is recognized by Hawkshaw, who keeps silent, and by Moss, who gets the ticket-of-leave man discharged. As a navigator (a labourer at work on the navigation canals was so called before the word was shortened to navvy) Bob comes to the Bridgewater Arms for supper. He discovers a plot to burgle the bill-broking office and scribbles a note of warning. "But", he asks himself aloud, "who'll take it?" A drunken navvy, who has been reading the note over his shoulder, declares, "I will". Bob, astonished, says "You?" Hawkshaw says, "I" (pulls off his rough cap, wig and whiskers, and speaks in his own voice), "Hawkshaw, the detective!" In the last scene, a churchyard, there is a fight, and Hawkshaw is saved from being strangled on a tomb by the sudden arrival of the low comedian.

The Olympic won by a short head. Two months later Hazlewood's *The Detective*, from the same French original, opened at the Victoria. Taylor, who always feared that managers might employ hacks to do their stealing for them, accepted £150 as payment outright for this masterpiece among melodramas. At the Olympic Henry Neville carried off the honours as Bob Brierly; at Wood's Museum, Chicago, Frank E. Aiken made a stir in the same part; and in New York five versions were acted in English and one in German—*Der Mann Mit Dem Freischein*—with *The Ticket-of-Leave Woman* to follow. Emily St. Evremonde, the heroine's friend who sings the sensation scene of "The Maniac's Tear" at the Bridgewater Arms, was the part that won the hearts of New York. Both in England and America Hawkshaw did not run away with the play until years later on tour and then no leading man would accept Bob Brierly. In 1863, when leading gentlemen gladly played Bob Brierly, the detective was left to players of lesser note, and that these did not make their names in the part shows that audiences were still under the spell of falsely-accused innocence.

Propaganda had not had time to invest the word "detective" with romance. Dickens, with the eye of a trained journalist, was the first in England to see some of its possibilities. Some of his short stories and sketches were about them, and his tale of a pair of white gloves, in particular, deserved to become a classic. But the next appearances of detectives on the stage made it clear that Hawkshaw was not considered worth imitating. They are decidedly penny plain, even when efficient. In *Black Sheep* (Olympic, 1868) Tatlow speaks confidently of setting his men after a fugitive. They will telegraph to all the ports, send to all the stations, and catch him if he tries to leave London by train. Tatlow makes inquiries and watches diligently, but the mystery is solved not through any ingenuity. Considering how up to date the criminals are in this play, its authors must have been blind to the possibilities of police work when they used portraits in lockets as the means of discovering the truth. Crime detection was ridiculed in *Time And The Hour* by Palgrave Simpson and Felix Dale (H. C. Merivale) at the Queen's, Long Acre, in the June of 1868, for Sparrow, a clerk who wishes to be a detective, cannot see evidence thrust under his nose. A Scotland Yard detective who is mentioned never appears.

The influence of *The Ticket-of-Leave Man* can be seen in the Prevention of Crimes Act of 1871, which limited the power of the police over convicts out on licence. How Bob Brierly set a fashion was evident in 1868, when C. H. Stephenson's *The Convict* was played at the Pavilion and Henry Neville's *The Convict* at the Royal Amphitheatre, Liverpool. Henceforward convicts were always sure of public sympathy.

7 Murder Puzzles

The Mystery Of A Hansom Cab

LORD BYRON was the first to write a murder mystery for the English stage. His claim, though overlooked in many industrious attempts to trace the beginnings of detective fiction, cannot be disputed. His tragedy of *Werner*, begun in 1815 and published in 1822, presents the now familiar " Sealed Room " where somebody is done to death, nobody knows by whom, while suspicion falls heavily upon the innocent Gabor and one of two others :

> No bolt
> Is forced; no violence can be detected
> Save on his body . . .
> I took upon myself the care
> Of mustering the police.

But though first in the field he cannot be credited with originality. His drama, according to the preface, was taken entirely from the " German's Tale, Kruitzner ", published many years before in " Lee's Canterbury Tales ". Byron adds that these were " written (I believe) by two sisters, of whom one furnished only this story and another " ; he adopted the " characters, plan and even the language, of many parts ".

The next murder mystery that I have traced was a drama written by Franz Grillparzer, Vienna's leading dramatist. He was born in 1791 and spent most of his eighty-odd years in the Austrian civil service. *Sappho*, and a trilogy of *The Golden Fleece*, were among the many poetic dramas he wrote that were destined to be headaches for Austrian schoolgirls of the future. But it is his first play, *Die Ahnfrau*, staged in 1817, which the outside world welcomed most. As *The Ancestress ; or, The Doom Of Barostein*, it was acted at the City of London Theatre in 1837, and as *The Ancestress* it was written by Mark Lemon for the English Opera House in 1840. In New York the manager of the Old Bowery turned it into *The Ancestress ; or, The Ghost Of Destiny* in 1863 as a medium for Pepper's Ghost.

By now Poe's tales were being avidly read in Paris. Under their influence the indefatigable and resourceful Dennery (in collaboration) took Grillparzer's play in 1863 and changed it into *L'Aïeule*. Tom Taylor seized this and called it *The Hidden Hand*. This, designed on " who done it? " lines, was staged at the Olympic in 1864 (a date worth noting for not so very long afterwards both Dickens and Wilkie Collins were making criminological mysteries). The ancestress of the German and French titles has become Lady Griffydd, living in Dinas Arvon, feudal castle in Carnarvonshire, during the reign of James II. She is also known as the Grey Lady of Porth Vernon. Her daughter, now dead, was Lady Penarvon, whose child, Enid, must marry Caerleon. Enid's step-mother, the new Lady Penarvon, cherishes a secret passion for Caerleon and he loves her own daughter, Muriel. Meanwhile Madoc, the shepherd, prowls around swearing that his mission in life is to anticipate the dowager's every wish. When Muriel suffers from arsenic poisoning there are thus three suspects. Lady Griffydd is ruled out because she is, through paralysis of her legs, unable to move. But when suspicion is removed in Act II from Lady Penarvon and from Madoc early in Act III, the final disclosure may be foreseen. Taylor's title already belonged to a popular American feuilleton; when his play went to New York in the May of 1865—at the Winter Garden Mrs. J. W. Wallack played Lady Griffydd—it was called *The Grey Lady Of Penarvon* and it lasted a fortnight.

In " East Lynne " the sub-plot is a mystery—secret consultations between Lady Isabel's husband and the suspect's sister cause the jealousy which begins the tale. Mrs. Henry Wood published the novel in 1861; the next year she brought out " Mrs. Halliburton's Troubles ", where she introduces mystery into her main plot when the hero, suspected of having killed his brother, cannot clear himself because he was, at the moment of the crime, secretly closeted with a Quakeress. The identity of the actual murderer is not disclosed until the end; it is, therefore, a genuine detective story in the pioneer class. What the public thought of it is shown by these figures : while " East Lynne " sold 860 thousand " Mrs Halliburton's Troubles " came third in her list with 235 thousand. Other authors were pleased to copy, but while they merely dabbled in crime, Emile Gaboriau,[1] though not such an innovator as he has hitherto been held to be, settled down in Paris to make of it a regular trade. He began in 1866 with " L'Affaire Lerouge " just at the time when the craze appealed to Dickens and Wilkie Collins. Together they wrote *No Thoroughfare*, a melodrama of embezzlement and attempted murder, staged at the Adelphi in 1867. The plot consists of crime, some attempt to conceal the identity of the criminal, and a

[1] This was his real name, even though it does so aptly recall Gabor in Byron's murder-mystery, *Werner*.

E

little weak detection, though these strands are obscured by the unconscious resolve of each author to tell a separate story.   In the Dickensian
prologue, foundlings drink real soup while an agonized mother,
heavily draped in black, tries secretly to discover which one of them is
her secret son.   When Act I begins at the wine-merchant's the audience
has to understand how the wrong foundling has, by the strangest of
coincidences, made Vendale, the genuine foundling, his partner.   Pay-
ments for champagne have gone astray and Vendale must cross the Alps
in order to link Dickens' story with Wilkie Collins' thriller, which
begins at a Swiss inn where Obenreizer, whose ward Vendale loves,
drugs him and tries to steal his papers.   On an Alpine precipice Vendale, drugged again, falls into the abyss and is rescued; here a snow-
storm created the effect of a sensation drama and there was a run of 151
nights with Webster as a cellar-man for comic relief from Fechter's
grim Obenreizer.   At Mrs. F. B. Conway's Park Theatre, Brooklyn,
on 6 January, 1868, *No Thoroughfare*—minus foundlings—was produced by Louis Lequel, who noted, " If two St. Bernard dogs can be
obtained and used, the effect would be greatly enhanced; they should
carry cloths and a canteen, as in pictures ".

Immediately after this Wilkie Collins brought out the detective story
that became a classic of its type—" The Moonstone ".   This novel may
be unique as a tale of a crime committed by somebody who is entirely
unaware of his guilt, and it certainly belongs to that very small minority
of crime mysteries which are about theft, not murder, but the case
Sergeant Cuff has to tackle has complications since copied a thousand-
fold.   The great yellow diamond, prised from the forehead of the God
of the Moon at the siege of Seringapatam, is sought by its priests.   They
are obviously suspect—proof of innocence to modern readers but not
to those of 1868.   There is a tin case hidden by an eccentric housemaid,
and an opium addict who is thought guilty even by the woman he
loves; the moonstone goes back to the idol.   Thus the detective-story
established its definite form in the years when Dickens, despite failing
health on his last American tour, was writing " The Mystery of Edwin
Drood ".   After his death in 1870 the Surrey finished it for him.   *The
Mystery Of Edwin Drood*, by W. Stephens, was acted there in 1871.
The Britannia followed suit the next year with a version by G. H.
Macdermott, *lion comique* of the halls.

On the stage the idea persisted that audiences must not be mystified.
The principle was enunciated in 1871, when Wilkie Collins dramatized
his novel, " The Woman in White ".   As a book it was tinged with
Gothic mystery—a usurping baronet who forges an entry in a church
marriage-register, a woman who escapes from the lunatic asylum

where he has imprisoned her, and Count Fosco's secret society, which assassinates members who betray its trust. The reader was kept guessing but not the audience. A critic (Dutton Cook) agreed with the change, since while it is allowable to perplex and mystify a reader to almost any extent, " it is found advisable to enlighten a spectator concerning the secrets of a plot at the earliest possible opportunity ". This argument was soon proved to be wrong-headed. When " The Moonstone " at last became a play, at the Olympic in 1877, it was rendered meaningless by all-open-and-above-board treatment. There was nothing for the audience to look forward to, once it had been kept too well-informed, apart from the pleasure of hailing, in the fat and genial Count Fosco, a new type of villain.

To make matters worse, another crime play, in the same district of London that selfsame season, clearly demonstrated the effectiveness of the " who-done-it? " treatment. For Paul Meritt had written an admirable example of the detective-drama; it had been brought out at Edinburgh in 1876 and was now, a year later, with a change of title from *Grace Royal* to *The Golden Plough*, at the Adelphi. One title referred to a hostelry in the eighteenth century and the other to its hostess, and the reason the story had to be put in costume is because her morals—not as good as they ought to be—had to be viewed with a more tolerant eye than could be bestowed upon a character in modern dress. Sir Francis Claude had once been her lover and the Rev. Martin Preston, a schoolmaster with long fair hair, is their son; he wishes to marry the niece and heiress of Sir Francis, who answers, " I will make it impossible for her to marry without losing everything ", and is next found dying from a knife-wound as a figure with long fair hair escapes. Martin declares that he is guilty solely to prove that he is no coward— he has been taunted—but after his arrest, his mother sees a man with long fair hair at large. Who it is might surprise any audience.

With a novel called " The Leavenworth Case " in 1878—seen as a play at the Theatre Royal, Halifax, seven years later—Anna Katherine Green set herself up as a writer of crime mysteries. Her novel of 1883 was the first to be labelled " A Detective Story ". The most popular was Fergus Hume's " The Mystery of a Hansom Cab ", published in Melbourne in 1886, before it broke all English records as a best-seller. The dramatized version at the Princess's in 1888 gave the plot away, and what was left after the puzzle had been removed, barely lived up to its label of " Sensational Drama " despite character tags on the programme. Cabman No. 1,104 of Melbourne (whose licence is as untarnished as his harness) is hailed by a young man who leaves a corpse inside his cab. Policeman X 43 (the servant's friend, the burglar's foe) is baffled, but a detective discovers that the young man was visiting a dying woman, first wife of the heroine's father, whose existence proves the second marriage to be a bigamous one and the heroine illegitimate. The murder has been committed by " the canker which insidiously eats its way into the heart of society " in order to seize the dying woman's marriage lines for blackmail.

There was a fresh development in 1887. In " Study in Scarlet ", a tale by Conan Doyle, there appeared a detective of compelling interest to people without any desire to solve problems of crime. Poe's influence on Doyle was noticeable in mysteries of the sealed-room kind, in murders committed by zoological means and in the reading of cryptograms. But all such ingenuity was appreciated afresh because it exhibited the personality of Sherlock Holmes.

8   Secret Service

Diplomacy

WHAT Vidocq was to the detective police Fouché was to the secret police. Secret Service, since it means crime without the criminal, makes a distinct appeal, for here sympathy is for the law-breaker; a sergeant strict in his arrest becomes the representative not of law and order but of evil. Fouché, that merciless agent of the Terror whose cold-blooded, scientific zeal for probing into secrets won him the post of Minister of Police, was trusted by nobody and respected by everybody. Whoever ruled France was his master. Robespierre, Napoleon, Napoleon's conquerors, and Louis XVIII in turn were ready to employ him : they knew he was unscrupulous, they knew he was faithless, they knew he was expert, they knew he would serve their purpose as long as it served his own. Fiction could invent nothing so inhuman. It could merely make use of his name.

He had been dead not many years when Melesville and Duveyrier used him as a character on the stage. Their play became *Secret Service*, an after-piece in two acts by Planché at Drury Lane in 1834. Miss Murray, who was the heroine, went with it to the Walnut Street Theatre, Philadelphia, after which it took its place in stock throughout the United States. The title then signified secret police. "How questionable", runs the introduction to the American edition, "it appears to the American patriot whether such a system is at all necessary for the good of nations or individuals." It denounces the extraordinary ability of " the contemptible informer ", Desaunais, and the false friend, Fouché, and consigns them " to the infamy they have so justly earned ". Nothing of this occurs in the " beautiful drama " itself. Fouché is a faithful friend to Michel Perrin, who has been turned out of his curacy and is lodging with his niece and her betrothed, Bernard. The moment the Minister hears that his old tutor is in want, a post is created with no other duties than dining out. Desaunais, misunderstanding the situation, asks Perrin for news of what he has seen and heard, and by chance the answers incriminate Bernard. A plot to assassinate Napoleon is disclosed and the ringleader arrested. Perrin asks the prisoner whether there is none to fear for him, " No kindred—no mother?" The prisoner breaks down, the curé frees him, the conspiracy is cancelled, and Perrin flings down his wages of shame after Fouché has apologized for causing a respectable man to be branded as an agent. From this detective *malgré lui* some prejudice against police spies may be assumed. But the story is of interest chiefly because of the use to which it puts a scrap of paper—a list of names passed unknowingly from hand to hand until at last it comes under the eye of Desaunais. Although an incriminating letter had often been dropped by guilty lovers at the feet of the last person on earth they would wish to read it, the list in *Secret Service* begins the tornado of political documents, plans of fortifications, blue-prints of inventions, sealed orders and rough drafts of international treaties, to be lost, stolen or mislaid, sold, traced or photographed, for ever.

In Philadelphia, in the years when Planché's *Secret Service* was played at the Walnut Street and Arch Street Theatres, Poe was writing his " Tales of the Arabesque and the Grotesque " for the *Gentleman's Magazine*, of which he was assistant editor. Possibly a hint from that play set him thinking of " The Purloined Letter ", which in turn has often been held responsible for all the stealing and concealing of private papers for years to come upon the stage. When the evidence is examined *Secret Service* is the more open to blame. It inspired *Plot And Passion*, by Tom Taylor and J. Lang at the Olympic in 1853, where secret papers stolen from a hollow walking-stick cause Fouché's downfall at the hands of a female spy who has fallen in love with her intended victim. Here is the father of several plots that would make the name of Sardou famous in years to come. Robson, an astonishing little genius who usually acted in burlesque and sang comic songs, was Desmarets of the Secret Police.

When his first play was hissed at the Odeon in 1854 Victorien Sardou was in his early twenties. He went back to journalism and planned, according to Brander Matthews' account, " a series of semi-scientific tales after the manner of Poe's ". Six years later, when he was in such demand in the theatres that his plays were presented at the rate of one every three months, he is supposed to have been prompted by " The Purloined Letter " to construct *Les Pattes De Mouche*. Here the letter is hidden by a lover under a statuette, where it is found, not by his mistress, but by his enemy. It is used for lighting a cigar and thrown half-burnt out of a window, where an entomologist picks it up to wrap a little beetle in. Another lover snatches it to scribble a hasty note upon. Who should receive it but the husband of the first woman? But he reads the second message, not the first. The idea that a compromising

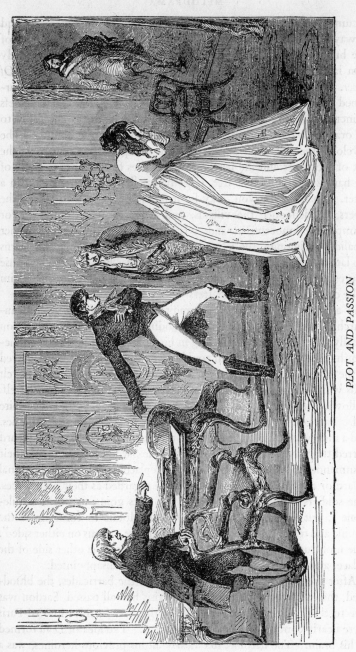

PLOT AND PASSION

Olympic, 1853 : Desmarets of the secret police denounces Madame de Fontanges to her lover in the presence of Fouché

document should, after a note has been scribbled on the other side, find its way into the last hands meant for it, will be found in the text not of Poe but of Planché, yet nobody noticed this when Sardou's comedy won lasting popularity on the English-speaking stage as *A Scrap Of Paper*. Not only in that play but also in others he made use of purloined letters in a way that " hand properties ", from lost handkerchiefs to incriminating daggers, had never been used before. The reply to his oration at the Academy spoke of his way with the letter. " The envelope, the seal, the wax, the postage-stamp and the postmark, the tint of the paper and the perfume which rises from it, not to speak of the handwriting, close or free, large or small—how many things in a letter, as handled by you, may be irrefutable evidence to betray the lovers, to denounce the villains, and to warn the jealous ! " For example, the innocent Fernande writes to the marquis the story of her squalid upbringing ; the letter is intercepted, and the marquis learns too late that marriage to her has " dishonoured " him. In " Playhouse Impressions " Walkley calls this trick Sardou's one indefeasible claim to be considered " a man of letters ".

In accordance with the stage tradition of Paris (ever since Beaumarchais invented Figaro as the embodiment of democracy), Sardou usually expressed political feelings in his plays. Throughout the nineteenth century no Frenchman could escape political fever, and he lived in the midst of it. A brief sketch of his career by Blanche Roosevelt ends with her translation of " How I Took the Tuileries ", by himself. Following the surrender of Napoleon III at Sedan, the Second Empire fell. Part of every French revolution was an attack on the Tuileries, and a mob was advancing to keep up the custom. The Imperial Guard barred the way. With a friend at his side Sardou set out to ask their commander to withdraw his troops and replace them with the National Guard or the Mobiles, whom the people regarded as their own forces. The soldiers from a distance saw " two ants going to storm a milestone ", but those two caused the Garde Mobile to come up at the double and form " a large passage with a hedge of guns on either side ". The mob rushed straight through, found itself on the other side of the palace, and walked off pitifully, astonished and disappointed.

After the siege of Paris, the Insurrection, the barricades, the bloodshed, the executions and the political crisis had all passed, Sardou was free to think of Secret Police. When the new fortifications of Paris were nearly complete there was a spy scare. The idea of *Dora* formed in his brain. The heroine, like nearly all his previous heroines, was a fresh, engaging, charming girl. Secret papers entrusted to her betrothed have been read—a perfume tells by whom—a personal matter

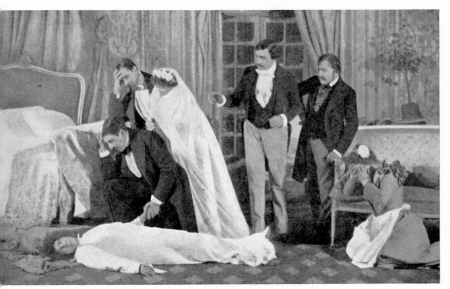

XXII   *The Lady of the Camellias:* The ghost of Marguerite consoles the mourning Armand

THE DIVINE SARAH

XXIII   *Theodora* (Paris, 1884)

XXIV *La Tosca* (Paris, 1887): Sarah Bernhardt

XXV *La Tosca* (Garrick, 1889): Mrs. Bernard Beere

HEROINES, FRENCH AND ENGLISH

XXVI *Fedora* (Haymarket, 1886): Mrs. Bernard Beere

XXVII *Adrienne Lecouvreur* (Paris, 1880): Sarah Bernhardt

VIII *Lost in London* (Adelphi, 1867): Adelaide Neilson as Nelly Armroyd

XXIX *Lost in London*: J. L. Toole as Benjamin Blinker

WAIFS AND STRAYS

X *Jo* (Globe, 1876): Jennie Lee as the crossing-sweeper

XXXI *Two Little Vagabonds* (Princess's, 1896): Sydney Fairbrother as Wally

XXXII *TWO ORPHANS*

Olympic, 1874 : 1. Helena Ernstone as Henriette. 2. William Rignold as Jacques. 3. Mrs. Charles V
as Countess de Linière. 4. Henry Neville as Pierre. 5. Mrs. Huntley as La Frochard. 6. Emily Fo
as Louise

upon which hang the destinies of nations.   There are no combats, no
prisons, no escapes, no encounters in the style of Dumas—nothing but
a paper-chase by well-bred people in what were known as surroundings
of ease and refinement.

In short, it is Drawing-Room Drama.   But it is still more emphatically Secret Service.   Clement Scott, who watched the play in Paris in
the company of Bancroft and B. C. Stephenson, saw "Constanti-
nople" in letters of fire.   There was always a Near Eastern problem,
there was always the Great Bear, and the three eagerly set to work.
On the English stage the title, *Dora*, had already been taken for a
popular idyll by Reade out of Tennyson, so their adaptation of Sardou
became *Diplomacy*, acted by the Bancrofts at the Prince of Wales's in
1878 and that same year by other notable companies, at the Haymarket, in the provinces and in America, with many revivals for half a
century.   The cup-and-saucer had had its day.   It was now the day
of the document.

What an astonishing change came over Sardou in mid-career may be
gathered from Brander Matthews' account of his work up to 1882.
Writing at that date this critic could agree with the playwright's boast
that his great respect for woman was evident in the way he had imbued
his female characters with common sense as well as tenderness and self-
sacrifice.   When "French Dramatists of the Nineteenth Century"
was printing, Sarah Bernhardt had brought to a close a long tour of
England and America with *Adrienne Lecouvreur*, *Froufrou* and *La Dame
Aux Camélias* ;   and when the book was being published Sardou had
begun to write plays for her—as he would continue to do until past the
age of three-score years and ten.   Whatever she might demand in the
way of tenderness and self-sacrifice there could be no denying that she
wanted nothing so cold-blooded as common sense.   Sardou had to
throw nearly everything overboard—everything except plots which
ticked round with clockwork made out of Secret Service.   Here is the
one link between the confiding and engaging *ingénue* who was for him
the old love, and the revived *femme fatale* who was the new.

After her return to Paris, Bernhardt appeared at the Vaudeville in the
December of 1882 in Sardou's *Fedora*, as a Russian princess.   When
her fiancé is killed she swears revenge upon Ipanoff, the Nihilist, who is
blamed.   In Paris, while luring her victim into falling in love with her,
she falls in love with him, but neither can escape the shadow of the
Secret Police.   "Sardoodledom" was Bernard Shaw's word for it.
Every man to his taste, every critic to his own objections.   When
Outram Tristram's *The Red Lamp*, at the Comedy in 1887, told the
story of a Russian princess who signals to anarchists in order to save

her brother from betrayal to the Secret Police, the comment of those who held that playwrights should always be told not to, was, " Nihilism is a subject that it would be perhaps best to leave alone ".

Though the decline and fall of the Roman Empire was too early a period for Secret Service to be mentioned direct, Sardou easily imagined such activities as typical of Byzantium and with this as his formula wrote *Theodora* for Bernhardt at the Porte-Saint-Martin in 1884. The empress, mocking the police, tells the emperor that an attempt is being made on his life. Conspirators steal into the palace that night. The one who is caught calls out, " Andreas ", the name of Theodora's lover. She holds the door to stop Andreas from entering. The captive, fearing torture, asks for death at her hands, and declares he will shout the name of his companion unless she grants the request. She holds one hand over his mouth as she pierces his heart with a gold pin from her hair. Unwittingly she causes the death of Andreas and then yields herself to execution.

Sardou's most thrilling play, *La Tosca*, was also his most effective example of Secret Service; and its villain, Scarpia, the Fouché of the Court of Naples, has become a by-word for ruthless extortion of confessions. When it was staged at the Porte-Saint-Martin in 1887, and at the Lyceum, London, the following year, Bernhardt appeared as Floria Tosca, a prima donna engaged to sing at an entertainment prepared prematurely to celebrate the supposed victory of Marengo. When later news tells of defeat and the festivities end, she is happy at having to stay no longer. But Baron Scarpia, at whose side she had been sitting, now follows her and captures her lover, Mario Cavaradossi, who knows the hiding-place of a political fugitive. While Floria Tosca beats her hands impotently against the door, she hears Mario's cries as the Luke's Iron Crown on his head contracts. She tears her hair, writhes on the floor and shrieks, then stands mute, motionless, paralysed. She kills Scarpia, lays him out on the floor with candles at his head and feet, and throws herself from the battlements because even in death he has been too clever for her.

Frequent charges of plagiarism were brought against Sardou. After winning every case which came into court he published " Mes Plagiarists ". He was safe in the quarter where he was most guilty, for (like the majority of successful authors) he stole from himself, by which is meant that he borrowed situations that had proved effective in his current play for use in his next. Shaw indicated the resemblance between the plots by naming them, as a collection, *Toscadora*. All those tigresses who kill and get killed for love were but a wardrobe for that lithe, shadowy—" an empty cab drove up and Bernhardt stepped out "—feline, coiled to spring with the heart-throb in the cry of her golden voice. Any number of actresses tried to wear the tiger-skin. All are forgotten. La Tosca remains because Puccini in 1900 made a gift of her to prime donne everlastingly.

Contrasts between common-or-garden crime and gilded murder disclose the secret places of the nineteenth-century heart. The duller industrialization became, the livelier glowed the mirage of blood-and-thunder to the strains of grand opera, but even glamour set to music was not equal to Bernhardt's unaccompanied. The dream of passion that is an integral part of hidebound propriety became tangible in her before the eyes of rows upon rows of the sober-minded. Through her performances the respectable playgoer could commit the splendid sin by proxy. Whenever Bernhardt killed and died for love in the slightly varied series Sardou supplied for her, audiences of timid souls found rest from their vain longings. Whole-hearted worship was given in the 1880s to this actress they called " divine " because her rages were Satanic. With the sudden cleavage of public opinion that was soon to set anti-romantics and romantics at each others' throats, the intellectual critics stopped their ears against the Siren. She outlived their denials and bewitched another generation—but not with Sardou.

9 Modern Life

Lost In London

WHY was a mirage so unreal as melodrama always merging into realism? The paradox flourished in Dickens' novels, where starving children, workhouses, debtors' prisons and all the murk of Victorian London were the fabric of romance. In the general scheme brigands had withdrawn in favour of convicts, and hussars in favour of detectives; there were prisons in the place of dungeons, and instead of the castle in flames there was the sinking ship or the oncoming express. Modern life was henceforth the favourite setting for melodrama.

This persistent desire to approach actuality nearer and ever nearer may be discerned in a score of plays. At the start of Victoria's reign that sturdy veteran, Fitzball, was tampering with modernity. In 1843 he brought out, at the Adelphi, the drama of *Mary Melvyn ; or, A Marriage Of Interest*. Her lover, believed dead, arrives during a party in " A Magnificent Apartment in Warley Castle ", and this is what they have to say to one another :

MARY (*recoiling*) Ah! touch me not—they told me you were lost, dead—touch me not, Frank, I am a wife!
FRANK Wife! Mary! Mary!
MARY Pardon—I die.

But she refrains. Amid thunder her husband soliloquizes, " Rage on—rage on—ye furious elements! Lend me your deadliest thunder, to avenge my wrongs—your fiercest lightnings, to direct my steps! Revenge! Revenge! " The storm breaks out afresh in the last scene, when Melvyn, tracking his wife to a solitary cottage, is shot by an assassin he hired to shoot Frank.

While Fitzball was declining—he died at the age of eighty-one in 1873—much of his play was purloined by Watts Phillips, as whose work it was presented at the Adelphi in 1867, under the title of *Maud's Peril*. It takes an original turn when the lover enters the house of the heroine the moment after a burglar has stabbed her husband, who then deliberately causes the innocent intruder to be charged with the crime. At the trial there is every prospect of a verdict of guilty, but the burglar's extortionate claims for blackmail cause the husband, on the point of death from a heart attack, to confess. There were many plays in this category. *Too Late To Save ; or, Doomed To Die*, long popular on tour in Great Britain and America, began at Exeter in 1861. T. A. Palmer, its author, wrote for the provinces and was seldom heard of in town.

The threat to chastity that had, in the drama of castles and brigands, sprung from *force majeure* or royal prerogative, became more sinister when produced by means—"ample means", said the Victorian punsters—of finance. For an outstanding example of this there was, also at the Adelphi in 1867, Watts Phillips' much-postponed *Lost In London*. That handsome young actor, Neville, played Job, a miner, and Adelaide Neilson, his wife, Nelly, who is abducted by a wealthy man of leisure, Gilbert. The news is brought down to the workings of Bleakmore Mine; Job, ascending in the basket, stands erect while all the miners uncover, and he points upwards. In an elaborate mass of built-up scenery Gilbert's "The Ferns", Regent's Park, is seen amid other villas in varied perspective, gleaming white in a "great snow effect". Windows and distant gas-lamps are lighted as broughams and "all the minor outdoor details which accompany the giving of a grand evening party" animate a handsome portico that has large practical doors. A lantern-bearer stands by the steps as visitors pass into the house. Snow falls more thickly. Lively dance-music strikes up and shadows pass across the blinds. Job sinks on the steps under the lantern. Indoors all exclaim :

Bright champagne !   bright champagne !   bright champagne !
Bright champagne !   bright champagne !   bright champagne !

before Signora Simondi's song leads to the chorus of "Tra ! la ! la ! Tra ! la ! la ! Laugh ! Laugh ! ha ! ha ! ha ! " Into this glittering scene Job forces his way. "What does he want?" The throng suddenly divides as Nelly, brilliant in diamonds and lace, utters a wild cry and covers her face with her hands. Job tells them, "My wife !" and takes her home. In the last scene their poor cottage's wide window gives an extensive view of a sunset over London. As Nelly dies the City is bright with moonbeams. The author adds the note, "It is required that the silvery light of the moon should fall suddenly upon the figure of Nelly, flooding it as with a glory". Job raises one hand to heaven. "I shall find her *there*," he says, "though lost in London." Her death seems directly due to public demand. For a hundred years or more, dramatic critics had preached that nothing but death should come of a woman's lapse from virtue, and *Lost In London* obeyed this ordinance in defiance of the law of the land and the practice of medicine. The fate of the character compares curiously with the fate of the actress. Like that heroine, Adelaide Neilson came from the industrialized North. In a village near Bradford she had been known as Lizzie Bland—too well known, for her mother had been seduced by a handsome Spaniard and the child never escaped from gossips who had heard about it. This, even more than hard labour in a factory, drove her to run away to London, where she had no other lodging than a place on a bench in the Park, until pushed off by an old woman who claimed it as hers. Lizzie was rescued by an officer of the Carabineers. Putting her trust in a male who was (to her Yorkshire way of thinking) more like a young lady, she climbed into his cab and walked up wide stairs to his chambers. Life became pure nursery tale. He was a very young Heavy Dragoon; other subalterns, let into the secret, came to see his protegée and find her a place on the stage.

As soon as she had learnt to walk and talk at the Theatre Royal, Margate, she returned to town—an exquisite fifteen, with steadfast eyes that suggested assurance until you saw the depth in them. Her friends, almost in awe of her now, took the Royalty (which lent itself to amateur stars) and there she played Juliet. Nothing came of it, but a face of such ethereal quality was destined for fame—until a parson's son carried her off as his sixteen-year-old bride to minister to the sick and teach in a Sunday school miles from anywhere. She forsook that rustic happiness three years later to play in *Lost In London*, before she went with her husband to New York. She left him in order to win triumphs at Old Drury. Her beauty, likened by Ellen Terry to the ripeness of a pomegranate, for some fleeting years dazzled the stage. She took a holiday in Paris. One day she stopped in the Bois de Boulogne at a café to recover from pain; and as was not uncommon when little was known of surgery, she died suddenly in great agony. That was in 1880; her age was thirty-two.

Where Watts Phillips took his ideas from is evident when a backward glance is given to the Surrey. The title of *The Flower Girl; or, The Convict Marquis*, played there in 1858 and 1867, tells its own tale. Its author, T. Townsend, was responsible in 1860 for *Ralph Gaston; or, The Three Lives*, whose fashionable villain not only seduces a girl and leaves her to perish after the birth of her child, but also bears false witness against Gaston, her brother, to have him transported. A Surrey drama of 1864, *The Orange Girl*, by Henry Leslie and some lesser Nicholas Rowe, had a sensational climax by the Black Tarn, a flat piece

Mary Warner (Haymarket, 1869): Kate Bateman as
the convict

of practicable ice amid rocks beside a Druidical rocking-stone and pines,
out of compliment to which the title was soon changed to *The Frozen
Pool*. Sir Peregrine and Uriah lure Jenny across the ice until she
reaches a hole and falls in. "The bells fire for the New Year and we
are safe", Uriah boasts as she drowns. Then the moon, bursting out,
reveals the figure of Mrs. Fryer on the eminence near the rocking-
stone :

Mrs. F. No! Ruined, Uriah! Body and soul, ruined. (*Mrs.
Fryer tears at the practicable branch of the tree and screams*) "Murder,
Jenny," etc. (*All this as quick as lightning till climax.*)

Uriah Swift as thought, the gun! (*he seizes the gun from Sir Peregrine,
and fires*).

Mrs. F. (*having torn away the branch, places it under the rocking-stone,
using it as a kind of lever*) Useless, Uriah—my life is charmed
against your bullet. Oh, Heaven, give me a giant's strength.
Help! murder! Help! (*simultaneously with his reaching her, the
rocking-stone totters and slides off, cracking the whole of the ice—crash.
Mrs. Fryer leaps in after it*).

URIAH Too late! We must fly, or we are lost!—Two travellers have heard the screams—the report of the gun—and are coming as fast as their steeds can bear them (*rapidly descending*). Quick, Sir Peregrine; quick!

SIR P. Mercy of Heaven! Look there! (*the face of Mrs. Fryer is seen above the ice*).

MRS. F. My head above the ice! My hand close woven in her hair! Murder! Help! (*with her other hand alternately clinging to, and endeavouring to break the ice*).

URIAH Rouse, man! and away!

MRS. F. (*getting Jenny's head above the ice*) At last! At last! Thank heaven! (*she seizes the crowbar which Uriah has left upon the ice, and breaks her way towards shore*). Arms round my neck, Jenny! Cling to me, darling! Cling to me! (*Mrs. Fryer reaches the land, and drags Jenny out of the water in a fainting state.*)

Such evidence proves that Surreyside drama in the 1860s was like Adelphi drama, only better. Plays of the prisoners' van, once indigenous to the Surreyside, had taken root and thriven in the theatres of fashion. Again and again the "mirror had been held up to circumstantial evidence", crime had been shown its own features, delirium tremens its own image, and the detective policeman had been reflected (vain assumption) "in every variety of type".

Even the Haymarket, hitherto "distinguished for representations of a more refined class", was seized in 1869 with an attack of dramatic jail-fever. This was because Tom Taylor had written for Miss Bateman his realistic and sensational drama of *Mary Warner*. George, her husband, is charged with theft when missing banknotes are found in his possession. To save him she makes a false confession. Each believes the other guilty. When he visits her in prison they bicker. After her release she sinks very low in the social scale indeed. She is charged with "accosting" a gentleman who turns out to be, in the police-court, none other than George (a fine legal point for any magistrate). Meanwhile alcohol has rendered the real thief's constitution so pervious to virtue that he convinces George and Mary Warner of each other's innocence.

"More than the ordinary regard for realism of effect" meant vast steam-engines in full operation, the interior of Brixton prison, a squalid alley in Lambeth lit with real gas-lamps, a grimy interior "commanding the usual fine view of the illuminated clock tower at Westminster", a police-court with prisoners' dock, witness-box, constables, spectators and presiding magistrate all complete. No pains had been spared to impart vividness and reality to the play down to the "most repulsive particulars"—significant Victorianese.

Realism was usually called revolting. It is not easy to understand why people who deliberately went to have their feelings harrowed, afterwards complained bitterly in terms of "too". Perhaps they regarded the experience as necessary—rather like a visit to the dentist. Yet in fairness it must be reported that they found unalloyed delight in mild forms of realism, such delight that they paid the opera price of half-a-guinea a stall to see real bread and butter cut and spread; in fact they were as responsive to realism in pleasure as in disgust. Robert Buchanan observed how audiences thrilled with joy at the sound of the postman's knock, or the muffin bell, and rejoiced when they saw an actor, dressed like a real gentleman, open a real umbrella or smoke a real cigar. In the scene of a park at dusk, when the chairs for visitors were gathered together and put away by a boy in buttons, the scene was "recognized at once with delight, but the great point was the appearance of the *real boy* who after his real work was done, repeated it on the stage nightly".

To see the park on the stage was pleasant. To see the police-court was not. The very playgoers who insisted on seeing life's seamy side at the footlights knew that it was too grim for make-believe. Yet they did, during the period of national prosperity, flock as readily to dramas of crime as to cup-and-saucer comedies. They had the outlook which made puritans acquire a thorough-going acquaintance with the scandals of night-life.

On the other hand, flourishing trade did create a very natural optimism. Philanthropy promised a better land. Following the example of George Peabody, an American merchant who gave money and houses to the London poor, the City Corporation built a lodging-house for the poor; international and industrial exhibitions opened; slums were cleared to make way for new thoroughfares, railways, hospitals, embankments, viaducts and approaches to new bridges. Faith in Progress was shocked when disclosures were made that paupers were dying in workhouses through neglect. Strikes became frequent and unemployment increased until there was no ignoring the distress of the East End. There were also the bank failures of 1866 to bring poverty nearer home. But more and more exhibitions, and various associations for reforming and preventing, showed the general feeling of hopefulness in the most fashionable part of Town. What the most unfashionable part felt could find melodramatic expression because it had theatres of its own, vast in size, distinctive in character, not dependent on others for plays and players like the earlier theatres of the East.

F

The Britannia, under Mrs. Sara Lane, had for playwright-in-ordinary C. H. Hazlewood, whose plays ran into hundreds. His *Jessy Vere ; or, The Return Of The Wanderer* in 1856 had a baronet who secretly marries a vicar's daughter and finds her a bar to his social success; that was an old story but the sentiments were up to date. Jacob Thorne, a poor but honest labourer, asks, " Does not nature bless us with bounteous harvest, and flocks and herds in plenty? But man—greedy, grasping man—stands like a fiend between the food of life and his fellow creatures." The Hon. Arthur Fanshawe, heir to a baronetcy, joins in the man-hunt when Jacob is falsely accused :

JESSY   What has the man done?
ARTHUR (*slightly intoxicated*) 'Pon my life I don't know—something, I suppose, or if he has not, it's of no consequence; he's a poor half-starved devil, and such people are fit for nothing else than to afford folks like us a little amusement.

Yet the most popular dramatist was Shakespeare, " for the proper representation of whose works many talented performers are engaged ". This was also true of the Standard, Shoreditch, the Britannia's neighbour. As both places were rebuilt to house crowds of 3,000 a night the popularity of their performances, Shakespeare or melodrama, is manifest. John Douglass, who began as a pantomime child at Covent Garden, managed theatres at Gravesend and Chelsea while becoming one of the most popular of Jolly Jack Tars. In the 1860s he managed both the Standard and the Pavilion, Whitechapel.

" From Mayhew's cyclopædic work " was the strange derivation of an afterpiece, *London Labour And London Poor ; or, Want And Vice*, at the Whitechapel Pavilion in 1860. It was a local drama of real life with scenes of thieves' kitchens, station-houses and boozing kens. A wife is persecuted by a roué, cornet in the Guards; her husband is tempted to crime by the cadger chief. " It is questionable how far it is provident to rivet the attention of an uneducated audience by a vivid representation of the social aspects of the outcasts of society ", was a critic's judgment.

XXXIII   On the road to London

THE LIGHTS O' LONDON (Princess's, 1881)

XXXIV   The Canal, Regent's Park

"By reason of the elaborate changes of scenery to be effected, the indulgence of the audience is requested during the intervals between the Acts" (*vide* the programme)

DRINK AND DEGRADATION

XXXV   *The Lights o' London* (Princess's, 1881) : Mary Eastlake as Bess and
Wilson Barrett as Harold Armitage

XXXVI   *Drink* (Princess's, 1879) : Charles Warner as Coupeau

10   Brutal Realism

The Lights O' London

THERE can be no doubt that more and more realism was what the mid-Victorian public wanted.   It moved Dickens to describe in " Our Mutual Friend " Rogue Riderhood's trade in drowned bodies.   It sent the people who had gushed over the cutting of real bread and butter at the Prince of Wales's to gasp over the behaviour of stage crowds " picked from the streets " at the Princess's.   It became such an obsession with Charles Reade that he garnered hard facts until his study was a store of press-cuttings, carefully indexed, to ensure that every novel or play he wrote should be " real ".   Who then could object?   This public thronged to hangings until public executions were abolished in 1865.   Refined, cultured people went to inspect lunatic asylums in the same way that they went to Madame Tussaud's.   Nothing short of Jack-the-Ripper seemed able to make them shudder.   They could witness slum life in Tottenham Street and Newcastle Street unmoved, but the mere spectacle of a make-believe hospital ward was intolerably " gruesome " and a make-believe prison caused hysterics among strong-minded males.   Inside theatres there were protests.   Outside there were crowds eager to prod money through the pigeon-hole of the box-office.   To blame critics as hypocrites would be too easy a way out; they were like everybody else—unable to accept enjoyment as such.   Wholesome plays exercised a man's better nature.   Unwholesome plays exercised his excessively active righteous indignation, and a man liked, without knowing it, nothing better.   Nodding acquaintance with all the chapters written by Dickens about the seamy side of life would set young authors on the road to fortune.   Facts taken fresh from newspapers would be too realistic—though what " too " means is problematical, since such questions as " for whom? " or " for what? " are never anticipated.

When Reade wrote *Gold* for Drury Lane in 1853 he had acquired a well-documented knowledge of the mining fever in Australia.   When he acquired a still more extensive knowledge of penal servitude in England, he used the same plot for his novel, " It's Never Too Late to

Mend ", with chapters to serve as an exposure of the way prisons were run. Next he presented the old play with this new title and a brand-new prison scene in 1865 at the Princess's. No one could miss his faith in realism now. In Act I the farm boasted " all the details of Agricultural Life—The Farm Yard, Wall and Gate—The Straw Yard—The Duck Pond—The Barn—The Barley Mow—Pigeons, Ducks, Poultry, Animals, etc. etc." And in Act II the Model Prison, labelled " Abandon hope all ye who enter here ", exposed " the new system—Solitude—Silence and Starvation, represented by the Gaoler—two old systems—the Law and the Gospel, represented by the Chaplain—Despair and Death of Josephs under the new system—reformation by Robinson under the old system—Despair is the soul's worst enemy—' My last word to you, and perhaps my last word to you in this world, is, It's never too late to mend '."

Part of this meticulous care in representing actuality consisted of casting a lovely young actress for the boy, Josephs, who is kept at the tread-mill until he dies. The result was that a critic rose in his seat during this scene and loudly protested against its " brutal realism ". On the same spot some dozen years before, " Un-English " had been shouted at the French duel in *The Corsican Brothers*. At the Queen's, Long Acre, in 1871, Tom Taylor got into similar trouble for burning the beautiful Mrs. Rousby at the stake in his *Joan Of Arc*, though this time history was largely to blame. And yet, with all this susceptibility, combined with all this rigid attention to detail, the Princess's brought out a programme to mark a revival of Reade's drama in 1879 which read *It's Never Too Late To Mend* Gentlemen's and Youths' Clothing.

The death of another youthful victim of law and order was a more enduring theatrical sensation when *Bleak House* was at last firmly set upon the stage. To modern eyes there may be a resemblance between Oliver Twist and Jo. Yet a sharp line of social history divides them. One came with the blessings of a public already in favour of befriending outcasts. The other's welcome was chilled by suspicion towards any-one in rags. Nebulous horror evoked by the mere mention of socialism, with its " damning desire to shirk work ", caused a damming of the sentimental tear—except, of course, in working-class districts, for " Bleak House " had been dramatized in 1853 at the Marylebone, City of London and Pavilion. When Mr. Peabody's philanthropy eloquently expressed what an American thought of London slums, public opinion was shamed into a reversal of feeling. This was the general cause of sympathy for Jo; the particular was Jennie Lee. Her father, an artist, died while she was young and she walked on in the tights of *opéra bouffe* at the Lyceum. In the next piece, *Le Petit Faust*,

It's Never Too Late to Mend (Princess's, 1865) : The Australian Goldfields

she won a word or two of praise for the way she plied, in silken rags, her besom as a crossing-sweeper. She became a favourite of Strand burlesque, especially as Jack Sheppard, and then went to New York. At San Francisco she married J. P. Burnett, actor-playwright, whose aim in life was to write a piece exactly suited to her. She saw herself as Dickens' pathetic little crossing-sweeper.

So far *Bleak House* had taken rank on the American stage merely as one of the lesser works of Brougham, who had seen it as a vehicle for himself as Turveydrop. At the California Theatre the story became *Jo*. It was a success. Husband and wife came to England in the November of 1875 and acted his play as *Bleak House* at the Prince of Wales's, Liverpool. That Christmas Jennie Lee spent at the Surrey. In the February of 1867 she leased the Globe in the Drury Lane slums, and there *Jo* triumphed. The hoarse voice, the slouching, dejected gait, and the furtiveness of some hunted animal were acclaimed as " realism difficult to surpass " and yet not " too ", however illogical this may seem now.

The initial run of over a hundred performances gives an inadequate idea of Jennie Lee's success. With another supporting company, mostly changed although the author was still " Inspector Buckett of the Detectives " and Kate Lee still Guster, she started another run the next year, and from then on there would be no slackening in the demand. Nor would there be any slackening of the attempts at imitation, beginning in 1876 with *Bleak House* at the Pavilion, Eliza Thorne's *Bleak House ; or, Poor Jo* at Sheffield, and *Joe The Waif* at Greenwich. The next five or six years would produce *Jo The Waif; or, The Mystery Of Chesny Wold* at the Liverpool Rotunda, and James Mortimer's *Move On ; or, The Crossing Sweep* at the Fulham Grand. Burnett wrote *Midge* as a successor, but the public wanted *Jo* and nothing but *Jo* as far as this particular Jennie Lee (there was then another Jennie Lee on the stage) was concerned. She toured first the provinces, then Australia, Africa, India and China, with greater triumphs than ever awaiting her at Drury Lane.

More helpful feelings towards waifs and strays might reasonably be ascribed to one actress. There must still be taken into account a similar influence over a still greater public by the irrepressible Dennery. With another collaborator in 1874 he wrote for the Porte-Saint-Martin *Les Deux Orphelines*, which for blood and thunder was the best version of the Babes in the Wood ever acted. It is a melodrama of the eighteenth century in Paris, with view of the Seine, bureau of the minister of police, and cells in the Salpêtrière all complete. From the frou frou of silk and satin, the clatter of glasses and laughter, during a midsummer night's fête in a *petite maison au bel-air*, the scene changes to deep winter in the *parvis* of Saint-Sulpice. The evil Marquis de Presles has robbed Louise of her inheritance. Now she begs in the snow on the church steps. But she has faithful friends. Both Henriette, the other orphan who is her constant companion, and Pierre Frochard, the crippled knife-grinder, are resolved to protect her. When the helpless girls are sent to the Salpêtrière, Pierre discovers that his brother, the wild, burly ruffian Jacques, holds the power of life and death over Louise. In the garret of La Frochard (their horrific mother) villain and hero draw their knives for the finest duel in the whole struggle of virtue against vice. Nobody protested.

That September Oxenford brought out *Two Orphans* at the Olympic. In the October Paul Meritt and George Conquest put on *The Blind Sister* at the Grecian Theatre; in the November the East London followed with *The Blind Girl's Fortune*. What *Jo* was to one actress *The Two Orphans* was to pairs of actresses by dozens. In New York a version " specially adapted " for the Union Square Theatre (which Jennie Lee had just left on her way to meet fate) ran from the December of 1874 to the following June. Kate Claxton, the blind orphan,

The Two Orphans (Olympic, 1874) : Rignold and Neville setting a new standard for
realism in stage fights

bought the rights and toured the play until Hollywood turned it into
a tale of the Revolution, *Orphans Of The Storm*, and film-fans thought
the play " left out something ".

In Europe its popularity was not so constant, for its place was
usurped by the work of authors who came under its influence. That
scene in the garret, for example, was the making of one London playwright, G. R. Sims, who had another kind of fame, widespread among
people who knew nothing of his writings beyond his signature, as the
unintentional abolitionist of antimacassars. Though old people may
be bored by the statement, young people are frankly shocked to learn
that these protected upholstery from macassar oil on the flowing
manes of young Victorian lions. The nuisance was abated by a new
hair-restorer bearing the portrait of G. R. Sims. Infants who learned
to lisp his name before they heard of Shakespeare would always
associate him with shelves of bottles rather than shelves of books. Yet
he undoubtedly deserves honourable mention for his share in what
embittered critics called " the exposition of the gospel of rags ". It is
usually supposed that the task was handed down to him by Dickens,
for Ruskin's share has been overlooked. Something more tangible was
borrowed from *The Two Orphans* by the two dramas that made (in
this branch of human endeavour) Sims' name.

The first was *The Lights O' London* at the Princess's in 1881. In this,
trouble begins when Harold Armytage and Bess keep their marriage

secret. Old Armytage, suspecting seduction because the girl is his lodge-keeper's daughter, disinherits his son. Clifford, a nephew, becomes the heir at Armytage Hall, where he seduces the daughter of another retainer, Seth Preene. There is robbery with violence and Harold is the victim of circumstantial evidence. He is sentenced to hard labour but escapes. While hunted by the police he is given shelter in a showman's caravan until he finds his wife. They become outcasts, vagabonds of the casual wards. One evening in Regent's Park, when the " real " boy from the real Park has removed the chairs, they wander to " the Slips ". There the villainous nephew, angry at being asked to marry the girl he has ruined, happens at the moment to be throwing her father over the bridge into the canal. Harold dives to the rescue and Seth Preene swears, " You have saved my life. I will save yours."

The scene of the Borough on Saturday night exposes, " the dirt and degradation of London life, where drunkenness, debauchery and depravity are shown in all their naked hideousness ". The escaped convict is hiding in a garret, where he is found by his cousin. There is a deadly fight but it is interrupted by the police. Harold crawls along a roof, drops to the street below, and struggles among a yelling crowd until overwhelmed at last. When the scene changes swiftly to a police-station, with the same crowd surging outside, Seth Preene is there to confess how he and the villainous nephew were guilty of the robbery.

At the Princess's in 1882, Sims' *The Romany Rye*, founded on his own novel, "Rogues and Vagabonds", was pronounced " bad and mischievous ". From a fancier's shop full of real birds and real rabbits, the villain tried to abduct the screaming heroine. After her wedding a ship bore her away while the bridegroom was decoyed into Ratcliffe Highway in order to be " bashed " by hired murderers—the Thames was then well-stocked with " bashed bodies " through undetected crimes—who dragged him to a slimy cellar. There they bound him to a hook in a wall while an old hag (who reminded everybody of La Frochard) prepared to hocus him with a sleeping draught. But as he resembled her long-lost son, she let him merely pretend to be drugged before the scene changed to a beautiful picture of the moonlit Thames. The boat put out. He knocked out the bashers, reached the ship just as it was sinking, hacked his way through spars and shrouds, and swam with his bride to a lifeboat.

Late Victorianism showed at its best in Sims. His friendliness, his frankness, his air of well-being, made him the most popular of journalists. " Early in the 'eighties ", his autobiography mentions, " I

The Romany Rye (Princess's, 1882): with Wilson Barrett as Jack Hearne and Mary
Eastlake as Gertie Heckett

wrote a series of special articles—'Horrible London'." Plain records
give them a place in the history of London as the cause of " much
excitement " to improve matters. For a dozen years his pen was engaged on the business of pleasure until chance brought it back to a play
about waifs and strays—*Les Deux Gosses*, by Pierre Decourcelle, whose

faithful representation of a hospital ward was a triumph for realism at
the Ambigu in the February of 1896. Sims and Shirley went at once
to see it, wrote their English version which they called a "new and
original melodrama" partly because it left out the hospital—too
daring an idea even for Sims—and staged it at the Princess's on 21 May
as *The Two Boys* for a single copyright performance. When thrown
open to the public in the September it had the irresistible title of *The
Two Little Vagabonds*. At the start there is a matrimonial quarrel. In
the bitterness of his heart George Thornton apprentices his infant son,
Dick, to a burglar. But the boy devotes his time to caring for a sickly
companion, Wally, who goes home with him when the Thorntons
make it up; and now Dick's peculiar education comes in useful, for
he rescues his father from a blackmailer's den by helping him through a
skylight. On their way home they cross a canal by the lock and open
the sluice-gates; their pursuer, close upon them, misses his foothold
and is drowned. After that nothing remains except the death-bed
scene of Wally for the sake of tidying things up. It sounds just the
kind of play to make *East Lynne* more popular than ever, but this is
reckoning without current faith in the virtue of slumming. *Two
Little Vagabonds* ran for the better part of a year, and was revived after
two or three months. It was still more popular on tour.

There was profit in realism, no matter how the term was interpreted.
The real live rabbit gave pleasure; so did the unreal death of the actress
pretending to be a boy on the stage-carpenter's tread-mill. What did
these two have in common? Costume dramas were still flourishing
(and Shakespeare was popular when the real live rabbit appeared in the
Forest of Arden) despite the strong liking for modern dress. Hence
it was not romance that was out of favour. Playgoers were striving to
break away from melodrama. The more they tried the more they
sank, for realism was accentuating villainy and heroism. With a
prodigious effort virtue was, in fashionable theatres, bidden not to
triumph. But it did so still, by clear implication, because all that could
be set up in its place was a warning that the wages of sin is death. This
new and rather depressing kind of melodrama enabled people to feel
they were keeping abreast of the times—to them it was real. Yet
each attempt to bring imagination nearer to actuality caused angry
alarm. Zola never stepped beyond the bounds of melodrama. "The
wages of sin is death" is all he had to say. But in saying it he demonstrated that the unspeakable was speakable. Vizetelly, who translated
his novels, went to prison for giving it voice in England.

In *Thérèse Raquin* Zola offered Paris a masterpiece of the 1870s' brand
of realism. There is an old woman who becomes helpless and speech-

less on discovering that her son has been killed by her daughter-in-law, Thérèse, with a lover's aid. While the murderers attempt to enjoy the freedom and possessions their crime has brought them, she fixes them with a glare of implacable hate that changes to gloating over their misery. When this play, the classic of its period, failed in his own country, Zola expressed what he thought of the stage in criticism and essays. He wrote no more plays and he disowned *L'Assommoir*, dramatized from his novel by Busnach and Gastineau, which was played at the Ambigu in 1879. Sala went there, intending to be disgusted in print. On the way he stopped at an actual *assommoir* and found it rather worse than Zola's; since he published lurid details that were not in the novel, he was plainly of the same mind as the novelist. Self-deception was infinitely preferable to admitting that. A good word must not be said for Zola, but a bad word had to be said for the play, however much the public might like it. Sala " sat out " several scenes—the squalid garret with the abandonment of Gervaise by Lautier, the laundry with the " abominable fight " between Gervaise and Virginie, the Boulevard de la Chapelle with the blacksmith's speech about temperance, the restaurant garden with the double-wedding feast of Gervaise-Coupeau and Virginie-Poisson, the street with the fall of Coupeau from a roof, the grand dinner on Gervaise's saint's day, and the *assommoir* itself. The sordid characters on the stage had been drinking and smoking and gobbling for three mortal hours and a half. Everybody had changed his or her shabby garments three or four times over. To Sala it was a masquerade of rags. " I dare say that it was all very realistic; but so is Seven Dials on a Saturday night. Seven times had the curtain descended. . . . I was told that there was a beautiful scene coming of a padded room at a hospital, where the alcoholized Coupeau, in the saltatory stage of delirium tremens, dances himself to death. I thought I would not wait for the discovery of the remains of Gervaise in the hole under the staircase, and ' quite green '; so I went to bed."

To yawn would always be the best way out of the difficulty. Sala, whose bottle-scarred nose hung out like an inn-sign proclaiming good fare within, was more inclined to be shocked by the apostrophe in favour of temperance than by alcoholized antics, but he had to write for a public which regarded itself as a child playing with fire and chiding itself. All who read " L'Assommoir " discussed it as " too "—and hastened to the Princess's when Charles Reade's version, *Drink*, began its run there in 1879 of 222—this, the actual figure, is not meant as a pun—performances. There had been modifications to appease the censor, but still the trump card was a display of delirium tremens.

Charles Warner, recently seen as Robinson in a revival of *It's Never Too Late To Mend*, was Coupeau, and he won fervent praise for his acting in this scene. Since the sternest puritans were forced to admire it, there might seem no reasonable complaint against either Zola or the playwrights for having provided the actor with his opportunity.

Consistency was no obstacle. " What moral end is to be gained by the spectacle of two passionate women drenching each other with buckets of water, or of a man dying of delirium tremens, when these spectacles are merely the illusions of the stage, we confess ourselves unable to comprehend," was a pronouncement that ended, " Such subjects have no place in the legitimate province of art ". This view must not be called old-fashioned. It was new-fashioned by the standard of playgoers who admired O. Smith in a similar display. In *The London Stage*, Barton Baker says that in " one of the old dramas, I believe it was *Peter Bell* ", he played the part of a drunkard, and in one scene he had to upset a cup of liquor. With a cry of horror he cast himself upon the stage and ravenously licked up the spilled drink. Had it been weakly done it would have raised a laugh ; the way he did it sent a shudder through the house.

Similarly Warner now, in the words of another critic, " sent a sensible thrill of horror through the crowded and excited audience ". His voice, looks and gestures were " horribly realistic "—the unsteady walk, the thin yet bloated face, the wandering eyes, the lean, live fingers that clutch at nothingness and are never quiet. When his eager wife goes out, Coupeau is left alone with the supposed claret which Virginie has sent in. With trembling hands he unwraps the bottle and takes out the cork. Then a spasm of horrible delight thrills him as he finds it is brandy. He crouches at the other end of the room, putting all the space possible from table to wall between himself and the tempter. The doctors say it will kill him, " but then, doctors tell such lies ". He will just taste it. With gleaming eyes and convulsive fingers, he approaches the table and seizes the bottle. When his wife comes back it is empty and he dies raving.

Feelings were still more violently outraged by " Nana ", which Zola published in 1880 and which he assisted Busnach to dramatize a year later. Public modesty had recovered from the affronts put upon it by Dumas *fils*, whose daughter-of-shame had, at least, been repentant. This new one was as unblushing as Shakespeare's Bianca in *Othello*. There was an outcry, of course, because Nana was not in historical dress, and the only English adaptation to be granted the Lord Chamberlain's licence was a curious hybrid between Zola's novel and *La Dame Aux Camélias*. It was by a Mrs. Kennion, who called her work *Nina ;*

or, The Story Of A Heart and tried it upon Wigan before bringing it to the Strand in 1887. For the first time the demand for seemliness had to be taken seriously. *Nana* would stay under the ban until too old-fashioned to interest playgoers. (In time it would be filmed, but by then Zola's world would have shrivelled into printer's ink and paper.)

11

Drawing-Room Drama

Jim The Penman

SINCE it was the Bancrofts who brought the atmosphere of the drawing-room into the theatre, their cup-and-saucer comedies may be confused with the drama named after so peaceful a place. But while they were chiefly concerned with bringing its furbishings into the auditorium, the term " Drawing-Room Drama " refers to what occurs on the stage. It is the kind of melodrama on which the curtain does not rise until deeds of blood and violence are past—until, that is, the characters are living in well-bred retirement, surrounded by outward and visible signs of respectability, and so far removed from the sensational occurrences which have set the plot in motion that their gestures, movements, language, and manner are controlled by polite restraint. Here, then, is that retrospective method of telling a story which created such a fuss when employed by famous dramatists, but the " Drawing-Room Drama " is of more importance for another development. Special attention must be paid to its vogue in the 1880s because it modified the public's moral attitude. The change may appear technical if baldly stated, but when its effect on the susceptibility of middle-aged men in beards or waxed moustaches is noted, it reveals itself as far more revolutionary than most theatrical fashions of the day.

All that it amounted to was that criminals, while not unsympathetically treated even though in modern dress, could occupy the limelight instead of being execrated in minor positions. Twenty years earlier the Mathews' sponsorship of *Black Sheep* had been treated as the temporary lapse of usually reliable people, but the objective attitude to dishonesty shown in that play was now to become the mode. Since it follows so hard upon " Nana ", the influence of Zola may be seen in this, for people who are at first obstinate over small things do become more tractable after being rudely shaken by big things. Those old susceptibles had been shocked, and it had done them a power of good. Henceforward anything the drawing-room drama might do while maintaining an air of ease and refinement would be tolerated.

FIRE AND BRIMSTONE

XXXVII (*above*) *Jim The Penman* (Haymarket, 1886): E. S. Willard, who succeeded Arthur Dacre, as the forger

XXXVIII (*right*) *Captain Swift* (Haymarket, 1888): Beerbohm Tree as Wilding

XXXIX (*below*) *The Still Alarm* (Princess's, 1888)

XL *The World* (Drury Lane, 1880) : Ultra-sensational

FACING FEARFUL ODDS

XLI *A Run of Luck* (Drury Lane, 1886): (*L. to R.*) E. W. Gardiner, William Rignold, Harry Nichol
Sophie Eyre, Alma Murray, and J. G. Grahame

The next black sheep in Savile Row clothing would be positively welcomed.

So Sir Charles Young perceived. As men of title were rare in the theatre he had been overwhelmed with good advice directly he turned playwright. One manager wanted him to steal Wagner's plots, and another told him, belatedly, that he must provide a sensation scene. When he wrote his last play, the year before his death, he pleased himself. The title of this drama, staged at the Haymarket in 1886, was the nickname of a notorious social pest—James Townsend Saward, a barrister who was transported in 1857 for cheque forgeries which menaced the "entire mercantile community". The real names of contemporaries were ruled out by the censorship, but *Jim The Penman* was allowed to stay and the drawing-room drama, with Lady Monckton as leading lady, came into its own. Compared with this "romance of modern society" *Diplomacy* is rough house. The sole breach of good manners occurs when Captain Redwood, left alone in the conservatory, pretends to fall asleep. With an assumed slothfulness which enables him to eavesdrop, he is the new type of detective which always would, according to quite a number of authors, be new. Pressure is brought upon James Ralston, an international jewel-thief who is thought to be a City gentleman of some standing, to steal the family diamonds of his future son-in-law. When he relents, his chief accomplice (Baron Hartfeld, who was played by Tree) opposes him and a fatal heart-attack saves a lot of future trouble.

Once more a stage death challenges comparison with life, for this story makes less impression than the story of its leading actor. Dr. Arthur James paid a considerable sum in 1877 for a Kensington practice. The next year he sold out, left word that he had gone abroad for his health, and vanished—to reappear in America as an actor under the name of Arthur Dacre. With very little experience but great confidence in his good looks, he came back to London as a star and was welcomed at first. But when he tried to divorce his wife he was "the object of the execrations of the virtuous gods"; his petition failed. His wife divorced him, and he married a Miss Hawkins of Lillie Road, Fulham, who made considerable headway on the stage under the name of Amy Roselle: she was tender and winsome in her acting, she adored her handsome husband, and he shared her opinion. She suited herself to her husband's engagements. So much has been written about his "inordinate vanity" and insane love of histrionics in private life, that a letter of his, concerning his part in *Jim The Penman*, may help to explain his mentality (though as eight pages are covered with his writing it cannot be quoted in full).

Dacre wants the author to go over the part with him scene by scene and sentence by sentence. Neither in this nor in what follows—the discussion of terms—is there any sign of egotism until the last lines : " I have under consideration a joint offer for my wife and myself—as soon as she is well enough—I will give you an answer soon—but if I hear to-morrow I will throw it over to play in your piece." At length Amy Roselle signed a contract with Irving for the Lyceum. She seemed likely to be restored to her place on the West End stage. Instead she became her husband's leading lady, although even the provinces welcomed them no more. They went to Australia. At Sydney they took the leading parts in a New Zealand melodrama, *The Land Of Moa*, by George Leitch, in 1895. While they were rehearsing for the next season despair overtook him. One morning, in their hotel bedroom, Dacre shot his wife, wounded himself with the next bullet and then cut his throat. When the servants broke in, he was clutching the mantelpiece and crying " Oh, the pain, the pain ", until he died.

Sensation dramas at popular houses made no pretence of being at all like events off the stage, but the drawing-room drama did insinuate that what was happening to its characters could happen to anyone. Without such attempted justification, this type of play would have been seen as merely the last scene of melodrama long drawn out, in which case an audience might well consider it had been cheated. Careers of crime were over before the curtain rose—too late for anything but repentance. A play which took the place of *Jim The Penman* at the Haymarket, with Lady Monckton again as an inwardly suffering wife and Tree as another presentable rogue, illustrated this admirably. The author was Haddon Chambers, an Australian stock-rider who arrived in London at the age of twenty determined to starve until he had made his way as a writer for the stage. After eight years of journalism he " arrived " in 1888 with *Captain Swift*. The hero is a bushranger, friendless in London until he stops a runaway hansom and is invited by its occupant to a house where the hostess *happens* to be his mother, the butler his foster-brother, and the daughter's fiancé a stock-rider he once held up in Australia. If only there had been a prologue about his birth, several scenes of bushranging, and a real runaway cab, the long arm of coincidence—the author's own phrase—would have been not only pardonable but commendable as true to the very soul of sensation. Anyhow the play succeeded because it was a drama in the latest style. The detective arrives. Captain Swift escapes. He is still clever enough to avoid arrest by following the sleuth instead of being followed. But the love of two moderately good women (his newly-found mother and an heiress he has drawn away from his half-brother) is too much for him. He shoots himself. Why? Out of respect for any respectable audience's feelings.

Captain Swift with its simplified setting might be compared with H. J. Byron's *Haunted Houses ! or, Labyrinths Of Life. A Story Of London And The Bush !* billed at the Princess's in 1872. Its scenes included a cabman's lodgings, section of the brig " Eclipse ", landscape in Australia with war dance of aborigines, and the completion of some " deadly design " in haunted houses at Penge.

12

Play Panoramic
or Ultra-Sensational

The Great City

VERY little was needed to turn realism into a game. A thrilled audience thought the property railway-engine ran true to life; a bored audience said it ran true to the nursery. While *After Dark* was at the Princess's in 1868, Watts Phillips presented the Surrey with *Land Rats And Water Rats*, whose heroine, a beautiful Covent Garden market-woman (one idea never copied [1]), was placed inert upon the track. All the thanks he got for keeping up with the fashion was a critic's comment that the jerky express was "much given to shutting itself up telescopically". Boucicault was wiser: his *Rescued* put steam loco-motion to a fresh use at the Adelphi in 1879. The villain causes a swing-bridge to open because the passengers travelling towards the gap include the infant heir to vast estates. Down stage the heroine swings on a lever in the signal-box: up stage the distant bridge closes and a toy train rattles over a toy viaduct to safety. While Boucicault thus dropped the bound-and-gagged idea and stuck to the railway, Daly dropped the railway and stuck to bound-and-gagged in his drama of 1868, *The Red Scarf*. The hero is tied to a log that bears him almost to the mill with rescue music accompanying the shriek of the circular saw—which was so good a sensation that it continued on the stage, in other plays, long after *The Red Scarf* had been forgotten.

Realism was solely in the eye of the beholder. Scenes might possess this quality one year and lose it the next, and recover it when removed to some less pernickety theatre. So much depended not on what was viewed but on how it was viewed that almost any melodramatic spectacle of contemporary life could be acclaimed as the real origin of realism on a panoramic scale. Some have given all credit to *The Great City*, written by Andrew Halliday for Drury Lane at Easter, 1867,

---

[1] This rash statement must be amended. Covent Garden Market was represented by a ballet at the Empire, Leicester Square. "Covent Garden Market", said Sir Max Beerbohm, "is not like that. Don't you wish it were?"

because its beggars, police, paupers and swells showed the " extremes of St. James's and Giles's ", on top of which a real hansom drove up to the make-believe toll-keeper's box by the canvas Waterloo Bridge, and The Railway Station realized " Frith's celebrated picture ". If all this should be considered epoch-making, it was not acclaimed as such by Drury Lane, which employed Halliday in future upon costume dramas mostly based on Scott. Nor, according to outsize playbills sold in the streets like newspapers, did the Adelphi change. In the early 1870s its stage sparkled with stars of the early 1840s. Ben Webster himself returned to the footlights during the 1873 boom in *Wandering Jews*. The Adelphi came first with one by Leopold Lewis. Webster took a leading part. His legs gave way and he sat down suddenly on the stage. Characters who had sworn never to stretch out a hand to him even if he were drowning, helped him gently to his feet. After that he decided to go on tour. In 1875 he retired finally. His farewell benefit at Drury Lane had help from all London's leading players, and 2,000 guineas was the record result. Not long afterwards he was given up for dead : " Well, sir ! I felt a queer suffocating sensation; something was over my face. I snatched away the sheet—for such it was. I was alone. But there was a light in the room. So I got out of bed, put on my dressing-gown and slippers, and went down into the parlour. There, sir, sat my friends, drinking whiskey and water—my whiskey, sir—and saying, ' Well, poor old Ben's gone at last ! ' ' Am I ? ' said I. You may guess what a turn the fellows had. But I was not going to let off the doctor, you know. We guessed he hadn't gone far. I dressed quickly; and, true enough, we found him at a neighbouring pothouse, sitting with his back to the door, and eating tripe and onions, sir, with a gin bottle by his side, quite comfortable. ' A pretty fellow you are to send me out of the world before my time ! ' I shouted. We all thought he was going off in a fit then and there, instead of me."

In the July of 1882 Webster really did die. To the last he had kept his name on the Adelphi playbills, as sole proprietor, and his ghost seemed to reign there for a few more years because of the " grand revivals " of melodramas celebrated in his day. These included *Uncle Tom's Cabin* in the same bill as a Christmas pantomime, besides a ventriloquial performance by Lieutenant Cole, whose dummy added to the language the once-prevalent catch-phrase of, " Chuck it, Cole ". Old plays were still preferred to new even though new actresses were preferred to old. Lydia Foote, whose assumed surname concealed the unseemly reality of Legge, was glamorous enough to justify a revival of *Lost In London*. There was masculine glamour to match hers when

William Terriss appeared in a new version by Halliday of *Nicholas Nickleby*.

Obviously there was a temporary revolt against brutal realism. Perhaps a story of Tom Robertson's early struggles may show how this operated in an author's mind. On being shown into a nursery when a rice-pudding was on the table, he burst into tears—his own children were starving. Yet he wrote the scene of a roly-poly pudding in *Ours* without an inkling that hungry men before Sebastopol regarded food as anything but a joke. That was realism without reality. *Little Gerty, The Lamplighter's Daughter* turned this the other way round. It was adapted by George Lander from a novel, " The Lamplighter ", for the Prince of Wales's, Liverpool, in 1876. Gerty, an unwashed Cinderella unromanticized, is driven out of doors into the snow, though " The scene should not be painted as if covered with snow, as it would be out of place when it is used again in the last Act ". There is a preposterous plot with a fire at sea as its sensation. At last in " The Churchyard, as in Act I (no snow) ", the comic servant recalls how he caught gold-fever in California and there heard a confession, and so gives Gerty's father back his good name. It is about as far-fetched as a story could be, but when the child confesses to having eaten " the make-weight " [1] any audience would know there was such a thing as hunger. This, of course, was Jo's doing. Dickens at third or fourth hand was more natural than " naturalism ".

Should plays mean anything or nothing? There was no harm in meaning nothing, for excitement was valued for its own sake : scenic marvels had been more important than morals ever since Boucicault began. But what was indignantly called " the play panoramic or ultra-sensational " went further. There was a time, mourned an old-fashioned critic like a child with more cake than it could eat, when one sensation scene was sufficient for any play, but now one was needed for each act. The lament deserves its place in the history of grumbling.

As one more glimpse of realism, *The Still Alarm* by Joseph Arthur, an American drama brought to the Princess's in 1889, is peculiar. From the programme it would seem that the performance was meant to demonstrate (a) the use of fire-escapes in public buildings and (b) the social welfare of firemen. " Surely ", D. L. Murray comments, " one of these cases where the title makes a play." What read like a terrify-ing hint of cataplexy, the mesmeric state 'twixt waking and sleeping caused by a sudden shock of fear, merely meant that villains had put the bell out of order.

---

[1] When loaves were sold by weight a slice of bread had to be supplied with one that was underweight.

13 " Grecian " Dramatists

New Babylon

THE comic servant of the evil land-lubber in Jerrold's *The Mutiny At The Nore* was played at the Coburg in 1830 by an actor born Oliver and christened Benjamin, who called himself Conquest. He made good the boast by gaining control of an extensive pleasure resort on the way between Sadler's Wells and the Britannia. Resolves to " elevate the masses " left many marks on London midway through the nineteenth century, and more than one such enterprise developed from the sale of strong drink. In the grounds of the Eagle Tavern an opera house was built with the name of the Grecian. From 1851 it set out to rival the Wells with Shakespeare before finding its proper level with melodrama. It was now under the Conquests.[1] Benjamin Oliver lived from 1804 to 1872; his wife, Columbine and ballet-mistress, from 1803 to 1867. George Augustus, their eldest child, was born under his father's management at the Garrick, Whitechapel, in 1837, and narrowly escaped burning with that theatre in his boyhood. After starting his stage career as a beetle he went to a school at Boulogne and sat, he used to say, on the same bench as Coquelin, whose father kept a tuck shop.

At the age of twenty George Conquest married the most promising pupil of his mother's academy for dancers. The skill he acquired from pantomime he gave fully to Shakespeare before bestowing the experience gained in both upon melodrama. Yet another source of knowledge, altogether different, was his. Ever since his schooldays he had collected French plays; he read them all and remembered them; Tom Taylor and Boucicault together had not such a comprehensive knowledge of plots from France. He was often first with the latest Paris fashion. *L'Ange De Minuit*, by Barrière and Plouvier, staged at the Ambigu on 5 March, 1861, appeared in English at the Grecian on 20 May, 1861; John Brougham's version did not reach the Princess's until

---

[1] " Conquest, the Story of a Theatrical Family ", by Frances Fleetwood, was published in 1953.

the February of 1862, following an autumn season in New York, where it had been presented at Barnum's under the same roof as a real live hippopotamus. It was the very mildest of Faust stories. A doctor is granted all his heart's desires on condition that he does not cure patients wanted by the Angel, but when either his mother or his wife must be the next victim he appeals to heaven. The double-crossed Angel, before departing, gives him her blessing.

" Grecian " drama, though it owed much to France, took its stamp from the leading author's determination to be the leading actor and from his desire to reveal one or other of his two special powers. In pantomime both came into play. In melodrama one might be enough. Either he made a phantom flight (which meant that he leapt, sprang or dived through star-traps in stage or scenery) or else he transformed himself into some surprising, unexpected, possibly unheard-of creature— on a visit to Wallack's he came a cropper while impersonating a twenty-five-foot worm. He was the most agile and inventive of actors. In the trap-door class there is *Hand And Glove ; or, Page* 13 *Of The Black Book*, by George Conquest and Paul Meritt, Grecian picture of contemporary London life in 1874. Conquest was Hand, a detective, who watches through a hole in the ceiling what his partner, Glove, is plotting with the poisonous Colonel Raven. There is a quarrel in the room below over some evidence that will prove who murdered a lady. When backs are turned, Hand harpoons the papers with a toasting-fork, reads them and puts them back. The police arrive to arrest falsely-accused innocence in another room of this cross-section. Hand " comes through ceiling " like a little god-in-the-machine and puts things right.

In his expansive moments Paul Meritt, who was of Slav ancestry, told various picturesque but discrepant stories of his origins, claiming among other things descent from the Polish national hero Jan Sobieski. He was a clerk in a carpet warehouse until stage-fever took him to the Grecian, where he stood at " Exit " in the interval with pass-out checks for playgoers who wanted to drink at the Eagle. In this way he became the local dramatist, and an object of interest up and down the City Road because of the reedy falsetto voice which issued from his enormous bulk. " In and out the Eagle " was not his habit. Food was his failing. Even when the standing of a man-about-town was his for the asking he could not resist the eating-houses where he could buy pease pudding and then walk, picking it out of its paper, down the Strand. He took his stage name during his Grecian life, when his job was to string to-gether accidents and offences, crimes and catastrophes, hero and heroine, persuasive and persuaded villains, and newly-married comics, before the time came for dialogue to suit the stage-carpenter's convenience according to whatever prison or precipice, rail-smash or shipwreck, waterfall or earthquake, heaven or hell, needed to be brought out of the scene-dock before the moths got at it. Keeping pace with energetic scene-shifters was hard work. Another stage-struck, would-be author, tall, lanky and hook-nosed, was allowed to help. Inspired by the manager's example of turning Oliver to Conquest, Metzger suggested to his new partner, " I'll be Meritt and you be Success ". But the newcomer, not liking this strong smack of the Brothers Knockabout, stuck to his own name of Henry Pettitt. There was nothing of the stage in his upbringing apart from a childhood's prank at Sadler's Wells, where he went on in a crowd and got badly knocked about through fighting too realistically. He was a writing-master before making the change in his career that led to a fortune of nearly £50,000. From a school at Camden Town he set out on his travels, first as advance agent for a circus in which he played Tybalt in *Romeo And Juliet* on horseback. As business manager of an opera company he was kept so short of funds that he stole the proprietor's Christmas goose so that the singers should not go without a Christmas dinner. Such adventures did not teach him stagecraft, nor was he born with it, since his father was a civil engineer. Yet as soon as he entered the Grecian as its treasurer, at the age of nineteen, Pettitt turned dramatist. With Meritt he wrote *British Born*, which was so full of patriotism that it was immediately bought by Belasco and presented as *American Born* in San Francisco.

When rebuilt in 1877 the Grecian was advertised as " one of the largest and most beautiful theatres in London, and capable of holding nearly 5,000 persons ". The opening piece by Conquest and Pettitt was *Bound To Succeed ; or, A Leaf From The Captain's Log Book*, a tale of Muscular Christianity (so the programmes said) from Tasmania to Tasmania Dock, with the manager as an inventive genius and his son as " a nervous gentleman ". When offered £21,000 for his theatre (by an aspiring impresario who soon parted with it at a loss to the Salvation Army), Conquest transferred to the Surrey and made that birthplace of melodrama the scene of its renaissance. The old house, keeping up its old habits, had been burned down in 1865. The new house had a proscenium of a size worthy to frame the most awful disasters the new proprietor could think of, but before his arsenal of terror-striking appliances could start production, Meritt and Pettitt had been inveigled into exploiting Grecian drama for somebody else's benefit. Drury Lane was now under the command of a young actor, Augustus Harris, son of the Augustus Harris who had staged grand opera at Her Majesty's and Covent Garden for many years. Outwardly they were unlike, for the father, long-haired and clean-shaven, suggested a German musician, while the son had the affably expansive smile of a salesman. But opera, very grand and foreign, was for both the greatest of life's glories. From this both derived their ideas of stage-management, which they bestowed upon the drama lavishly, extravagantly and sometimes deplorably.

Augustus Harris *père*, as senior manager of the Princess's in 1860, prevailed upon James Anderson, a leading tragedian of the day, to play Macbeth amid " new effects ". When Duncan was being murdered the witches exulted in a transparency high up in the castle wall; their platform gave way, all were injured and one of them died. Then Banquo's ghost appeared in a transparent pillar where the lighting set his wig on fire. Under the same management, *Les Couteaux D'Or* of Paul Féval became *The Golden Daggers* by Edmund Yates, when Fechter appeared at the Princess's in 1862. Its sensation was a duel in punts on the Thames. The pleasant picture of moonlit water represented by steel gauze was spoilt when the punts would not move an inch without dragging the metal net after them.

The younger Harris regularly produced similar effects. Sometimes there were blunders bad enough to wreck any ordinary management. But his was not ordinary. " Seldom ", states the *Dramatic Peerage* of 1892, "can one chronicle so brilliant and successful a career "—when he was at the age of forty. The dazzlement began only twelve years earlier and was to last, because of his early death, only four years more. " Napoleon " and " colossus " were the compliments he earned in that brief period, chiefly it would seem because he made Drury Lane pay. But there was something else, taken for granted now but shining new then. His was the spirit of what became known as " big business ". Instead of interesting himself in the theatre either for its own sake or as a means of self-aggrandizement, he eyed it like a gamester; his zest came from faces startled by his wild extravagance, his reward the punter's joy in having backed his fancy. At the start it was his father's death which kept him from shouldering his way into high finance. Then he consented, for the sake of ready money, to play Shakespeare's Malcolm at Manchester in 1873. After three years of acting he showed such a flair for " front of the house " that he suddenly became the manager of an opera company, and then just as suddenly took over sole responsibility for staging the Crystal Palace Christmas pantomime of *Sinbad the Sailor*, a tale whose very nature is " panoramic or ultra-sensational ".

But Meritt was before him. He had taken the cue from *Formosa ;*

Youth (Drury Lane, 1881)

or, *The Railroad To Ruin.* Though this had a prosperous run at Drury Lane in 1869, it was not until ten years later that its style became the model for spectacular melodrama, naval, military, sporting or just catastrophic. Meritt adopted it at the Duke's in 1879 as the design of *New Babylon*, described by D. L. Murray as the perfect melodrama, "It has every character, every situation, every sensation". Its pictures of real life showed a Collision on the Atlantic, Tattersall's with its Sale of Horses, Cremorne with its Dancing Platform and 10,000 Lights, Goodwood on the Grand Race-Day, the Thames Embankment with its Electric Witness, and Seven Dials by Night.   These were still drawing crowds to Holborn when Harris had to prescribe a cure for the listless tendencies of Drury Lane.   There in 1880 Pettitt, Meritt and he together created *The World* out of a notion taken from the Grecian's *Rescue On The Raft* a dozen years earlier.   They " treated melodrama very much like a pantomime ".   A ship was blown up, there was a mutiny on board, a raft disturbed the peace of mid-ocean with dead and dying, a man was incarcerated in a lunatic asylum on a false certificate, a villain who desired to compromise a woman's honour met a just fate in tumbling headlong down a hotel lift-shaft, and Harris as the player of this part bore hissing with " delightful indifference ". Clement Scott praised the authors for discovering the golden rule that had guided the pens of Charles Reade, Dion Boucicault, Wilkie Collins and all the most popular writers of drama or fiction.   " Believe me," he solemnly averred, " it is not cant, or humbug, or claptrap, to deal in generous sentiment; it is human, it is nature.   The mask of affectation and the veneer of cheap satire are rudely torn off when a popular play is represented.   People don't want to be told when their hearts and better natures are touched; they feel it."

So they were again made to feel it in *Youth*, the Drury Lane drama of 1881, by Paul Meritt and Augustus Harris, with the latter as hero. The Rev. Joseph Darlington once sinned with Mrs. Walsingham.   Now he casts her off and she revenges herself upon his son, who is arrested at her soirée and sent to prison.   There he is saved from death by an " illiterate fellow " who in a manly manner declares that no brazen bully shall kill his pal.   The " Departure of the Troopship " leads to " The Defence of Hawk's Point " (Rorke's Drift) and " The Son's Return ", where Clement Scott found " more nature " in all the manly and generous actions between man and man.   To another critic *Pluck; A Story Of £50,000*, by Pettitt and Harris in 1882, was " one of the worst plays of its kind which has ever been placed on the stage of a West-End London theatre ".   The heroine who claims the £50,000 is to travel by the 9.15, which the villain decides to wreck.   Harris has him arrested for fraud and forgery, so that he comes to the station handcuffed.   Railway lines curve across the stage with a practicable wooden bridge, signal-posts and other accessories (which is precisely how the scene had been set for the body-on-the-line episode in *Land Rats And Water Rats* at the Surrey).   The approaching engine is heard to the breathless excitement of the audience—" excitement dispelled when presently a property train, resembling nothing more impressive than a child's toy on a large scale, puffs in at a rate of four miles an hour, stops, goes on again, prances, and falls into two palpably pre-arranged segments amongst much explosion of squibs, yelling of supers, and manipulation of all the noise-creating instruments under the command of the prompter." Harris rescues the heroine just before a train from

For Ever (Surrey Theatre, 1882)

the opposite direction falls to pieces with business as before. Later a mob wrecks a bank, windows of real glass are really broken, and in the " memorable snow-storm of 1881 " somebody finds his child dying in the snow. In 1882 the Surrey eclipsed this with *For Ever*, by George Conquest and Paul Meritt, which made the most of its reputation for creating strange monsters (and old playgoers in years to come would recall this with laughter when bed-ridden and in pain). It was Beauty and the Beast over again, but more intense. Zacky Pastrana, the monkey-man, would stop at nothing to sacrifice himself for the damsel in distress. " But what ", she asked, " what can I do for you? " and a voice from the gallery advised, " Lady, chuck him some nuts ". Even that did not lessen the pathos when he uttered the simple words, apropos of nothing, just before the curtain fell, " For ever ". Finality-mongering was very active at a time when everybody was singing Tosti's " Goodbye " and " Nevermore ", and this play came at exactly the right moment for everybody except another of those poor long-suffering critics. This one saw " suggestiveness " in the " unwhole-some " love of a demi-savage for a young and pretty girl, since, " The better such a part as the erratic man-monkey is acted the more offensive it becomes ". There were seven acts with a unique climax to their synopsis of scenery. A grand panoramic effect of moving streets and houses ended in Eternity prolonged by " !!! "

Revolting realism was tried in 1883 at Drury Lane when preparations for hanging Harris were made in *A Sailor And His Lass*, in which Robert Buchanan had a hand. " This last Drury Lane monstrosity is really too much for us ", complained another of those debilitated critics, although he had seen the country with a real cow, the docks with real rain, and a real horse. The sailor was Harris and the lass a farmer's daughter with the real cow. Her ruined sister and baby are being taken by Harris to start life afresh in a new world. But a gang of dynamiters, having persuaded the farmer to blow up a London street in one sensation scene, now disguise themselves as sailors in order to scuttle the ship in another. Harris floats to safety on a few spars only to be sentenced to death at the Central Criminal Court for a murder actually committed by the farmer. In the scene of the condemned cell Harris hears that his last moments have come. There are shrieks and sobs, he is pinioned, there is a procession to the scaffold, and the black flag is hoisted. The trap-minder is asked, " Are you ready? " The order, "Pull ", is given and then retracted—the farmer has confessed. The public were not amused.

Because he liked " monosyllabic titles " Harris wanted to call his next effort *Humanity*. But as the Standard had staged three years earlier a drama called *Humanity ; or, A Passage In The Life Of Grace Darling*, he chose the title of a piece by his father instead. Accordingly the autumn drama for 1885 at Drury Lane, written by Pettitt and himself, was *Human Nature*. Captain Temple, the hero, comes home from service abroad to find that Cora, once his mistress, is now his wife's paid companion and turns her out of the house indignantly, whereupon she makes him believe that his wife is Paul de Vigne's mistress. Captain Temple, fighting in Egypt, leaves the zareba at night to bring in a fugitive. It is Paul de Vigne and he confesses conspiracy with his last breath. As Cora is murdered by her angry husband, everything ends happily for the parts played by Henry Neville and Isabel Bateman. The next year, in *A Run Of Luck*, Harris and Pettitt caused their heroine to be decoyed to a house of ill-repute, and the filly, named after her, to be seized as security for debts. Both are freed so that they may win in a canter.

Meritt, odd man out, sent Harris reproaches that filled several pages, until he found cause for satisfaction. To Sims he said, " I read my last letter to Harris to you, didn't I? Well, that's a fortnight ago, and he hasn't replied. My boy, I've knocked him speechless!" Opposite "sole lessees" on Surrey programmes the name of Meritt (business manager) was coupled for a spell with Conquest (stage manager). Meritt was appreciated there.

14 William Terriss
and the Adelphi

The Bells Of Haslemere

FASHIONABLE theatres like the Haymarket could have their drawing-rooms, and family theatres like Drury Lane their Turf, but the Adelphi wanted nothing better than fore-ordained triumphs for virtue. Falsely-accused innocence was fresh enough for every new plot. It was the staple of the Adelphi drama even before that theatre engaged the perfect hero for such plays, perfect because he made it seem a matter of such urgency for us to have faith in him. That hero was William Terriss. Like the stuff he acted, he was middle-aged with the looks and the spirit of youth. He was born in 1847. His father, George Lewin, was a barrister, and his mother was the niece of Grote, then a famous historian. Several schools, hundreds of miles apart, are supposed to have had a share in William Lewin's education, though at fourteen years of age, when his father died, he became a midshipman.

At seventeen he came in for a little money and retired from the Service to spend it. He went in for tea-planting at Chittagong but it was too monotonous. He suffered shipwreck with ten days of terrible exposure on the inhospitable shore of Holy Gunga before being taken off by a ship bound for England. He refused the chance to go on the stage; that was unthinkable. Instead, he tried the wine trade but as that was too monotonous he apprenticed himself to an engineer's shop at Greenwich, and found that too monotonous too. Next he took a berth on his uncle's yacht for a Mediterranean cruise, and on the way was cheered by a crowd who mistook him for a prince of the royal blood. In the autumn of 1867 he at last consented to act. As Chouser in *The Flying Scud* at the Prince of Wales's, Birmingham, he had a speech but forgot it. When asked for the words he said, "It's all gone", and was afterwards known to the rest of the company as " All gone ".

He left for London, where his tale is continued by Squire Bancroft. " I had been constantly told by a maid-servant that a ' very young gentleman had called ', and that he seemed very persistent about seeing me.   One day the girl informed me that the ' young gentleman ' had in a most determined way pushed past her, bounded up the steps, and walked into our little drawing-room, where he then was."   Bancroft was disarmed by the frank manner of a handsome young fellow who had resolved " not to leave the house until I had given him an engage- ment ".   After two seasons he married and went to seek his fortune in the Falkland Islands.   Monte Video was in a state of siege.   The emi- grants, unable to land, transferred to a coasting schooner for the thousand miles to Stanley.   Through foul weather the voyage lasted twenty-four days instead of ten, and rations were reduced to two bis- cuits and half a pint of water a day.

After six months of sheep-farming Lewin took passage for himself, his wife and their baby, Ellaline, in a Swedish whaler which had put in for repairs.   Off Gibraltar their ship was lost in a fearful gale.   Pas- sengers and crew drifted in open boats in the Bay of Biscay for two days and nights until picked up by a ship bound for Falmouth.   Now the traveller was at last reconciled to " raddle his face and go for hire upon the stage ".   He played Robin Hood in Halliday's *Rebecca* ("Ivan- hoe ") at Drury Lane.   Yet he had not had his fill of wandering. With an introduction to Mr. Tattersall, nephew of Mr. Tattersall of Tattersalls, he went to Lexington, Kentucky, to try his hand at horse- breeding.   It was too monotonous.   He went to New York, lost all his belongings, and came home steerage.   At Drury Lane he was given parts in Halliday's *The Lady Of The Lake* and *Richard Cœur-de-Lion*.

When *The Belle's Stratagem* was revived at the Strand in 1873, he played Doricourt, and a record run for this old comedy was the result. After that he was Romeo at Drury Lane.   With neither training nor inclination, with nothing in his upbringing or family tree to account for such natural aptitude, the hero of real life became the hero of the stage as a matter of course.   That he should have done well as Robin Hood may not be so very remarkable.   But mannered comedy and tragic poetry are distinct techniques which Terriss never had mastered.   Even if others had taken audiences by assault, though less astonishingly, in other generations, comparisons show that those who won fame in a night when Kean and Wallack laboured step by step, were invariably beautiful young women: handsome men could not do likewise until the rowdy, masculine and chivalrous pit was pushed into the back- ground by the upholstered half-a-guinea, feminine stalls.

With his start in life as a midshipmite, his shipwreck and his terrible exposure, Terriss is the Jack Tar up to date.   But he has altered.   He is not jolly.   He suffers a lot more, which is a sign that the century has grown sadder and wiser. There is no ignoring the nostalgia which was part of the maudlin fog now enfolding English life. A Frenchman described the most popular of juvenile entertainments—Nigger Minstrels—as a company of undertakers rattling cross-bones while singing songs about the dead, which was true. Similarly melodrama's heroes, like the glum villains of the drawing-room drama, suffered heavily, particularly when the Adelphi's limelight became sacred to William Terriss and Jessie Millward. For the Christmastide of 1885 they appeared in *The Harbour Lights* by Sims and Pettitt. Lieutenant Kingsley, of H.M.S. "Britannic", and Dora Vane have nothing to disturb their happiness apart from the fate of her life-long companion, Lina—victim of a gay young squire who is murdered in circumstances that cause all three to be suspected in turn. Through this turmoil Lina falls from a cliff down which Kingsley climbs to the rescue: a " clever mechanical change " showed the whole descent and the arrival of the lifeboat with the perilous tide. Although a run of over 500 performances established this as a landmark among melodramas, it seemed to take less hold over old playgoers' memories than *The Bells Of Haslemere*, by Pettitt and Sydney Grundy, which opened at the Adelphi in July 1887. It was designed to exploit homesickness. William Terriss, hoodwinked, goes on business to America with forged greenbacks that he utters, and he is consequently wanted by the police. While hunted through the brakes and swamps of the Mississippi by bloodhounds, he comes across a very sick crook who recovers his health in order to turn Queen's evidence—but not before the villain has tried to drown his own wife in a mill-race from which Terriss rescues her.

Several naïve tales left their mark on playgoer's memories because Terriss enacted them. Another was *The Fatal Card*, by Haddon Chambers and B. C. Stephenson, at the Adelphi in 1894, which begins in Colorado with an attempt to lynch a scoundrel who is rescued by the hero; this links itself with the murder of a miserly banker in circumstances that seem to fasten the guilt on his son; and all ends well when a villain is destroyed by an infernal machine which brings the walls of his laboratory tumbling about his ears. *One Of The Best*, by Seymour Hicks and George Edwardes, the Adelphi drama at the end of 1895, made Terriss undergo the military ceremony of degradation recently suffered by the innocent Captain Dreyfus as the climax of the greatest military scandal ever known until then. More interest was taken by the Press in the moral turpitude of the young-woman-in-love who was the real culprit when her political treachery, theft, burglary and perjury caused the hero to be publicly degraded. Early in 1897, at the height of his popularity, Terriss played Douglas Jerrold's Jack

The Bells of Haslemere (Adelphi, 1887)

Tar in a revival of *Black-Eyed Susan* (Surrey, 1829). The Kendals
employed W. G. Wills to alter the salty old play into *William And
Susan* at the St. James's in 1880; Sims and Pettitt stole the plot for
their military drama of *In The Ranks* at the Adelphi in 1883; and Pettitt
had used it again in *A Sailor's Knot* at Drury Lane in 1891. Terriss at

H

the Adelphi in 1897 had the novel idea of presenting it under its own title.

The next author to be billed at the Adelphi was William Gillette, who began at Madison Square Theatre in 1886 as actor-author with *Held By The Enemy*, which was presented in London at the Princess's the next year. This was melodrama without a villain. A Confederate girl, after falling in love with a Federal soldier, tries to save her Confederate fiancé from being shot as a spy by declaring that he is being victimized by her new lover who is trying to rid himself of a rival. It is the prisoner himself who denies the story. He is supposedly shot but actually concealed. The Federal tries to smuggle him to safety in a coffin. At length the General orders it to be opened : there is a corpse inside, for the spy has died during the argument. Ten years later Gillette again chose espionage in the Civil War as his subject in *Secret Service*. This time a Federal spy learns a military secret from the Southern heroine, but keeps it to himself in the belief that all is not fair in love and war. In this the author made his first appearance on the English stage at the Adelphi in 1897 before handing over the play, in the summer, to Terriss and Jessie Millward. They regarded it, at first, as a stop-gap and it was withdrawn.

This was to make room for *In The Days Of The Duke*, by Haddon Chambers and Comyns Carr, which had a prologue, dated 1800, to show Terriss as the victim of a most thorough villain [1] who first seduces his wife, then causes him to be branded as a traitor, and finally murders him. In a scene of 1815 Terriss is the son who kills the villain's accomplice in a duel. Jessie Millward, the heroine, receives a written confession, but since it tells the truth about both the parents of her betrothed, she keeps it secret. The ball at Brussels on the eve of battle was "brilliant beyond all description", and on the field of Waterloo the villain, dying from his wounds, clears the father's good name.

Towards the end of November, *Secret Service* was revived. Three weeks later, while it still filled the bill, the grotesque figure of a madman, an actor named Prince who had been a member of the Adelphi company, haunted the alley by the side of the theatre between the Strand and Maiden Lane. While rehearsing in the provinces he forgot his lines, wildly commanded the theatre to be closed and stalked out when not obeyed. In his black hat and Inverness cape he arrived at the stage-door of the Adelphi. He came night after night; on 16

---

[1] The villain's misrepresentation of fact became too much for one young playgoer. "I leapt up in my Eton collar", D. L. Murray recalls, "and shouted 'LIAR' at the top of my voice".

XLII and XLIII   William Terriss as Sir Kenneth in *Richard Coeur de Lion* (Drury Lane, 1874) and as Dudley Keppel in *One of the Best* (Adelphi, 1895)

ADELPHI IDOL

XLIV and XLV   William Terriss and Jessie Millward in *The Harbour Lights* (Adelphi, 1885) and *The Fatal Card* (Adelphi, 1894)

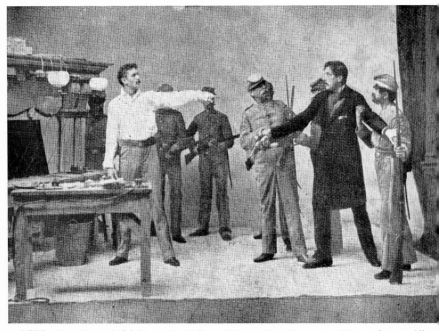

XLVI *Secret Service* (Adelphi, 1897): William Gillette as Lewis Dumont. " Arrest that man ! "

SOLDIERS WITHOUT GLORY

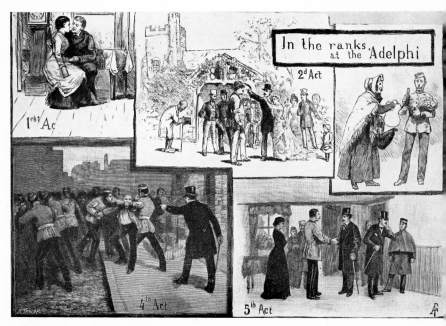

XLVII *In The Ranks* (Adelphi, 1883): Realism applied to military life

December he had some mysterious " hand property " under his arm and the stage-hands chaffed him, as they had done before. That evening (according to the book J. B. Booth wrote for her) Jessie Millward drove up in a hansom to the pass-door in Maiden Lane, where she noticed Prince. There was, she said, " something in the man's face that frightened me, and instead of waiting to open the pass-door I rushed to the stage-door ". While dressing she heard Terriss put his key in the pass-door, and then there was silence. " Something has happened ", she cried and rushed down the stairs; Terriss was leaning against the wall, near the door. " I had just reached him when he swayed. ' Sis ', he said faintly, ' Sis, I am stabbed '. I put my arms around him to support him, when we both fell to the ground on the bare boards at the foot of the staircase leading to our dressing-rooms. . . . He opened his eyes, and faintly squeezed my hand. ' Sis ! Sis ! ' he whispered. And that was all."

With other leading players *Secret Service* resumed its run at the Adelphi for the Christmas holidays. Gillette continued his London season in 1898. On returning to New York he impersonated Sherlock Holmes so successfully that throughout the rest of his career he felt there was no pleasing the publics of two countries unless he constantly reappeared in the part. As he grew old he went to live on a farm. Some old friends came with the purpose of leading him back to the stage. He was still refusing when he bade them good-bye at the gate. As he shook his head a goat looked at them and made the noise that goats make at all times and in all places. " You see," said Gillette with a break in his voice, " here even the animals love me." [1]

---

[1] In fairness to Gillette the author of this book wishes to add that he once took comfort, when hopelessly lost in a blinding, deafening hill-fog, from blundering into an old goat.

15   Wilson Barrett
and the Princess's

The Silver King

"STOP! You that have wives or mothers or daughters, remember there is a lady on the stage." This appeal quelled a riot at the Princess's in 1875. The audience which had come to see *Heartsease*, by James Mortimer, strongly objected to the nature of the story. It had been taken from *La Dame Aux Camélias* and the heroine was unchaste. Now this outburst was strange because never in all theatrical history has there been such a time for fallen heroines as the boom they enjoyed in the 1870s. While Mortimer took henceforth to farce and comedy as though wishing to turn over a new page, a whole rabble of playwrights exploited Magdalens so thoroughly that they might have been accused of living on immoral earnings.

One of them was W. G. Wills, king of Bohemia. Some called him picturesque, some slovenly; smudges of paint on his face and rolls of MSS. in his pockets advertised his callings. "A poor painter who writes plays for pence", was the label he gave himself, but as a specialist in children's portraits he received a command from the Queen for the likenesses of little princes and princesses which should have sent his fees on commission soaring. Even Paris in the 1840s never boasted a more ardent romantic. He used to tell how he was so overwhelmed, on first sailing up the Thames from Dublin, by the sight of the Tower of London that he burst into tears. What he felt then was what he could always feel about any sentimentally hallowed scene of history, and by writing costume dramas he gave this emotion full vent. His success, for an author with little stage experience, was astonishing. He sold *Buckingham* to Neville, and *Mary Queen Of Scots* to Mrs. Rousby. But the subject which lay nearest his heart was Jane Shore, particularly as she appeared in the old play by Nicholas Rowe which affected him deeply, so deeply, in fact, that he sought to turn his grief to good advantage by transforming the work into a play of his own. His biographer,

Freeman Wills (author of *The Only Way*), says that Rowe's play "possessed little (if any) literary merit, and my brother made no use whatever of it". Nevertheless Rowe was named as part author of the new play, which certainly took its outline from his : King Edward has just died, the Princes are in the Tower, Hastings wishes to protect them and also to inherit Jane Shore's favours, Gloucester has resolved on killing the Princes and Jane Shore on protecting them—the difference is that whereas Queen Anne's playwright saw her as a poor, weak woman, Queen Victoria's makes you feel that but for the obstinacy of history on this point it might be Gloucester who would need our pity. Still the lack of novelty in so old and familiar a heroine told against her. Although Wills became more and more in demand, his MS. of *Jane Shore* aroused no interest, and no offers, until the studio of the poor painter who wrote plays for pence was visited by a young actor, Wilson Barrett, whose good looks were eminently those then fashionable—a somewhat classical, very muscular archangel, which was partly to be explained by his early training as a blacksmith's apprentice.

With his brother, George, he had made his first appearance before the public in comic duets at the Grecian, but when his magnificent presence won the admiration of Caroline Heath he acted with her, learnt all about acting from her, and married her. He was playing Archibald to her Lady Isabel in *East Lynne* at the Surrey when he went to see Wills in the Fulham Road; the young husband of Miss Heath, zealous for her interests, had decided that the time had come to find her a new play; and after witnessing her tear-compelling powers as Lady Isabel he knew what kind of a play that play should be. On turning the pages Wills could not sell, Barrett realized that nothing was there for himself but the little-more-than-a-walking-on-part of Master Shore, but he knew that Mistress Shore would prove for his wife a grief-stricken goldmine. The author had prepared an alternative happy ending. This was swept aside.

Directly Miss Heath showed herself in the character, Barrett's choice was justified. At Leeds, early in 1875, the new *Jane Shore* was received with rapture, and at the Princess's a year later that audience of fervently righteous but utterly inconsistent souls launched the production on a morbidly triumphant career to outlast the actress's lifetime. With resources which included a real penny loaf, the famous penance became no mere matter of words but " Old Cheapside (Winter) by Night " all in white and snow falling on Miss Heath's low-cut evening dress that trailed a long silk train of black. Already " hath a woman lost her life " for offering aid, but John Grist swears not by his halidom but by his " halliday " (out of compliment to Andrew Halliday's historical

dramas) that he will lie there in his own blood an' he not give her food.
" Exit Grist into his house, hastily returns with loaf. She flies to him,
ravenously snatches it, and, dropping at his feet, tears it to pieces.
Ruffians interfere, Crowd cry out, ' Strike him down! '—Grist is
thrown down, and one of the Ruffians drives Jane back; she falls on
the snow—Enter Shore, armed—he strikes dead the Ruffian who had
thrown back Jane, and rescues Jane, supporting her on his arm."

Dropping at a wronged husband's feet, as Augustus Egg indicated in
his painting of " The Suffering Husband " at the Royal Academy (now
at the Tate), was the correct procedure for erring wives. What
galloping in imitation of a horse was to comedy, crawling on the stage
was to tragedy. This had recently been added to the lore of etiquette
by " Idylls of the King " when Arthur comes to confront Guinevere:

> . . . prone from off her seat she fell,
> And grovelled with her face upon the floor,
> There, with her milk-white arms and shadowy hair,
> She made her face a darkness from the King.

It may seem more like Warner's big scene in *Drink* than romance, but
as four or five actresses sent audiences into ecstasies by such means, there
can be no denying it was currently correct. Caroline Heath was not
the first to try it, but when she seized the penny loaf and bit it, she added
a paroxysm to the effect. Henceforward she was identified with the
character and it took years from her life. In London her husband
handed over the part of Shore to Charles Warner and contented himself with management. At the Princess's in 1876 it had one long run
and in 1877 another. In the provinces it stayed in constant demand and
Caroline Heath went on continually from tour to tour as Jane. After
ten years of it, increasing fits of mental depression hastened her death.

Meanwhile Wilson Barrett had won praise as a Shakespearean actor
with Madame Modjeska. She also appeared with him, and under his
management, in *Juana*, by Wills, at the Court in 1881; while she played
the wife driven insane by jealousy to do murder, Wilson Barrett was
the priest who, for love of her, confesses to the crime and is about to be
bricked up in " a living tomb " when she recovers her wits and speaks
the truth. But this was not his type of play. His mission in life was
melodrama, to the greater glory of which he transformed the old
Amphitheatre at Leeds into the aptly-named Grand, where the founda-
tions of his fame as the champion of virtue were profitably laid. Here
he received the oft-rejected MS. of *The Lights O' London* which has had
to be described in an earlier chapter because the works of its author,
George R. Sims, belong to the study of " Brutal Realism ". It ran for
over 200 performances at the Princess's when Barrett played it there in

Jane Shore (Princess's, 1876) : Caroline Heath as the penitent

1881–82, and was succeeded by *The Romany Rye*, also by Sims, in the following June, when Barrett did almost as well.

That style of " diluting Zola at Aldgate pump " aroused the emulative instincts of Barrett's business manager, Henry Herman, an Alsacian with a glass eye in place of one lost in the American Civil War. " Daddy " was Herman's nickname because he seemed to be past the age for enjoyment, but that was not how he saw himself. Into the whirlpool of winning and spending that then made London life, he threw himself with wholehearted zest, one day entertaining all-comers and the next reduced to bilking a cabbie whose whip, he swore, had cut out his eye—here, in his hand, for witness. Very frequently the more grotesque a man's shape the more he hankers after the gorgeous. This was the state of Herman's soul, and the theatre of the 1880s, which wanted imagination in bulk, had a use for him. Cataclysmic and supernatural devastation was always present to his overwrought vision; the only difficulty was that he could not put pen to paper except when making up accounts, and so preferred that in authorship someone else should undergo the hard labour of putting it to paper. He found the very partner he needed in an industrious young man named Jones.

So many stage careers had been the result of chance, or inexplicable natural aptitude or environment, that some reward for perseverance instead was overdue.   Henry Arthur Jones was a farmer's son.   At the age of ten he went to school in the summer between six and seven o'clock before breakfast, sold milk until it was time for more lessons between nine and four, and sold milk again until he went to evening classes.   At the age of twelve he was packed off to an uncle, deacon of a Baptist chapel, who kept a shop at Ramsgate, where Henry Arthur worked fourteen hours a day.   The next year he became a commercial traveller.   At sixteen he wrote a drama.   At eighteen he entered a theatre for the first time; it was the Haymarket, where five hours of entertainment sandwiched Kate Bateman's agonies between two farces. Every evening he went to the play.   He would see a successful drama six times, " till I could take its mechanism to pieces ".   He fell in love with Adelaide Neilson as " a glorious Rosalind ", and when he had done clapping and shouting for her at the fall of the curtain, hurried to the stage-door and patiently waited to see her into her four-wheeler.   By treating her cabman to a pint of beer, he learned where she lived in order to stand for an hour or two outside her window.   He gained a foothold on the stage with a one-act play at Exeter, where Mrs. Rousby's husband " was willing to play the leading part if I would take half the dress-circle ".   He quickly advanced to other " subsidized productions ".   At last he received payment of £50.   This was for *A Clerical Error*, acted at the Court in 1879 with Wilson Barrett as a vicar. Jones next dramatized a novel, about an attempt to repudiate a Scotch marriage, which had for hero a clergyman whose attitude to the heroine recalled *The New Magdalen*.   At this critical moment the young play-wright was invited to collaborate with Herman.

The century was closing in conscience-stricken grief—a sense of guilt everywhere.   It inspired the poem of qualified fidelity to Cynara as well as manifestoes of vegetarianism, and convicted of sin every soul from Swinburne's " luxurious Dolores " to addicts of tobacco, not to mention anybody so unnaturally inclined as to wear clothes while posing before the camera.   Such widespread shame could not be kept secret.   Wilson Barrett sensed it.   He wanted a play about it.   Falsely-accused innocence was not enough.   He was tired of holding his head erect to look the whole world in the face; he wanted to raise his eyes to heaven and cry, " Repentance !   Pardon !   Peace ! "   In other words, he coveted the torments of the damned which had made Mrs. Wilson Barrett the idol of galleries awash, so to speak, with tears.   Accordingly he approached Herman and Jones with the words (according to the report of that genial critic, Chance Newton), " Look here, boys, the sort of play I want is *East Lynne* turned round. That is, with a man in the position of Isabel Carlyle; lost to the world for a while—reported to be killed, like her, in a railway accident, if you like—and returning secretly in disguise, well-off though totally unable for a time to see or succour his suffering wife and children." The idea of self-accusation was to be exploited as never before.

Together they supplied him with *The Silver King*, which opened at the Princess's on 16 November, 1882. Wilfrid Denver faces ruin in a skittle alley. Ware, his wife's former suitor, taunts him and he swears revenge. There is a swell mobsman, the Spider, with such a respect for his calling that when preparing to crack a crib he dresses as though for the opera. His gang are already at work when Denver arrives full of alcohol and threats, only to be chloroformed. On recovering his senses he finds his revolver at hand; a shot from it has killed Ware. Believing himself to be a murderer, Denver tries to cover up his tracks by taking a train and jumping from it. Part of that train is destroyed by fire after a collision and Denver (who has prayed, " Oh God, put back Thy Universe and give me yesterday ") reads the newspaper reports and realizes that he has the chance to start life afresh in a new land. Three years and six months pass. Nellie Denver is hard pressed by her landlord, the Spider. Her child comes home with a purse, the gift of a stranger whose hair turned silver while he mined silver in Nevada. In the disguise of an aged half-wit the stranger wanders into the riverside warehouses where the gang is quarrelling and there he learns the truth about the murder. When the Spider is brought to account, the exile is at last free to declare himself to his wife and children and there was no doubt from the start of a run of nearly 300 perform-ances that a masterpiece had arrived among melodramas. It gave the public all the sin-laden misery that it hankered after in outbursts of a soul's distress that have been cited regularly ever since.

Since *The Silver King* is as guilty as Sims of expounding the gospel of rags, Barrett was ready for a change of repertoire. So far, despite the variety of his costumes, he had not seen how classically his features would suit a backcloth of pagan temples. The time was still to come when an old cleaner, arrested by his portrait in *décolleté* armour, would shriek, " 'Er? I knoo 'er when she were Connie Gilchrist ". But once a toga had been draped upon the blacksmith's manly and generous form his destiny was fixed. Herman decided this. He had been play-ing with scissors and paste, which always fascinated him, and had made a scene-model of Rome; a simple mechanism made all its columns topple in bits as though snapped by an earthquake. Long before *The Silver King* went into rehearsal, Herman was showing his new toy to

Barrett and receiving orders for a play to suit that earthquake. This time Herman's Cyclopian gaze fell upon Wills, who had been working with Barrett upon a great tragedy (about Boadicea's daughter) for a great actress who retired from the stage rather than act in it. The unemployed poet was swept off to Margate, where he was thrown scraps of plot every morning in bed with his breakfast. Since Herman carried out his share of the bargain by constructing a plot which consisted of " The Last Days of Pompeii " added to " The Wandering Jew ", the play was finished in six weeks. *Claudian* opened at the Princess's in the December of 1883. For killing a priest Claudian is doomed to perpetual youth while tribulation afflicts everyone else. When he takes to his heart Almida, after her lover has been flung into a torrent, Herman's earthquake turns the whole city into ruins by moonlight. Claudian invokes the spirit of the murdered priest, who lets him choose between life and death; because the lovers have survived, the sinner decides to die. Here was another study of " Repentance, Pardon, Peace ", and it had nearly as long a run as the other.

Now Wilson Barrett decided upon authorship himself, and adopted the simple method of using a plot whose effects had already been demonstrated. He took his idea this time from Frank Harvey, author-actor-manager, who had brought his touring company to the Olympic in 1881 with *The Workman; or, The Shadow On The Hearth*, in which Bessie, the heroine, bears the reproach of the wrong done by her sister, and her husband is driven frantic before he discovers that her infamy is self-sacrifice. Once some obvious objections had been removed this made an excellent story for Barrett's use—with no acknowledgments. In *Hoodman Blind*, which he wrote in collaboration with Jones [1] for the Princess's in 1885, the wife is not to blame for her husband's jealousy. There is a cold, calculating villain who steals her hooded cloak. Her double, a gypsy, is bribed to wear it while being embraced by her lover for the husband to see.

With her wide staring eyes and small taut mouth, Mary Eastlake gave such an impression of emotional intensity, first as one woman and then as the other, that *Hoodman Blind* was her triumph. In both parts she made sure of the audience's sympathy for which Barrett laboured in vain as the too credulous husband. In his next play—*Clito*, at the Princess's in 1886—her part could win no sympathy. She was a hardened sinner of the classic age as imagined by Barrett in league with another young playwright, Sydney Grundy. Athens at the height of

---

[1] In *The Lie*, acted by Sybil Thorndike and Mary Merrall at the New Theatre in 1923, Henry Arthur Jones made still better use of this idea of a woman blamed for her sister's sin.

its luxurious decline was their subject. As a critic said, "Woman's infamy and man's guilty weakness are shown to us in all their nakedness". Clito, the sculptor, goes to Helle's house to upbraid her. She falls at his feet and promises to be his wife. Meanwhile she has lured her innocent little foster-sister into the power of a voluptuary who kills the poor child when she cries for help. Clito revenges her. Helle again falls at his feet, begging him to save her from the mob. Both died, Barrett more especially, for though Miss Eastlake grovelled on the ground, beating the floor in the agony of her terror, she "touched the utmost limits of realistic acting", and realism was still considered "too".

16 Parsons in Love

The New Magdalen

ONE more reference has to be made to *La Dame Aux Camélias*. That Marguerite Gautier was reviled unfairly has already been suggested. The outcry against her reveals more bias when she is compared with the heroine of Wilkie Collins' *The New Magdalen* at the Olympic in 1873. Here the penitent, trying to expiate her sins by serving as a nurse in the Franco-Prussian War of 1870, steals the papers of a woman thought to have been killed and personates her. The idea seems to be that if she sincerely regret her sexual delinquencies, any offences against the criminal code are too trivial to be worth mentioning. According to the current view of woman's duty this was but fair. Men need not be chaste but they must be honest : women, since they must be chaste, need not be honest. Though never officially sanctioned, this nice balance expressed itself every now and then. In *Not Registered* (Royalty, 1882) a post-mistress stole money from a letter and relied on the audience's sympathy. In *The Power of Love* (Prince of Wales's, 1888) the appeal was for a very nice young lady who merely tried to poison her father. In *One Of The Best* (Adelphi, 1895) the pardonable offences of a virgin included robbery, treason, espionage and readiness to let the innocent suffer for these crimes. " Foolish little creature " was the right attitude towards dishonest but prepossessing females.

But *The New Magdalen* has other importance. When the heroine's plans are upset by the return to life of the woman whose place she has taken, she finds a champion. He is a clergyman. To label him " infatuated " would be to meddle because that is not the story as it was written or as it was received. The clergyman understands her, because of that he loves her, and because of his love he is ready to sacrifice himself for her. The hero who had the right to preach as well as the right to fall in love was a new inspiration to the drama. To be photographed in a " dog-collar " was every actor's ambition at this sudden blossoming of Episcopalian romance—Belasco was rarely photographed out of it. W. S. Gilbert's " pale young curate ", whom maidens of the noblest station, forsaking even military men, would gaze upon while

rapt in admiration, was no figment of idle thought but a shrewd caricature of the times (and the parson in Shaw's *Candida* needs this as
reference).

While *The New Magdalen* was the most popular of plays it happened
that "The Church and Stage Guild" was formed in 1879. According
to *The Theatre* magazine, damsels more or less known to histrionic
fame made speeches before canons and curates on racy subjects and
originated savoury discussions. An important member of the Gaiety
company, who had hitherto generally succeeded in keeping her name
out of the programme, was put up to discuss the conduct of "noble-
men, men of high position and soldiers, who stand at the stage-doors to
tempt girls who are perfectly innocent". She suggested that a fire-
hose should be directed at the heads of these aristocratic Lotharios.
"Fled gilded duke and belted earl before me", the fair young curate
sang.

Here the Vicar of Wakefield comes into the story. When W. G.
Wills wrote *Olivia* for the Court in 1878, older versions of this part of
Goldsmith's novel were revived and new versions dramatized, besides
which a very similar father-and-child episode appeared—this time
wearing modern dress—in Henry Arthur Jones's *Saints And Sinners* at
the Vaudeville in 1884. A minister's daughter, loved by an honest
farmer, elopes with a heartless military man. She returns and is forgiven, but a vindictive deacon swears to reveal her shame unless he is
assisted in fraud. The minister tells his congregation the secret and
goes away with his daughter to starve until the farmer makes an honest
woman of her, upon which the father returns to his chapel, having by
the same ceremony been made an honest preacher of.

There was still novelty enough in religious romance for a critic to
talk of the "rather daring experiment of choosing a clergyman for the
hero", when Wilson Barrett wrote *The Golden Ladder* in collaboration
with Sims for the Globe in 1887. The Rev. Frank Thornhill, to save
his future father-in-law from disgrace, hands over his fortune and goes
to Madagascar as a missionary with his bride. There some unusually
resourceful villains poison the wine he is sending to the sick, and he is
likely to be shot but for the defiance of French authority by the English
skipper who takes him aboard. Back in England, a false message from
a dying woman lures him by night to Hampstead Heath, where he is
saved from death by his wife, who shoots one of the villains and is
sentenced for attempted murder until pardoned. The prison was
"fearfully harrowing" and "too" painful to some, but Barrett found
a champion when the author of "Alice in Wonderland" wrote "The
Stage and the Spirit of Reverence" for *The Theatre* in 1888. Villainy

had been hissed in *The Silver King* to show that, " Those who thus hiss
—evil as their own lives may be in some cases—yet have their better
moments, when the veil is lifted, when they see Sin in all its native
hideousness, and shudder at the sight ! " On the other hand, there was
an example of the sympathy shown by playgoers for what was pure and
good in *The Golden Ladder* when the greengrocer said he had called his
child Victoria Alexandra, " because they're the best two names as is ! "
The applause in Lewis Carroll's ears seemed to say, " Yes, the very
sound of those names—names which recall a Queen whose spotless life
has been for many long years a blessing to her people, and a Princess
who will worthily follow in her steps—is sweet music to English ears ! "
The hero of *All Is Not Gold That Glitters* brought down the house by
declaring, as factory-owner, that he could not sleep in peace if he
thought any man, woman or child among his hands went to bed cold
and hungry. What, asked Lewis Carroll, did it matter that the
" hands ", so tenderly cared for, were creatures of a dream? " We
were not ' reverencing ' the actor only, but every man, in every age,
that has ever taken loving thought for those around him, that ever
hath given his bread to the hungry, and hath covered the naked with a
garment." Preachers of this manly type were thoroughly typical of
the state of the world after many years of inspissated melodrama.
" Right-thinking " was all.

Another stage pastor makes full confession to his flock in *Judah*, the
Jones drama at the Shaftesbury in 1890. Vashti, a faith-healing, fasting
girl, is brought to cure an earl's daughter. Judah Llewellyn, a Welsh
minister, discovers she is a fraud. In order to save her he perjures himself and for ever after his soul is in torment with the reproach from his
conscience of, " Liar ". When his congregation presents him with a
testimonial and the deeds of a new church, Judah and Vashti tell their
story and offer to leave, but are persuaded to stay. In *The Dancing
Girl*, the Jones drama which Tree put on at the Haymarket in 1891,
Drusilla, who cannot be called the heroine since she lacks the moral
fibre for it, comes home to the Quaker colony on the island of St.
Endellian, Cornwall. In London she is the shameless dancing girl of
the Duke of Guisebury, whom she despises; she will not even become
his duchess when he has no money for more debaucheries. With his
last remnants of credit he gives a party in trappings of magnificence
which he purposes to use as his funeral pyre. Drusilla is about to dance
before his guests when her father comes to fetch her. She dies, the
Duke marries a good woman, and melodramatic instincts have overwhelmed an author when trying to achieve something better.

So far Jones had favoured the view that the modern mind, as one

XLVIII and XLIX *The Silver King* (Princess's, 1882): Wilson Barrett as Wilfred Denver and Mary Eastlake as his wife

POPULAR TRAGEDIAN

L Wilson Barrett as Wilfred Denver

LI Wilson Barrett as Claudian (Princess's, 1890)

LII *Olivia* (Court, 1878): Ellen Terry and Hermann Vezin (centre) as the Vicar of Wakefield and daughter. The children are Edith and Gordon Craig

CHURCH AND STAGE

LIII *The Golden Ladder* (Globe, 1887): Wilson Barrett as the Rev. Frank Thornhill

LIV *Judah* (Shaftesbury, 1890): E. S. Willard as the Minister Judah Llewellyn, and Olga Brandon as Vashti Dethic

critic put it, revolted from " special maleficence " no less than from
" special providence ". But when the spirit of Shakespeare descended
upon him he broke into blank verse and forgot the modern mind. *The
Tempter* should have been his greatest religious drama. Unfortunately
it became memorable instead for his greatest display of bad temper.
Tree, who staged it on the grand scale at the Haymarket in 1893, was
blamed for turning poetry into pageantry. William Archer, who
(among many others) found fault with it, was answered in one of the
finest examples of invective in the language, inspired by that righteous
indignation which was now the white man's burden everywhere.

The greatest of all Jones's unacknowledged masterpieces was yet one
more with a clergyman as hero. For the third time he made a plot
turn on repentance in the pulpit, and each marks a stage in the development of the relations between salvation and sex. The vicar of 1884 has
to make public his daughter's shame : the minister of 1893 has nothing
worse on his conscience than a lie told under the influence of love : the
parson of 1896, hero of *Michael And His Lost Angel* at the Lyceum with
Forbes-Robertson in the part, is honestly guilty. The married woman
who mocks Michael's faith, rouses him. To escape her he goes to his
hermitage on an island and sends away the only boat. She arrives and
cannot leave. In a church scene, staged like a pageant, he publicly
brands himself as a sinner and exiles himself. But he feels no regret,
and when his lost angel dies, he cries out that he is ready to suffer all
things " only persuade me I shall meet her again ". *Michael And His
Lost Angel* was bound to fail. Women in bulk would not stand for a
hero who has to be seduced ; that was a sop to male vanity. They were
drawn to the opposite type with an increasing frankness which caused
the term " seducer " to change to " hunter " by a slow and gradual
process barely perceptible at the time. To find pleasure in tales of
sexual doggedness was not a new vogue. That it had always been so
throughout the age of virtue triumphant was not to be overlooked, for
" Clarissa Harlowe ", Richardson's novel of 1748 about chastity lost
through foul drugs and violence, was twice dramatized in 1890—by
Wills for Miss Bateman on tour, and by Buchanan at the Vaudeville.
Although melodrama had caused impassioned villains to demand
marriage (even when heroines were not heiresses) there was usually
some insistence that their attitude towards women was an implacable
desire for possession in some shape or form. Such villainy looked more
and more commendable once the heresy spread that woman was the
hunter.

There must be an epilogue to this chapter. Twenty years later a
playwright in Boston became bedridden. His solace was an ardent

friendship with Doris Keane. Both had had a little success on the stage and many disappointments. Together they planned *Romance* to present her as a prima donna of the 1860s, mistress of a wealthy banker who is leader of fashion in New York. At his house she meets the young rector of St. Giles's; they wish to marry until she blurts out the truth about herself and rushes away. He comes to struggle with her for her soul, loses his head and struggles for her body until she begs, " Please let me be good " (which became one of London's catch-phrases). The play opened at Maxine Elliot's Theatre, New York, in 1913. In the autumn of 1915 Doris Keane brought it to London. Zeppelin raids began soon after, and it might have been withdrawn but was transferred instead to the Lyric in Shaftesbury Avenue. There it broke all London records for melodrama and for all plays other than farces up to that date, with a run of over 1,000 performances. " Cabotinage ", said a critic who had seen all stage clergymen. Tawdry that belated specimen of sex-and-salvation undoubtedly was. But no one who saw it in the London of doused lighting is ever likely to forget it. Scene by scene it stays bright in memories which have lost sight of some hundreds of other plays.

17 Sex and Salvation

The Sign Of The Cross

WITH the stage clergyman came the Biblical title, another whim revealing the general hankering after a show of religion. While a few people, like Bradlaugh, who was called The Atheist, as though unique, were supposed to be disturbing religious rest, very many more were determined on a period of religious zest. There was a great to-do about making this part of everyday life. Preachers wanted to be men of the world, and men of the world, from the Prime Minister to dramatic critics, wanted to be preachers. There was nothing singular in Wilson Barrett's love of sermons as moral limelight, though in this he surpassed all other actors. Playwrights, long accustomed to adorning their dialogue with sentiments, now praised virtue at still greater length. But any nearer approach to sacred things was dangerous. Something remained of the spirit which caused the outcry over Holman Hunt's sacred pictures simply because he represented the form of Christ.

The new craze is cynically explained in Filon's "Modern French Drama". After Louis Napoleon's fall in 1870, the Pope had directed the priesthood to act as mediator between the old aristocracy and the new ruling classes so that the daughter of M. le Ministre sits at a charity meeting side by side with a La Tremouille, and his son has his coat cut after the fashion prescribed by the Prince de Sagan. This was called "the new spirit", or better still "the return to religion". Mysteries after the manner of Oberammergau were acted in booths at the fairs. While a "strait waistcoat" was demanded for Tolstoy when he frightened society with his Christian ideal in its pristine severity, religious emotion was enjoyed as an artistic sensation like any other. Their Christianity was a Christianity à la Baudelaire, lulled by bells and soothed by incense, seeing in the Magdalen only another "dame aux camélias", whose golden hair, borrowed from Flemish art, awakened beautiful dreams. To be in the fashion Sardou wrote *Gismonda* for Bernhardt. She first killed a man with an axe and then, as a saint, headed a religious procession.

London playgoers were nervous at first. There was some reluctance

to quote Holy Writ despite the successes won by *The New Magdalen*
and *The New Babylon*.   For strict Sabbatarians even *Saints And Sinners*
had been too previous.   They hooted the first of its 182 performances,
said Jones, " on the count that it dealt with religious matters, and that I
had made its personages quote Scripture on a Sunday morning "; to
offset this he published unsolicited testimonials from the clergy in his
programmes.

Books had an advantage over plays in being privately consumed.
Consequently the printed page revealed tendencies before they could
be expressed publicly.   There was always a time-lag for the theatre,
and where religious matters were concerned it was unduly long.
Novelists who wished to assist the world's salvation had their task made
easy for them by the affinity between sacred and classical subjects.
Lytton's " The Last Days of Pompeii " had founded a whole school of
fiction.   Whyte-Melville, retired captain, Coldstream Guards, who
served with the Turkish army in the Crimea, wrote " The Gladiators "
in 1863.   Lew Wallace, a major-general in the American Civil War
and then Governor of New Mexico, wrote " Ben Hur " in 1880.   If
power could be measured in fiction as it is in electricity, Lew Wallace
would be called a generating-station.   On the other hand, a rival claim
could be made out for Robert Buchanan, with whom originated the
" powerful " novel of modern life.   In literary history he has a
peculiar place as the author of an essay, " The Fleshly School of
Poetry ", which attacked Rossetti and Swinburne, drew answers from
both, and eventually prompted a fit of penitence peculiar in the annals
of criticism.   That such an ineradicable fuss should have been made
over it hints at the spirit of a young ladies' seminary in literary England.

Buchanan was granted a Crown pension at the age of thirty and
while thus subsidized set a new standard for popular fiction in 1881 with
the religious solemnity of his, " God and the Man "—the story of
two farmers' sons of the Fens, enemies since their youth when one
seduces the other's sister, then rivals in love and in the end allies against
privation in the Arctic, where the seducer is buried by the man he
wronged.   When dramatized for the Adelphi in 1883 the story lost its
devout and irrelevant title and was called *Storm-Beaten* (taken from
another novel Buchanan had written twenty years earlier); his powerful novel did not make a powerful play because his stage dialogue missed
the hypnotizing effect of his ponderous prose.

As novels " Ben Hur " and " God and the Man " were beginning to
exert an enormous influence upon the imagination of the masses.
Each inspired imitators who successfully created awe in the unfledged
mind.   The powerful novels of the 1880s and 1890s, were not cold print

when opened by the trembling hands into which they were intended to fall. Buchanan's emotional violence overwhelmed the young generation that was being brought up in an atmosphere conducive to religious mania. The breaking down of the old taboos against the display of sacred forms in profane places meant that the promise of heaven and the threat of hell dogged the footsteps of the young from dawn to dusk. At the same time the more freedom the stage had to represent the good-woman-who-had-sinned, the more fear and hatred there was of sex. Music-hall singers who extolled animal enjoyments were called disgusting.

Morality had come to mean nothing but sex, and the control of adultery was to be regarded as the be-all and end-all of religion. If stage heroes were presented as being in Holy Orders their illicit amours would, not illogically, wreck whole lives, but stress on the importance of the Seventh Commandment did not end there. As the nineteenth century was ending, authors who understood their public insisted on the close relation between sex and salvation or sex and damnation while avoiding the old term " sin " in favour of the new term " love ". Novelists of the kind called powerful made much of this. Their peculiarity lay in hints that they had been appointed to expound heaven's warnings against all the sinful lusts of the flesh—hearts included. Their books with Biblical titles refrained from humour, upheld the moral laws, indulged in portents, and maintained a gravity of language as though signifying the birth of a new, vaster and more fearsome Apocalypse, with themselves as sidesmen.

This was not to be Buchanan's mission in life. Having lost his money in the theatre he looked to the theatre to reimburse him. While he was vainly trying to do so, as author in whole or part of thirty or forty melodramas, he let the mitre of religious romance pass to another earnest provincial of his own frame of mind only more so. Thomas Henry Hall Caine was born in 1853 at Runcorn, Cheshire, and went to school in the Isle of Man, which to his prospecting eye revealed its rich lode of romantic ore. Though meant to be an architect, he was destined to champion what he called " The Little Manx Nation ". For a time he wrote for the *Builder* and the *Building News* before he came to London at the age of eighteen and turned novelist with " The Shadow of a Crime " and " A Son of Hagar ". In his beard and cloak and flowing locks, he seemed to be dreaming of fame, though all the while he kept an eye, a wild blue eye in fine frenzy rolling, on big business.

Belles lettres were his first concern, for he had known Dante Gabriel Rossetti. Next, to quote what happened to some of his characters, nature whispered in his ear the secret of sex. It came to him with all the force of revelation. When it inspired his story, " The Deemster ", London's limelight fell upon the somehow strangely familiar domed forehead and pointed beard. It was another Shakespeare—the Manx Shakespeare. Wilson Barrett was impressed. Together they turned the novel into *Ben-My-Chree* for the Princess's in 1888. Dan, the bishop's son, is hated by his uncle, the Deemster, whose daughter, Mona, is the only one who loves the outcast. Her brother, witnessing Dan's escape from her window, insists on a duel with knives and is killed. Dan is found guilty, but in the Isle of Man the Church has the last word and the bishop saves his son by passing on him the sentence of being cast off from the people—no one must speak to him and he must speak to no one on pain of death. The Governor, unable to make Mona his wife, accuses her of being Dan's mistress. She comes to church to swear her innocence but her testimony alone is not enough. Dan takes oath before the altar, thus dooming himself to death, and Mona falls dead in his arms.

Belief in the sacred duties of the stage wavered at the Princess's in 1889. Wilson Barrett had possessed himself of a panorama of riverside scenery in Tasmania. Forgetful of his allegiance to virtue, he persuaded Hall Caine to write with him a drama of escaped convicts to be pursued by the hero in a boat while the landscape unrolled its beauty spots. In order to get the characters transported there a husband has had to accuse himself of attempted murder ; actually the shot has been fired by his wife to escape the consequences of a past so lurid as to make a hollow mockery of the authors' choice of title—*Good Old Times*. When the public proved indifferent to the panorama Barrett did not jump to the obvious conclusion that piety paid. He gave a trial matinée of *Nowadays*, a tale of the Turf by himself with a villain so determined that Thunderbolt shall not win the Derby that he elopes with it to London ; it is brought back to Epsom and does win. Sport failed as the thriller had done. Manx virtue had to be tried again.

To be a Shakespeare without being a poet makes the theatre of particular importance. Hall Caine clung to it with a pertinacity that is altogether admirable in a land which has an almost heraldic veneration for the bulldog. No other novels have been dramatized and re-dramatized so often as his. His *The Bondman* (as distinct from Massinger's, Betterton's, Cumberland's and Bunn's) was staged at Bolton in 1892, and then took a rest in readiness for the next century. His *The Manxman*, story of a Manx girl who cannot make up her mind whether to live with her husband or the father of her child, was dramatized by Wilson Barrett, with music by the composer of *The Geisha*, at the

Nowadays (Princess's, 1889)

Grand, Leeds, in the summer of 1894. For the moment Hall Caine must be set aside, for Barrett, while acting *The Manxman* on tour, planned a yet greater drama, a " deep study of a social problem " with a secret no one could guess to the end. Though this particular play seemed to vanish into thin air, Barrett's ideas indicate the spirit of the times. He had a great moral urge to teach " those who are growing up, not merely the broad lines of right and wrong, of honesty and dishonesty, but something more ". He had, unlike earlier generations of melodramatists, " no faith in the innocence that arises from ignorance ", and could not blame a girl for falling into a trap " into which her own inclination or feeling may have drawn her, when the knowledge of the existence of such traps has been kept carefully from her ". When warned that this was delicate ground he answered, " If we *are* wrong, then it will be necessary to amend the texts and the Commandments over the altars, and to alter words used by every Church in Christendom ". But the epoch-making point was never raised. Barrett, harassed by a huge burden of debts, forgot his unborn masterpiece and went to America, first handing over *The Manxman* to the villain of his company, Lewis Waller, after re-dramatizing it so that the baby's father should become better fitted for the centre of the stage than the baby's mother's husband. Thus re-moralized the story was acted in 1895 at the Shaftesbury, where it caused Bernard Shaw to ask " Who is Hall Caine? "

Since the celebrated novelist was amassing one of the largest fortunes ever made from authorship and was to see his prosperity acknowledged with a knighthood, whatever his private feelings suffered from this question could go into the advertising account. What concerned him more was the ever-increasing rivalry which might have reduced his royalties had the public not been omnivorous. Sex-and-salvation fiction, down to pornographic love stories with prefaces by broad-minded bishops, could not cope with the demand. Shameless people might read such novels as Grant Allen's courageous " The Woman Who Did ", which was well boosted by public protests, but the masses stayed respectable and read Hall Caine.

Public taste had progressed, as though the nineteenth century were a girl at school, from highwaymen to gypsies, then to bigamists, then to convicts, and now to erring clerics. *Fin de siècle* was the glamorous label for the mentality of the sixth form, free to read about nocturnal encounters between man and woman out of wedlock and regard this as being grown-up. The new phase is marked in the output of Ouida, otherwise Louise de la Ramée. She was born at Bury St. Edmunds in 1839, and published a novel a year from the age of twenty-three for half-a-century. Among such early efforts as " A Dog of Flanders " and " Two Little Wooden Shoes " is a novel of the Foreign Legion— " Under Two Flags ", which she wrote in 1867. Though it became one of the best among romantic melodramas, its stage history is staggered : one version was acted at Norwich in 1870, another at Dundee in 1882, another at Cork in 1902, another at Stratford in 1909, and another at the Lyceum in 1912.

Under the title of *Firefly* it was staged as an equestrian drama at the Surrey in 1869—merely an echo of performances in Boston the year before when the heroine had been played by Charlotte Crabtree, who under the name of Lotta had won fame in the roaring camps whose miners expressed their worship not in bouquets of roses but in bags of gold-dust, so that at her death in 1924 she left an estate of five million dollars. At the California Theatre in San Francisco, Ouida's story was lavishly mounted with the Foreign Legion on the march and under fire, before Lotta mounted a real horse in front of a panorama to show the desert ride. Cigarette, the *vivandière* who obtains a reprieve for the legionary she loves and arrives just in time to fling herself between him

LV and LVI *The Dancing Girl* (Haymarket, 1891): Beerbohm Tree as the Duke of Guisebury and Julia Neilson as Drusilla Ives

OUTCASTS

II *The Dancing Girl*: Fred Terry as John Christison

LVIII *The New Magdalen* (Olympic, 1873): Ada Cavendish as Mercy Merrick

LIX *The Sign of the Cross* (Lyric, Jan. 1896) : Franklin McLeay as Nero cursing the Christians

LX *The Christian King* (Adelphi, 1902) Wilson Barrett as King Alfred

FRIENDS, ROMANS, COUNTRYMEN

LXI *The Manxman* (Lyric, Nov. 1896) : Wilson Barrett as Pete

LXII *The Daughters of Babylon* (Lyric, 1897) : Wilso Barrett as Lemuel and Maud Jeffries as Elna

and the firing party so that she is killed by the bullets meant for him, is the female equivalent of Sydney Carton and no drama of the Legion has yet equalled hers. With sex, which merely whispered to Hall Caine, Ouida was on familiar terms. Her novels " adopted an unhealthy tone " and became almost infamous for amorous Guardsmen. Then religious titles dominated her library list from " Santa Barbara " and " The New Priesthood " to " The Silver Christ ". Another was added in 1880 when her novel " Held in Bondage " was turned by James Willing, at the Olympic, into *Delilah ; or, Married For Hate.*

With " The Soul of Lilith " in 1892, " Barabbas " in 1893 and " The Sorrows of Satan " in 1895, Marie Corelli scrowged through the sanctimonious scrum. Her elbows expressed the lively and endearing spirit of a little street-arab ; and though her contemporaries may not have regarded her so affectionately they are not to blame. If she were criticised by far too high a standard, it was because of her power of stamping upon an impressionable public mind the seal of herself as a grande dame. That is an understatement. In showmanship she had no equal. Hall Caine could present himself as Shakespeare's double, but Marie Corelli could do better—she was Shakespeare's guardian and by the way she dressed hinted at the addition of the word " angel ". She sent to Venice for a gondola and gondolier so that Stratford saw her afloat like a better and brighter Swan of Avon. Where Shakespeare had his Birth-place she would have her Death-place. Her Will ordered that Mason Croft should be maintained out of profits from her two dozen novels in perpetuity. In time there were no profits. In 1943 newspapers set apart columns, ill-spared from war news, to describe how her home was being sold by auction. She bequeathed to the nation (and the nation declined) this monument to the self-appointed spinster pontiff who declared Barabbas to have been loyal and Satan saintlike. When Lewis Waller appeared in *The Sorrows Of Satan* at the Shaftesbury in 1897, Shaw himself expounded her gospel of " Electric Christianity " which bestowed the power of making trips round the solar system, living for ever, playing pianos at the dictation of angels, and knocking people down by means of electric shocks without apparatus.

It should have been plain that Wilson Barrett, too good a man of business to let others reap where he had sown, was not going to stay out of all this. What handicapped him in the early 1890s was lack of funds. All the profits of his seven fat years at the Princess's had been lost by a well-meaning friend when demonstrating how money should be invested in something sounder and safer than theatrical enterprise. Barrett parted from Mary Eastlake, whose " inability to keep the tears back from her eyes " had meant as much as his manliness to the Princess's. But he filled her place. While in New York he saw Maud Jeffries in Daly's company and engaged her as his leading lady. In " Master and Men ", one of his many volumes of lively reminiscences, J. B. Booth describes how on his American tour of 1895 Barrett travelled by train through wild districts where a mark was blazed here and there on prominent rocks. He was told by the negro attendant, " When de assayer find a likely spot for minerals he make de mark on de rock—de sign ob de cross ".

Within a very short time *The Sign Of The Cross* opened at St. Louis and had no success. Barrett re-wrote and wrote again, trying his play in every town, until he came back to England and tried his luck at Leeds. Sex-and-salvation had reached its zenith, for the quality of " power " had been transferred from the page to the stage now that religion had been dramatized as an aphrodisiac. Passion is innocently excited by his heroine, the Christian maid, Mercia, in the pagan breast of Marcus Superbus, one of Nero's prefects. She is brought to an orgy at his house where the guests deride her. Chivalrously commanding " Hence, all of you ", he attempts rape, but is confounded in his wickedness when she confronts him, a halo of light round her hair, with a cross. In the dens beneath the Colosseum she awaits death in the arena. If she will forswear her faith, Superbus will save her by making her his wife. With the shriek of a mangled Christian boy ringing in her ears, she refuses. Superbus decides to die with her, philosophizing, " If that thy faith be true, what is this world—a little tarrying place—a tiny bridge between two vast eternities : that we have travelled from, and that towards which we go ". Hand in hand they walk to their " bridal ".

Rumours of the impending masterpiece came first from America and then from Yorkshire as Marcus Superbus advanced on London for its opening at the Lyric, Shaftesbury Avenue, 4 January, 1896. " Innumerable clergymen, a famous Dean and at least one Bishop " hymned his praises to the skies. They led the public to the footlights, for no critics could growl louder than his lions. Archer likened the simpleminded padres to children at their first pantomime, but considering how " power " had evaporated from the imaginings of Caine and Corelli when transferred to the stage, Barrett's achievement is worth examining. How was it such old materials could be regarded as new? Critics played their part, for Archer uttered a *cri du cœur* in protest against its sanctimonious bloodthirstiness.

Bestiality, sexuality and Christianity are not in *The Sign Of The Cross*. Yet the compound of all these three was what its audiences saw.

There can be no denying that something was there which is no longer there.   What its performances did to the public in 1896 can be likened to chemical action.   The shriek of Haidée Wright when eaten alive as the mangled Christian boy, the spiritual agony of Maud Jeffries when running the risk of rape, the nobility of Barrett when preferring lions and love to lust and luxury, had meaning.   They registered on the critic who raged, as powerfully as on the gallery boys and girls who now by their firesides recall how that excitement burnt them up.

Excitement was what each playgoer found in the play.   Yet it was never mentioned in unsolicited testimonials.   Writers of these spoke as though they had mistaken the Lyric for something between cathedral crypt and lecture hall.   The Rev. Canon Thompson of Cardiff called Mr. Barrett " a thoughtful, refined, and scholarly man ".   Gladstone saw the show at Chester.   " A great service to the best and holiest of all causes—the cause of Faith ", was the residue when his feelings subsided.   " And I rejoice to hear ", ran his letter of thanks for free tickets, " of the wide and warm approval which the piece has received, most of all because its popularity betokens sound leanings and beliefs in the mass of the people."   Making full allowances for differences of opinion between generations, particularly propinquitous generations, that is still curious.

Actors who continually play one part for a year or more tend to confuse its identity with their own.   Barrett, after some hundreds of performances of *The Sign Of The Cross*, saw himself as Superbus. Formerly he had haunted Rotten Row in a velvet coat, a slouch hat and a Quartier Latin tie after the manner of *The Silver King*.   Now he attended Church Parade dressed with simple dignity in top hat, frock coat, flannel shirt open at his Roman neck, and hair, grey at the roots, antiquely flaxen, while in deportment he was as much Superbus as on the stage.   " When I was brought to the presence ", said W. E. Holloway—an actor of the richest experience—" I felt almost impelled to drop on one knee, the way I was ushered into his dressing-room and the way he sat on a dais and extended his hand were so rarified.   When he knew of actors who went hungry he would make an appointment at his house, then excuse himself on account of pressure of business and ask them to pass the time breakfasting at his table, where they could eat heartily unobserved."

There was no need to find a successor to *The Sign Of The Cross*— no need for Barrett to act again.   But the spirit of Shakespeare was as rampant within him as it was in Caine and Corelli, and he wrote several more dramas, though none of them excited public interest.   At the Lyric in 1897 he wafted the plot of *The Octoroon* to Ancient Assyria, where it became a new play, *The Daughters Of Babylon*, with a heroine held up to auction and freed by a sentimental courtesan who denounced the villain while Barrett carried a lamb to show a Christian spirit even in a century B.C.   *Man And His Makers*, by Wilson Barrett and Louis Napoleon Parker, staged at the Lyceum in 1899, scoffed at science. A Q.C. loves and is loved, but the girl's father, who believes in heredity, knows that the Q.C.'s father was a drunkard, and the match is forbidden.   The Q.C. takes to drugs and is ruined.   He sleeps on a bench in the Mall, where the heroine, descending from a ball at the Duchess's in Carlton House Terrace, lays her cooling hand on his temple and in ten years he is a judge and the father of a happy family.

One criticism rankled.   Barrett was distressed by the charge that *The Sign Of The Cross* had plagiarized " Quo Vadis? "   Witnesses for the defence included an old stock actor, George Graham, who saw a still greater similarity to " Pomponia; or, The Gospel in Cæsar's Household ", which he remembered as a serial in the *Sunday at Home*. But Barrett had a better way of confounding his critics.   He went abroad to see Sienkiewicz and obtained his permission to dramatize " Quo Vadis? "   Unfortunately a version by Stanislaus Strange opened first at McVicker's Theatre, Chicago, and was brought to the Adelphi in the May of 1900.   Barrett, a month later, mounted his play at Kennington.   "It was ", wrote George Graham, " a riot of solid masterpieces, such a profusion of different sized rostrums as I had never seen before."   Both productions were soon forgotten while Marcus Superbus still held the stage.

" Counsel in overflowing measure ", on many subjects from virtue to sea-power, marked *The Christian King*, Barrett's celebration of King Alfred's millenary, at the Adelphi in 1902.   His last play, *Lucky Durham*, was about a love-child who comes back a millionaire.   When it was being tried out at Liverpool in 1904, Barrett had to undergo an internal operation which lasted for four hours.   He died, pleading, " Hold me up, hold me up, I'm going."

THE LIGHT BEYOND

LXIII (*left*) *The Sign of the Cross* (Lyric, 1896): Wilson Barrett as Marcus and Maud Jeffries as Mercia: " The Master has spoken. You cannot harm me now "

LXIV (*right*) " Thus, hand in hand, we go to our bridal. The light hath come. Come, my bride! Come— to the Light beyond ! "

LXV and LXVI *Dan'l Druce, Blacksmith* (Haymarket, 1876): Marion Terry as Dorothy. Forbes Robertson as Geoffrey Wynyard

INNOCENTS

LXVII *The Squire* (St. James's, 1881): Mr. and Mrs. Kendal as Lieut. Thorndyke and Kate Verity

LXVIII *Little Lord Fauntleroy* (Prince of Wales' 1888): Annie Hughes as Cedric Errol

18 Melodrama Mocked

Gilbert and Sullivan

PROVIDENCE was undone. From the moment Wilson Barrett spoke of the risks run by innocence cracks appeared. According to the robust faith of his fathers nothing urged Providence to greater efforts than the defence of innocence, which therefore ran no risks. Trivial though this may seem it indicates how the entire pageant of virtue triumphant, universally vast no matter how insubstantial, was fading. If the change be dismissed as one affecting mere entertainments the answer is that the drama of democracy had not until now been mere entertainment. It had, as a means of self-expression, kept hope alive for the masses throughout the sordid age of industrialism, even though it had proved itself to be an illusion which left some with the feeling of having been duped.

There was no rude awakening. The first doubts came in gentle comic operas as romantic in manner as the fustian they ridiculed. Their author, William Schwenck Gilbert, was yet another barrister-official-journalist-versifier-playwright. For the Haymarket in 1876 he wrote *Dan'l Druce, Blacksmith*, a melodrama on the subject of an old miser with an adopted daughter, for which he gave the credit to George Eliot's " Silas Marner ". Sir Jasper, fleeing with a babe in his arms from the Ironsides—after a battle in which the baby seems to have taken part—leaves it in a miser's cottage and escapes with the miser's hoard, after scribbling, " Grieve not for thy gold—it hath taken this form ". The miser exclaims, " Heaven has worked a miracle to save me ". Two years later, in *H.M.S. Pinafore ; or, The Lass That Loved A Sailor* at the Opera Comique, Gilbert looked down from philosophic heights upon melodrama, turning to laughter the tale of infants changed in their cradles. In *The Pirates Of Penzance ; or, The Slave Of Duty*, at the Opera Comique in 1880, his jest was a hero as much in honour bound to a pirate king as the hero of Fenimore Cooper's " The Red Rover "—long popular as a play as well as a novel. The author's ability to mock the tricks of his trade was not so remarkable as his audience's avidity to smile with him at one end of the town and weep with Sims at the other.

From its very beginnings melodrama had been accompanied by so-called " burlesques " which de-emotionalized all its plots without as much as pin-pricking them.   What was serious on one stage became fun on another, not by the exercise of a critical or disillusioning wit, but by substituting song, dance, puns and horseplay for emotion.   Such entertainments of comic relief, badly needed by a public which became easily overwrought, never justified their label.   There was no genuine burlesque until Gilbert's comic operas exposed the absurdity of melo-drama both in the theatre and in real life.

Other signs that the polite world might be, very slowly, coming to its senses had been appearing for some time past in the kind of fiction it read.   Unmelodramatic novels had proved popular ever since Darwin's influence had been felt, but to find distinct traces on the stage might be difficult apart from the unscrupulous character in Alphonse Daudet's play, *La Lutte Pour La Vie*, who justifies his misdeeds by calling himself a " strugforlifeur ".   That came many years later. Passions that raged in 1859 demanded silence, and it was then that George Eliot expressed the scientific view of life in fiction.   As assistant-editor of the *Westminster Review*, Mary Ann Evans, from Nuneaton, met George Henry Lewes and " entered into an irregular connection with him " according to the phraseology of their bashful generation—in other words they lived together.   In the novels she wrote under the name of George Eliot, the hard-headed reasoning of the Midlander applied biology to story-telling.   Instead of proffering heroes or heroines to be praised or villains and vampires to be con-demned—the view that Dickens was still upholding magnificently— she expounded a new idea of sin : wickedness was damned, not be-cause of the eagerness of Providence to punish the evil-doer, but because the consequences of evil-doing were unavoidable.   That this was a distinction with a vital difference the whole trend of fiction would show.   Providence could no longer be relied upon to save an erring wife or any others who liked to sin and repent.

Why not ascribe melodrama's decline to a cause within itself—that craze for realism which must surely bring it into withering contact with reality?   But melodrama's unreality thrived on realism.   The greater the outward show of actuality the more thorough the deception. Providence was never so impressive to the gullible as when thwarting the express at that sixty miles an hour which on the stage was agreeably represented by half-a-dozen jerks.   There were, of course, several other kinds of realism.   But neither Dumas *fils* nor Zola could dispel faith in a Providence who waited behind the scenes to punish or reward in order of merit.   That they belonged to the old order became

Hermann Vezin as Dan'l Druce, Blacksmith : " Hands off!   Touch not the Lord's Gift "

evident as soon as Thomas Hardy's novels made his meaning clear.   In the early 1870s he was writing one a year.   What he signified can be understood when Wilkie Collins' " The New Magdalen ", normal evidence of public taste, is compared to Hardy's novel with a clergy- man in it—" Under the Greenwood Tree ".   To see here the differ- ence between the new world and the old might be strained, but the two novelists undoubtedly faced in these opposite directions.   Collins' love story followed the accredited and approved pattern of two souls destined for one another, and Hardy's simple country gossip plainly inferred that marriages, far from being made in heaven, might be decided by a silk umbrella.

"Far from the Madding Crowd" pleased everybody. Six years after its publication in 1874 Hardy assisted Comyns Carr to make a play out of it. They were forestalled by an unacknowledged dramatization called *The Squire* which pretended to be an original play. Though literary piracy was frowned upon, playwrights still picked up novels as unconsidered trifles. Pinero, an actor-playwright, deciding to "waft the scent of hay over the footlights", stole Hardy's zephyrs. Out of materials gathered in Wessex he wrote *The Squire* for the Kendals—inheritors of the Bancroft tradition because Madge Kendal was Tom Robertson's sister—at the St. James's towards the close of 1881. The resemblance was so strong that it would be simpler to regard it as a free adaptation. The version by Hardy and Carr departed from the original further still. In their plot a gypsy vowed revenge (like the one in *Maria Marten*) because his sister had been seduced by Sergeant Troy. He cowered behind hedges and came in and out of doors or windows for three acts, bent on the murder which would bring the true lovers together again.

Lest "Far from the Madding Crowd" should seem to set the standard for novels in the 1880s, another that was then avidly read deserves notice. Mrs. F. H. Burnett's "Little Lord Fauntleroy" was thought a beautiful work. It was dramatized by E. V. Seebohm in 1888 at the Prince of Wales's with Annie Hughes as the grandson from America—almost a legendary figure now in velvet suit, lace collar and long flaxen hair—whose winning ways soften the hard heart of the old Earl of Dorincourt until he forgives the boy's mother for marrying his son.

19 Male Magdalens

The Profligate

MELODRAMA of a kind which made no pretence at being anything else but melodrama became despised. Both people of fashion
and people of taste avoided it. They flocked to those comic operas at
the Savoy which expressed exactly what they had begun to think of
the old world and its ways, but they had also crowded to most of the
many plays of H. J. Byron,[1] who saw life precisely as the Surreyside
saw it although he cared less for sensations—that he could manage this
style when he chose was proved by the floods in *Guinea Gold ; or,
Lights And Shadows Of London Life* at the Princess's in 1877—than for a
lighter style where he could pun as much as he pleased. Such pieces
were comedies because the plot was slight and the dialogue facetious,
but to enjoy them the audience had to accept stereotyped artifices as
natural. *Partners For Life*, staged at the Globe in 1871, is typical of his
long list; husband and wife part because he is annoyed at finding that
she is wealthy; both pretend to be single and not to know one another;
they fall into each other's arms when they meet as fellow guests, and
cause a scandal. This treatment was so well liked that H. J. Byron's
Our Boys ran at the Vaudeville from the January of 1875 to the April of
1879. A rich butterman's son and a baronet's son starve together in
an attic rather than marry in accordance with their fathers' wishes;
then there is trouble with the brides of their own choice because a
bonnet, left in their attic by an aunt, provokes suspicion. A critic was
pained. "This rather unpleasant imbroglio", said Dutton Cook
apropos the bonnet, and then again, " amusement is excited by inhar-
monious and injudicious means ".

Nothing pleased this supposedly sophisticated town better than
melodrama which successfully pretended to be something else.
Ohnet's *Le Maître Des Forges*, at the Gymnase in 1883, was the type.
As *The Ironmaster*, by Pinero, it was acted by the Kendals in 1884 at the

[1] He was Lord Byron's second cousin but probably inherited his literary
talent from a great-grandfather who was a rascally quack with a gift for writing
advertisements.

St. James's, already established as the theatre of Mayfair. This story of a woman of good family who weds the industrialist in a fit of pique and insists on a *mariage blanc*, had the air of " social problem " about it. That meant diluted melodrama. The heroine, rushing between the pistols of her aristocratic old love and her commercial husband, receives a slight wound; it was gloomy and that made it fashionable, for the new intellectual drama which quidnuncs talked about would of course be gloomy—the drama of ideas from *The Robbers* to *Leah* always had been because it had always come from the other side of the Rhine where brains worked solemnly. The Franco-German frontier had been so great a wall against the free passage of thought that German plays came to London by way of New York. The barrier broke down when Harris presented at Drury Lane a German company, maintained by the Duke of Meiningen, which excelled in the handling of stage crowds. Thirty-odd years earlier there were riots when foreigners acted at Drury Lane. Now, however small the financial rewards, the talk of the town was flattering. "Managers", said Harris, "flocked to Drury Lane along with the general public." They were willing to borrow from other Continental cities besides Paris.

As a cosmopolitan Henry Herman was aware of what interested playgoers abroad. Fresh from the success of *The Silver King* he persuaded Jones to join him in tackling a similar subject (with the difference that it would now be a woman who innocently committed the crime) in a drama, by " the leading playwright of Norway ", called *A Doll's House*. It had caused a great stir in Germany even though the author, in Herman's eyes, seemed raw to the theatre, for he had strayed uncouthly from what Clement Scott had set down as the bounds of human nature. The partners soon put this right. While changing outlandish names into simple English ones, they corrected the " sympathy " so that the public would know whom to side with, and appealed to chivalry with their new title of *Breaking A Butterfly*. This redecorated masterpiece was billed at the new Prince's Theatre (later called the Prince of Wales's), mid-way between Leicester Square and Piccadilly Circus, in the spring of 1884. There was a brilliant cast with Kyrle Bellew, an exceptionally handsome actor from Australia, to play an elderly husband who confesses to the forgery committed by his thoughtless little wife, and Beerbohm Tree to represent the jilted lover who hopes to get her into his clutches by holding the incriminating document over her defenceless head. When a kind-hearted friend of husband and wife turns burglar for their sake, all goes well.

But all did not go well in the newspapers the next morning. Just as luck would have it this play, out of all the hundreds that had crossed

Partners for Life (Globe, 1871)

the Channel, was not to be freely adapted with impunity. That forthright Scot, William Archer, wrote as if the play were considerably more sacred than Shakespeare. Though the Bard's text could be altered at will, Ibsen's had to be respected. *A Doll's House* was not a title to be changed even though people might associate it with Christmas pantomimes; and the unthinkable ending, where the well-meaning wife walks out, deserting her children and slamming the door behind her, was not to be improved upon either. What was worse, the public, knowing little and caring less, stayed away and the play vanished within the month.

It was irksome to note Archer's inconsistency. When criticizing *The Squire*, he had defended the mangling of Hardy's meaning on the grounds that " the resemblance of the play to the novel, or rather the importance of the resemblance, has been exaggerated ". As much might well have been said in defence of *Breaking A Butterfly*. Both adaptations changed new lamps into old, as the critic ought to have gathered from his own summing up, " Mr. Pinero might—by the grace of the Lord Chamberlain—have made his play moral; he has only made it conventional ". As a puritan, Archer understood Ibsen's argument that those who practise virtue must be ready to perish for virtue; for the same reason he did not understand Hardy's cosmos

K

where man-made institutions like virtue were dwarfed. New thinkers occupied very different territories. Archer was trying to find his way about Hardy's Wessex with a map of Norway.

Enough was known of Ibsen's plays for Archer to declare that they could no more be introduced into the West End than the " marriage customs of the Zulus ". Yet they were praised with a reverence that any playwright might envy. Obviously the Norwegian drama could not be rendered acceptable by some ingenious compromise; on the other hand, there was nothing to prevent a London playwright from making the Norwegian manner his own. English plots, if shrouded in conscientious and unnatural gloom, had the chance to share in this intellectual awe. The foreign way was to raise problems outside the pale of polite society; the English way was to bring them within the pale by showing how they affected people of some standing instead of humble provincials.

How this would work out could be tested by adapting an argument now agitating authors and audiences abroad: whether pre-nuptial chastity was equally incumbent on both parties. The debate was highly significant of the moral questionings of the 1880s. It was provoked by *A Gauntlet*, written by Ibsen's closest rival, Björnson, to protest, through his indignant heroine, against the time-honoured belief that a bridegroom was entitled to have had a past; the play caused a stir at Hamburg in 1883, followed by a storm in Norway. In Denmark, Edward Brandes' *A Visit* showed how the husband of an unchaste bride decided that females were as much entitled to free pardons as males, and in Germany Sudermann's *Honour* examined the problem as seen through the eyes of a brother. In Russia Tolstoy's *The Power Of Darkness* presented profligacy on a monstrous scale; the farmer who has the outlook of his bull or boar, ravages the countryside.

Whatever their differences all these were at one in condemning the laxity of male morals, and the point of the attack becomes clear when the behaviour of bachelors in popular dramas is studied. In these, judging by the London stage, the blame for sexual indulgence was so very one-sided that the male felt in duty bound to revile his partner in adultery afterwards. The hero of *Human Nature*, the Drury Lane drama of 1885, brushed off his mistress like mud. *Sister Mary*, at the Comedy in 1886, went further—naturally, since it combined the imaginative powers of Wilson Barrett and Clement Scott. " Pretty " was a critic's adjective for its singular story of the morose Captain Leigh who takes to drink after becoming an unmarried father, as though entitled to usurp the unmarried mother's state of being ruined. He is reformed by the stage clergyman's counterpart, Sister Mary. After he has lied like any female vampire about the irregularity of his past—the mere fact that he has to do so shows there was something in the air—she promises to marry him; on learning the truth she changes her mind. When war breaks out in Africa, Sister Mary is a Red Cross nurse in a fort commanded by Captain Leigh while the mother of his child is in a doomed mission. Much is made of the soldier's heroism in leaving the woman he loves to rescue the woman he loves no longer, but he is soon free to marry the former because in the battle the latter is the first to fall (nobody asks who fired the shot).

Since that was "pretty" a retort was needed—a situation which must be borne in mind if justice is to be done to a scrap of almost forgotten history. It was in 1887 that Pinero wrote *The Profligate*, which may look like answering one melodrama with another melodrama until we see how the need for it arose. All that the overwrought scenes set forth is the remorse of a husband who meets the girl he once betrayed, but this was something that had to be said, and now, when playgoers knew there was an intellectual aura arising out of gloom, was the time for saying it. Two years passed. At length, in the April of 1889, a play had to be found for the opening of a new theatre, the Garrick in Charing Cross Road. *The Profligate*, with John Hare in the title rôle, was an instant success and ran for over 100 performances; it went on tour for the summer, which was then the "dead season" in town, and returned to the Garrick for the autumn—only to find that its moral was neither denied nor accepted but merely taken for granted. But it had done its work—heroes would still cast their mistresses aside, but the incident would not be called pretty. Even that achievement was ignored very soon. As early as the autumn of 1889 mockers had begun to quote passages from the dialogue about the way a man's wild oats thrust their ears not only through the floor-boards of his home but also between the paving-stones over which he walks with the wife who fondly imagines that he has been *good*.

Paris also tried change. The Théâtre Libre, in 1887, began in a narrow, very muddy and dimly-lit alley—the Passage de l'Élysée des Beaux Arts—and the fashionable world had to ask the way at a wine-shop at the corner. "A comparatively unknown actor named Antoine" was the manager. He was soon famous for his violently dictatorial methods, his contempt for all established theatrical ways and his devices for making his performances look like happenings in real life. But what he insisted upon still more emphatically was that they should be unlike happenings in real theatres. At his club he staged *La Puissance Des Ténèbres* de M. le Comte Leon Tolstoi. As a remarkably opposite treatment of the prevailing idea he put on *Les Fossiles* by the Vicomte François de Curel. The Duc de Chantemelle marries off the girl who is with child by him to his dying son, in order that the direct descent may not be extinguished. However that might shock or startle it could be comprehended by minds accustomed to nothing but melodrama. Ibsen's *Les Revenants*, another study at the Théâtre Libre of a profligate father, a dying son and the sowing of wild oats, was different.

20 The Truth about Virtue

Ibsen

" THE conscience is very conservative," Ibsen said—so conservative that its instinctive revolt against what was " revolting " could not be overcome.   Venereal disease spread through immorality : therefore, the subject itself was immoral : so conscience argued, condemning the healer along with the sinner.   When *Les Revenants* was first played in London as *Ghosts*, Victorian sensitiveness expressed itself in language that leaves very much the same impression on the mind as the gramophone record of a shriek.   This has become a commonplace of theatrical history.   Its whys and wherefores are still, and always will be, worth investigating anew.   So severe a shock cannot be fully apprehended at once.

Ibsen let his plays speak for themselves.   Critics in all countries took it upon themselves to explain those plays for him (or to him).   Where nobody has succeeded to date, nobody is likely to succeed yet awhile, but here a not dissimilar task must be undertaken.   Those plays are not part of our subject, but their effect upon it unavoidably is.   They were acid to alkali.   Their most resolute champion said that to imagine them in the regular run of London plays was impossible.   There was direct antagonism.   They destroyed the melodramatic faith.   They obliterated Providence.   They made no compromise with virtue triumphant.

" Virtue? " Ibsen could be imagined saying, " I'll give them virtue."

For many years he had been stage-manager of a Norwegian theatre where melodrama had regularly followed melodrama.   And having listened to everlasting sentiments upon the one subject, he set his mind to see the truth about it.   No dramatist before or since saw it so starkly. He stated his resolve in his poetic drama, *Brand*.   Here is the first of the stage pastors, totally unlike all others.   Here is the man of God, utterly unheeding of all else.   The cost of virtue can never be too high.   All must perish for it.   So the great preacher Kierkegaard was testifying and Ibsen's theme at first was as simple as that.   Yet his plays were called social dramas, welcomed by social reformers and interpreted as answers to social problems. Their dramatic spell was so great that they could have been interpreted as answers to any questions. But in cold blood, away from the theatre, logic cannot work out how *A Doll's House* solves the difficulties of marriage. Feminists took up a " serve him right " attitude to the husband without reckoning that the wife who slammed the door behind her was the one to suffer. From the sociological point of view Ruskin had already argued, " The woman's power is for rule ". From the practical point of view Barrie would do better with *The Twelve Pound Look*, where the wife buys a typewriter before she leaves home. This was not Ibsen's reasoning. His Nora is so intent upon virtue that she insists upon suffering for it in order to put herself to the test. She has the soul of Brand, set like his on the destruction of her material self. The play is not a marriage settlement and the fact that it was accepted as such merely proves how intent London was on Social Reform.

Virtue unrewarded is Ibsen's subject in those plays which first made his name. For its sake in *Rosmersholm* the lovers drown themselves; in *Little Eyolf* the parents refuse to be comforted; in *The Master Builder* ambition cannot rest short of death. Virtue here is Ibsen's idea of virtue. What the world respects under that name he vivisects. Female virtue inspires him in *Hedda Gabler* to a psychopathological examination of physical chastity. The virtuous wife and virtuous lover in *Ghosts* share, solely because of their virtue, the profligate huband's guilt for the disease which dooms the son. What immediate influence did these scientific demonstrations have on the popular stage? They took effect in the way a family Bible would if brought down heavily upon a sinner's head; he might be expected to benefit from such teaching but not to find in it any means of grace. Playwrights mended their ways in a safe and profitable compromise which proved how little they understood a genius essentially uncompromising. " The wages of virtue is death " was nailed to his door. Plays on the New Model all proclaimed, as though excited by a great discovery, " The wages of sin is death ". Even Ibsen's most ardent champions were unaware that this moralist wore his rue with a difference. William Archer constantly strove to expound him like a Shorter Catechist; the difference between them cries aloud when the puritan critic comments, " Not an altogether pleasing anecdote ", on the origin of *The Master Builder*. Ibsen, chuckling over his wine, boasted of an adventure with " a spice of devilry in it ", when he met a Viennese girl who said she preferred to lure away other women's husbands than to have one of her own. " She did not get hold of me," said the old fellow, " but I got hold of her—for my play." His last play disowned all his interpreters, who retaliated by dismissing it as incomprehensible.

The "New Spirit" was not one spirit but several—irreconcilable and united only in hatred for the old. This stirred a prophet in Russia, Tolstoy; a novelist in England, Hardy; a painter in France, Cézanne; and in Italy an actress, Duse, who overthrew melodrama exactly as Ibsen had done. She was the child of strolling players, born in such a wagon as the one dragged through mire in Scarron's "Roman Comique". In their company she played blood-and-thunder; when she won fame her repertoire ranged from La Dame Aux Camélias to La Tosca; yet before an Ibsen heroine came her way she was playing in his manner. She was praised by all the greatest critics of her time, whether they belonged to the new school or the old. But it is an anonymous article in The Theatre which best measures her achievement. Since the art that conceals art is for popular purposes no art at all, she steadily lost ground as people discovered, in acting that attained its highest and purest form, "nothing to startle or excite". In England players had to dazzle, convulse or frighten; her greatness would eventually be shown, "in the absolute inability of anyone who has once seen her to ever again accept the old-style acting as supreme". Whoever went away complaining, found something missing when next he saw his more conventional favourite. Duse had raised the standard of acting, and the day of brilliant jugglery was past. Her art was so perfect that it gave the effect of truth and was "accepted as nature".

In Duse's repertoire Ibsen's females found strange playmates. La Dame aux Camélias, Froufrou, Fedora and La Tosca were as natural to her as Nora, Desdemona and Hedda Gabler. In Germany she found Magda, heroine of Sudermann's Heimat, which was acclaimed as a masterpiece by champions of the Frei Bühne. It sketched a Prussian officer's household. The daughter rebels, runs away to study singing, is left by her lover with a child, becomes a prima donna, returns at the call of homesickness, meets her lover and thanks him for making a woman of her. "Honest" or "dishonest" had become immaterial in her eyes, which was hailed as a new thought though public opinion had decided long ago that prime donne were above the law. In London, Duse found Paula, heroine of Pinero's The Second Mrs. Tanqueray, acclaimed as a masterpiece when played by George Alexander and Mrs. Patrick Campbell at the St. James's in 1893, though what it boiled down to was Paula's resolve, simply because her former lover came back as her step-daughter's fiancé, to shoot herself. English society, it was implied, required from its women what German militarism required from its men. The most casual survey of Mayfair would have exposed the lie. In a society renowned for well-preserved men and well-kept women, highly respected Paulas battened on their pasts while lovers, once ruined, came rushing back to fling newly-made fortunes at their feet and be ruined again. Male ruin meant recent loss of cash, property, credit. Female ruin might mean recent acquisition of cash, property, credit. But Paula marched by the side of Froufrou in the crocodile of expiatory heroines who made triumphal progress through the world's tears.

In these trans-ocean performances Mrs. Campbell proved herself the most temperamental *femme fatale*, with her air of mystery and slumbering passion. But it was still Bernhardt who embodied the secret dreams of the disillusioned, dying century. In Paris she passed from management at the Ambigu to proprietorship of the Porte-Saint-Martin, next of the Renaissance, and then of the Théâtre des Nations which naturally became the Théâtre Sarah Bernhardt. From the prosaic Secret Service of Sardou she ascended to the poetic romances of Rostand—melodrama in its most delicate forms. In his *L'Aiglon* she made Napoleon's son her part no matter who else should try to step into his thigh-boots. In her repertoire the little subaltern mixed oddly with what Walkley described as the embodiment of Oriental exoticism : " The strange, chimaeric, idol-woman : a compound of Baudelaire's Vierge du Mal, Swinburne's Our Lady Of Pain, Gustave Moreau's Salome, Leonardo's enigmatic Mona Lisa ". Alligatress, strangled dove and mating tigress are among the things James Agate mentioned while writing about her. At three score years and ten she had a leg amputated. That did not end her career, and when she played the drug-stricken youth in *Daniel*, at the age of seventy-five, there was one critic who swore she had never acted more brilliantly (at which some of the old guard who could not separate acting from physical magnetism objected).

She made French the language of cosmopolitan drama, though it was not solely by virtue of her magnetism that the spotlight from the firmament fell no longer on ballerina and prima donna. *Fin de siècle* expressed itself in majesty of histrionics; the departing glory of the nineteenth century was a blaze of great Thespians. She-tragedies stalked the earth in dignified gloom—and yet they were not the quintessence of it all. The old world chose not one of these actresses but an actor for its champion. An era was ending in a joust at the footlights— Ibsen versus Irving.

LXIX *The Ironmaster* (St. James's, 1884): Mr. and Mrs. Kendal as Philippe and Claire

LXX *La Dame Aux Camélias* (Lyric, 1893): Eleonora Duse as Marguerite Gautier

SOPHISTICATION

LXXI and LXXII *THE SECOND MRS. TANQUERAY* (St. James's, 1893)
Cyril Maude as Drummle, George Alexander as Tanqueray and Mrs. Patrick Campbell as Paula

LXXIII *The Fate of Eugene Aram* (Lyceum, 1873): Henry Irving as Aram and Isabel Bateman as Ruth Meadows

RETRIBUTION

LXXIV *Dante* (Drury Lane, 1903): Henry Irving as Dante and William Mollison as Cardinal Colonna

LXXV and LXXVI   As Mathias in *The Bells*, Act II and Act III (Lyceum, 1871)

HENRY IRVING

LXXVII   As Louis XI (Lyceum, 1878)   LXXVIII   As Vanderdecken (Lyceum, 1878)

LXXIX   *Trilby* (Haymarket, 1895) :   Tree, at piano, as Svengali

LEGENDARY FIGURES

LXXX   *The Only Way* (Lyceum, 1899) :   Martin Harvey as Sydney Carton

Crime Repentant

Irving

OPPRESSED racehorses, Nonconformist Romans, limelit parsons, grovelling adulteresses and suicidal philanderers—had these been the best melodrama could offer now, in the decline of the age, the old spirit would have died unlamented.   But romance, even as it revealed itself to be an insubstantial pageant, faded in glamour such as had never yet been seen, the glamour of Irving's final quarter of the century at the Lyceum.   Remorse, regret, repentance, always apparent in melodrama, were still more dominant now.   That doomed fabric set itself to illumine memory for ever with the blaze of its funeral pyre against the sunset.

No conscious resolve made these final scenes sombre, yet a kind of sublime intuition guided the master-hand.   Shadows of many a great exit recorded by history on the world's great stage come and go among them.   The Martyr King passes to the scaffold, Becket steps down from the chancel, Wolsey fades into nothingness, Louis XI on his death-bed snatches the crown, Coriolanus is betrayed.   Is it by accident that all these come together?   Or is it, though not of set purpose, by some unknown, unguessed-at, design?   Take it as blind chance and still that grand climax of the Victorian stage will overawe every inward eye.

Its beginnings are here and there in plays of the 1860s.   Bateman, having brought one daughter to London in *Leah*, now returned with another, Isabel, to appear in Mrs. Bateman's *Fanchette, The Will O' The Wisp*.   George Sand's " La Petite Fadette " had been twice dramatized in Paris and then by Charlotte Nirch-Pfeiffer as *Die Grille*, which went, like all good German plays, to America.   In 1857 it was acted at the Stadt Theatre, New York; three years later it became *Fanchon* in English at the St. Charles, New Orleans; other versions, called *The Little Fadette* and *The Cricket*, shared in its abounding prosperity. Naturally the Batemans foresaw a good season for their daughter in London, which had neglected this piece apart from one version, *The Grasshopper*, written for the Olympic by Ben Webster junior in 1867.

Some parts are child's play for those suited to them and impossible to anybody else; and here was one such. The witch's grand-daughter must be elfin to throw a spell over Landry, son of the farmer who embittered the old woman's life; Isabel Bateman seemed no such woodland sprite when *Fanchette* opened at the Lyceum on 11 September, 1871. There was some rivalry too from the Standard, where *Fanchonette; or, The Cricket*, yet another variant from America, appeared at the end of the month. Bateman, noting the success of Henry Irving as Landry, cast him for Jingle in Albery's *Pickwick*.

The public still ignored them and the Lyceum was about to close. In desperation Bateman let Irving have his own way. Here was an actor with much to show for his five years' experience of London. Yet what precisely was his professional standing, what kind of actor could his provincial training in nearly 600 parts be expected to produce? " Crummles ", is the answer. " A strong smack of the country actor in his appearance, and a suggestion of the type immortalized by Dickens in Mr. Lenville and Mr. Folaire ", Sir Squire Bancroft said of him—as a leading gentleman of the drawing-room theatre might be expected to say of a mummer who played anything from wolf or ogre in Christmas pantomimes to Gothic heroes of " twopence coloured " style. The list at the end of Brereton's " Life of Henry Irving ", despite some thirty small parts in Shakespeare, is dominated by plays that could not be called old-fashioned because they had never been fashionable. When he grasped his first opportunities in town, Irving wore the clothes of contemporary life both in drama and comedy, and was acclaimed by playgoers accustomed to the new natural style. On the other hand, directly he chose for himself he steadily looked backwards with faith in the past and no belief in the future. He was both praised for this and blamed for it. What matters is that it was so. He made a golden harvest of old customs, and emphasized his nostalgia still further by choosing characters who looked back. The recitals in which he had introduced himself to London included Hood's poem, " The Dream of Eugene Aram ". Now he set his heart on a melodrama which likewise lived over again a murder done many years before.

Paris had taken a fancy to *Le Juif Polonais* by Emile Erckmann and Alexandre Chatrian, which opened at the Théâtre Cluny in 1869 and was still running. In England it was classed as blood-and-thunder and translated as such for gaffs up and down the country. Burnand's version, *Paul Zegers; or, The Dream Of Retribution*, was put on at the Marylebone on 13 November, 1871, and failed. *The Bells*, Leopold Lewis's version, had been declined by Bateman. The author sent it to

Irving, who saw how the spine-chilling effect he caused at his recitals of verse could be magnified if he played Mathias, the guilty burgomaster, in this play. "You—a burgomaster?" was Bateman's comment but he consented. It suited Irving's purpose so admirably that he knew his hour had struck when the curtain rose on *The Bells* at the Lyceum on 25 November, 1871. It opened idly with gossip in the burgo-master's house, first about a mesmerist at the fair and then about the murder of a Jewish traveller in his sleigh fifteen years ago. Suddenly Mathias hears the tinkle of bells. Then, in a vision, the Jew drives past in his sleigh, turns his face, which is ashy pale, and fixes his eyes upon Mathias who utters a prolonged cry of terror—" The bells! The bells! "—and falls senseless. In his bedroom when some revellers have bade him good-night, Mathias dreams that he is on his trial for the murder, and dreams also that he is sent into a trance by the mesmerist and that in this trance he betrays his guilt by showing how he listened for the sleigh, how with a savage roar he struck down his victim, how he bore the body to the limekiln—" Go into the fire, Jew, go into the fire ". The dream ends. It is morning. The door is broken down by fearful neighbours. Mathias gasps, " The rope! The rope! Cut the rope! " As he stares vacantly about him, his hands clutch at his throat and he dies. Death from remorse at last takes on meaning. " First 'e bores yer. Then 'e paralyses yer ", as a galleryite once said.

That first night was recorded by G. R. Sims. He was present by accident. Nearly two years before this he had been to the Queen's in Long Acre to see Mrs. Rousby in Tom Taylor's *Twixt Axe And Crown*. Near him in the pit a " shortish, square-shouldered gentleman with long whiskers of a bright red hue " was thinking aloud. When the manager was brought he answered, " Shut up! I want to hear Tom Taylor's history ", and was dragged backwards over the benches and pushed down the steps into the street. Sims, who gave evidence which gained Lewis a farthing damages, renewed that friendship on 25 November, 1871, on catching sight of a pair of long red whiskers com-ing out of a public house in the Strand. Leopold Lewis, with a thick woollen comforter round his neck, followed the whiskers and a strong odour of rum. Together they went to the Lyceum. The audience was rather bored until the scene of the dream, when there was a burst of applause; but these two had no idea that *The Bells* would " take London by storm and be Henry Irving's stepping-stone to a fame that would be worldwide ". Leopold Lewis, while he did very little after-wards, retained a false idea of his own value as a dramatist until his death, at the Royal Free Hospital, in the February of 1890.

" Packed houses " warmed the air of the shabby theatre. Bateman, dipping his fingers into gold and silver cascading through the box-office window, expanded visibly and regularly supped parties after the play. Actors came and came again with their friends. Wills was brought and made such an impression that Bateman gave him a five years' agreement, beginning with a play for his daughter Isabel. What was good enough for the best actresses in the world would, he thought, be good enough for her. In Ancient Athens a tragedy about Medea had been popular. It had been adapted to nineteenth-century taste by Legouvé for Rachel; and though she had not acted it, Ristori had. At Wallack's Matilda Heron had played a version of her own with such success that E. T. Smith had bought the play in 1861 for Avonia Jones at Drury Lane. When *The Bells* ended its run of 151 nights in the summer of 1872, *Medea In Corinth* filled the gap until Wills had written another play at express speed so that the leading lady and the leading gentleman of the company could appear together. They did so that September in his *Charles I*—four dramatic scenes, each exhibiting a different phase of the King's character. It moved the audience to tears. It did as much to anyone with a respect for history without lessening the effect of the King's last meeting with his wife and children, a scene most competent actors could make effective.

The backward trend of Irving's thoughts fitted in with the ideas of manager and dramatist, for Bateman trusted only in what had already been approved and Wills liked his stories ready-made. Thus each for a reason of his own agreed upon *Eugene Aram*, and that play opened in the April of 1873. It adopted the current craze for the retrospective because Hood's verses already had this technique. When Eugene Aram is hiding in the churchyard, he tells Ruth as he is dying in her arms how years ago he tracked the evil-doer to the cave. Again Irving "paralysed 'em"; having imagined the murder, he "fell crouching before the phantom".

In Lytton's *Richelieu*, revived in the September of 1873, he relied on those moments when the cardinal "lay back in his chair, apparently dying, but watching, like an old fox, the action of the irresolute King and the trembling secretaries". *Philip*, by Hamilton Aïde, which followed in the February of 1874, is the tale of an innocent man suspected by himself of murder. This one was based on an episode from Balzac. On a parapet overlooking the Guadalquivir Philip shoots his brother, Juan, to defend their mother's hired companion, Marie. Years later when she is Philip's wife in Brittany, Juan arrives, tries to compromise her and hides in the oratory. Philip, reminding her of Balzac's story, orders the door to be walled up until she confesses who is there.

Charles I (Lyceum, 1872):
Henry Irving and Isabel
Bateman

To *Hamlet*, *Macbeth*, *Othello* and *Richard III* succeeded the crudest of all things brought from the theatres of the Boulevard du Crime. *The Lyons Mail* (Reade's version) had Irving's confidence. Even in its own day it had been hack-work. Now it was regarded as a rough draft, lasting little more than two hours in performance, although the mounting fears of Lesurques and bloodthirsty frenzy of Dubosc, if fully expressed instead of being merely indicated, would have provided action enough for three—but Irving preferred to speak volumes with a glance than half a page with his tongue. He was satisfied with an ending no better than a conjuring trick after great expectations had been aroused by Dubosc's bravado. In the final scene the villain takes no interest in the safety of his own neck : with an unshakable faith in his own skill to overawe and dupe all comers, he wishes to enjoy the spectacle of his victim's execution. He rents a balcony overlooking the scaffold. He drinks brandy and sends Fouinard out for more. Sheer sadistic delight overwhelms him. " There they are, there they are ! The cart at last. There's Choppard, there's Courriol, and there's the fellow they say is so like me. You're almost at home now, my gentle-men. Gee whoa ! Gee whoaa ! Get on, you brutes. Stand aside, stand aside, and let the cart come on. At last ! At last ! They're mounting the scaffold at last ! Damn that fellow why don't he bring the brandy. Oh, indeed, they're favouring the crowd with their last dying speech. No, they're not. Why it's Janette. Janette spouting. Curse me, if the people and soldiers aren't mixing together. Why there's Fouinard. Fouinard too. Has the beast turned traitor? My name ! They're pointing here ! They're speaking of me." Line by line approaches the crash where the megalomaniac, confronted by un-yielding reality, cannot believe it—a situation of such power that at other times it has arrested attention in the feeblest melodrama. Reade, as quoted by Craig, passes straight on to, " Nabbed—nabbed at last, but they shan't have me cheap ". As Dubosc opened the door Irving changed places with the actor who served as his double, swiftly donned the costume of Lesurques while out of sight, and reappeared amid cheers.[1]

Merely because *The Lyons Mail* had come from the Boulevard du

---

[1] Such prolonged popularity was won by French plays which employed " doubling " that the theatres of the Boulevard were credited with having invented the device. But it was tried at the Old Vic a few years earlier. When John Thomas Haines' nautical drama, *The Wizard Of The Waves ; or, The Ship Of The Avenger*, was given there in 1840, one actor played both Captain Faulkner, R.N., and the mysterious pirate who turns out to be his twin brother. Another example of doubling occurred in *Vanderdecken ; or, The Flying Dutchman*, by T. P. Taylor, performed at the City of London Theatre in 1846, with the skipper and his evil genius as a " dual part ". *Le Courrier De Lyon* had its first per-formance in 1850.

Crime Irving was likened to Frédéric Lemaître (who had not played it), as he in turn had been likened to Edmund Kean. The three actors were the beginning, middle and end of romantic frenzy. What was exultation in the first became triumphant zest in the second and declined in the third to remorse or profound melancholy. Since popular entertainment cannot exist except as the expression of its time, this rise and fall graphs the spirit of the nineteenth century. Interpret the signs as you please, seeing in the popularity of these dreams of fictitious crimes either a secret sympathy with evil-doing or some more complicated frame of mind which calls for a greater effort at discernment. But it is strange to note how few parts were inherited by Irving from Edmund Kean and Frédéric Lemaître, his predecessors in the tradition of romanticized murderers. He borrowed instead from Macready, Charles Kean and Fechter, actors unlike himself except in one significant respect—these three were, so critics said, gentlemanly. With that quality went opulence of scenery. In the 1850s Charles Kean had given a set form to management for leading actors of the century to copy. One method, the grand manner in scenery, costumes, lighting, pageantry, processions and stage crowds, served both for Shakespeare and for romance that was melodrama in excelsis. Charles Kean's curiously exact sense of the spirit of the age is proved by the way three or four of the plays he first brought upon the English stage were kept together by succeeding actor-managers as the nucleus of the romantic drama. *The Lyons Mail*, *Louis XI*, *The Corsican Brothers* and *Faust And Marguerite*, for fifty years mingled with *Hamlet*, *Richard III*, *Lear* and *Macbeth*, as though their equals in colour and form.

Whatever difference existed between *Louis XI* in 1854 and 1878 was vague. That elaborately established " character " left little choice not only in make-up or costume but also in the broad effects of piety, cowardice, malignity, cunning, superstition and sardonic humour. Charles Kean had " paralysed 'em " when he, as Louis, resurrected himself to reclaim his crown in death. Irving, master of the stillness of crouched tiger, coiled snake, compressed mainspring, could but make the same effect. But while Charles Kean's portrait of Louis XI exists for antiquarians, Irving's is dominant, proverbially sinister. Musty the play may have grown, but what he created out of it— shrinking, fearful in nerves and body, grovelling in superstitious dread, yet still maintaining his claim to the crown with fingers that clutch in their last flicker—that figment is plainer to the inward eye than the real Louis XI.

All who upheld the romantic tradition—actor, author, audience— were trying to make time stand still. Its most eager champions were aware of the ever-increasing speed of social change. Some parts of London's jungle had reached such a state of civilization that young women were employed in large numbers as clerks. Masculine breasts, still filled by the chivalrous desire to protect, also felt the fear of a decline in wages. Violence was necessary to romance; without it the sexes mingled in the cold light of equality. The London of taverns was being transformed into the London of tea-shops, not conducive to masculine swagger. Life's sobriety created faith in realism; the stronger it grew the more frantic grew the yearning for last glimpses of departing glamour. Minds not so affected might admire Irving but could not feel as the public did. *Vanderdecken*, by Percy Fitzgerald and W. G. Wills, staged at the Lyceum in the June of 1878, meant little to the critical. The Flying Dutchman, looking for a woman to save his soul, chooses Thekla, is killed by her lover in a duel, flung into the sea and washed ashore (by realistic waves) alive.

Thekla was Isabel Bateman's last appearance in the company. Bateman died in 1875, and his widow took control until his lease ended, when she took control of Sadler's Wells instead. From 30 December, 1878, Irving was the Lyceum's manager, and his first new production was Lytton's *The Lady Of Lyons*. As Pauline, Ellen Terry made her first appearance in the company. She was not a Duse, not a Bernhardt; possibly she laid no claim to greatness; no one can tell because to see her was to feel a personal devotion which made cool judgment unthinkable. At thirty years of age she was radiant with this spell, though possibly less radiant than later. Fault was found because she could not represent the wounded pride and stung resentment that had no part in her. If she had learned, as Pauline does, that the man she loved was an imposter, she would have flung her arms around him protectingly and laughed in the way of sympathy however little she thought of him as the hero of a play. Irving, who had acted with her in his early London days, offered her parts she had already made her own. Her Portia, at the Prince of Wales's in 1875, had been praised for bold innocence, lively wit and quick intelligence, grace and elegance of manner, tenderness and depth of passion beneath a " frolicsome exterior ". Was it Portia or Ellen Terry herself the critic so described? Her lightness of heart was to be the perfect foil to Irving's sable muse.

It was, Walkley wrote, in the romantic rather than the tragic repertory of Shakespeare, " in the figures painted from the rich fantastic palette of the Italian Renaissance ", that Irving walked confidently. Now he played Shylock, a figure other than the one Shakespeare drew; the very sublimity of his hatred and the unflinching fervour of his faith overwhelmed all that defamed him in the text; and Ellen Terry added her Portia to the legend. Here were two opposites, the saturnine and the blithe. Neither had exactly the qualities for *Romeo And Juliet*; their partnership lives—in that vague and curious thing, the inherited theatrical memory—as the perfect Benedick and Beatrice. Whenever *Much Ado About Nothing* is played they will be spoken of. Mephistopheles and Marguerite, Wolsey and Katharine, Becket and Rosamund, Lear and Cordelia, Dr. Primrose and Olivia, King Arthur and Guinevere fade as they recede in time. But the thought of so mordant a Benedick with so volatile a Beatrice will always be among those achievements of acting which playgoers speak of long, long after, as though they had seen them.

Yet above all his triumphs remained *The Bells*. Not thousands but millions of voices tried to mimic his cry, "The bells! The bells!" One of the first curiosities of childhood then was to learn what that cry meant. People who abhorred the theatre knew whence it came, what it portended. It spread his fame everywhere. It was, in a world proud of Lipton and Whiteley, his trademark. It told people who were contentedly ignorant of art and letters the kind of goods he had to sell and they were willing to buy such glorious stuff though they did not recognize in it the splendour of despair. Nineteenth-century romance, knowing itself to be not another Renaissance, vainly tried not to find itself a hollow sham. With all its hankering after threats of wild behaviour it was steadfast in its resolve to be unwaveringly demure. This conflict between wish and will resolved itself in a compromise. Wild behaviour was past. The bushranger or swindler could then, as the sinner that repenteth, claim sympathy on condition that he was about to die. What tinged this stolid, respectable ideal with poetic feeling was the foreboding twilight which stole over all romance before the night. Irving's remorse had more in it than repentance. It was regret for what the Martyr King called "yesterday, bright yesterday"; innocent or blood-stained, it was still to be desired.

Murders and remorse. Dim masses of scenery in the soft light of gas "floats". Heavy shadows outside the brilliant cone of the lime-light around the weird, lanky figure, shed from a lamp in which two gas-jets spluttered into flame upon a stick of lime. Violins in constant *agitato*. An audience—this audience, above all, though it enjoyed the joke of likening Irving to a creaking, rickety five-barred gate—responding in shudders or tears. When and where had there ever been finer *theatre*? Adverse criticism served the purpose of making this clear. Old James Anderson, once a babe in *Pizarro* who had the privilege of wetting the great John Philip Kemble's head, now spoke as a classic tragedian sanctified by many years of temperate approval. Irving, he said, had resurrected *The Iron Chest* more for his own gratification than the public's. The veteran commented that whereas Mathias in *The Bells* was a mercenary murderer for filthy lucre with the constant fear of gaol and hangman before his eyes, Mortimer in *The Iron Chest* was the worshipper of reputation whose crime arose through a sense of shame at its being tarnished by the blow of a ruffian. " When he came to tell the story of that fearful night, it appeared to me, the actor took more pains to vindicate the murder than the outraged honour that led to it. To my thinking the difference betwixt Mathias and Mortimer was not marked enough." It was true that outraged honour was not within Irving's range. It was as alien to his feelings as resentful pride was to Ellen Terry's. Passions born of vanity in the small mind never belonged to their gracious realm, where egotism, petty or monstrous, dwindled into something for amusement, since its tragedies became comedies, like Malvolio, when seen at a distance. The wide sweeping view was ever seen on the Lyceum stage. " What a panorama he has given us ! " Walkley exclaimed, citing Illyrian seascapes, Veronese gardens open to the moonlight, groves of cedar and cypress. Spaciousness of setting matched spaciousness of mind.

Of his plays from the Boulevard by way of the Princess's, *The Corsican Brothers* had the richest tinge of romance. The bare, leafless trees of the silent forest, the frozen pond, the slowly descending snow, the deep orange and red bars of the setting winter sun, echoed his own melancholy. Here is the unmistakable flash of Dumas in a romance not to be bracketed with any others. It dispenses with all the paraphernalia of last-minute rescues, love interest, happy or unhappy ending; it has no heroine to speak of; yet playgoers could not shake off their nostalgia over that silence, broken as the red light fades on the snow by the sharp note of steel upon steel till the last gasp of death.

Patina was the quality of Irving's art. Taking familiar characters that were proverbial or legendary, he gave them the indefinable gloss that time puts upon enduring masterpieces. Better an old play to make it clear the play was not there to be criticized—to keep minds focused not on plot or dialogue but on the thing seen. Better, almost, a dead play in order that discerning eyes should measure how miraculously he brought it to life. The greater the effort needed the more greatly his power could manifest itself. Around him was the setting for this gleaming gem. That was his strength now and would be his weakness. The better the setting the more meaningless it would be without him. He dared not fall out.

By all accounts Ellen Terry and Hermann Vezin gave a perfect

LXXXI and LXXXII *The Christian* (Lyceum, 1907) : Matheson Lang as John Storm and Alice Crawford as Glory Quayle. (*Left*) "God sent me to kill you, Glory". (*Right*) Glory hides her love to save John

CAINE ON SACRIFICE

.XXXIII *The Prodigal Son* (Drury Lane, 1905) : The Prodigal (George Alexander) refuses to reveal the name of the woman who has caused him to forge his father's name

LXXXIV *The Bondman* (Drury Lane, 1906): Jason (Frank Cooper) becomes Bondman to Michael (Henry Ainley). Father Ferrati (Austin Melford): " I'll leave you together. You don't want me "

WRECK AND RECONCILIATION

LXXXV *The Whip* (Drury Lane, 1909): The favourite is saved

performance of Wills' *Olivia*. They had done so at the Court and they did so again at the Lyceum when Irving was ill. But the play staged at its best was of less account than when it was used, against its nature, to serve the purposes of genius. Dr. Primrose as Irving played him could not, on Bernard Shaw's evidence, be reconciled to the story. Yet to prove this point the critic used such words as beautiful, dignified, perfect. It was a performance undertaken in defiance of his destiny. " Baa—baaa—baaa " Irving bleated softly at rehearsal (on Gordon Craig's testimony) in self-criticism of his way of over-painting a sanctity he could not believe in. Compare this with its opposite. " A more horribly evil-looking beast of prey than his Macaire never crossed the stage ", said Shaw, which disproves the statement, so often made, that he was biased against the Lyceum.

That Irving could create a character unlike any so far known to the footlights was demonstrated by Digby Grant, monument of class-conscious vanity in James Albery's *Two Roses*—which enabled him to reverse his usual mood by depicting an old scoundrel without any conscience or sense of guilt whatever. But Irving preferred old parts to new. The Devil, his dearest project, had been played by all manner of actors in all manner of plays—several, including Frédéric Lemaître, Charles Kean, Wallack and Phelps, in versions of *Faust*. There was a challenge to the shade of Macready in Byron's *Werner*; [1] another to Ben Webster in Watts Phillips' French Revolutionary melodrama, *The Dead Heart*; another to Fechter, who had appeared at the Lyceum in 1865 in a dramatization of " The Bride of Lammermoor " (Palgrave Simpson's *The Master Of Ravenswood*) when Irving put on yet another version, H. C. Merivale's *Ravenswood*.

At the zenith of his life his thoughts were valedictory. No mere accident made him choose characters renowned for the ending of their greatness. Cardinal Wolsey in the spring of 1892 was followed by Lear in the autumn, and in the spring of 1893 by Tennyson's Becket with his cry of

> Back, I say !
> Go on with the office. Shall not Heaven be served
> Though earth's last earthquake clash'd the minster-bells,
> And the great deeps were broken up again,
> And hiss'd against the sun ?

Throughout 1893 and 1894 he was playing Becket, with some other parts, in many cities of America and Britain. For some years past his thoughts had turned to the greatest sunset of all, the fading splendours of a vanished chivalry. The " Idylls of the King " could not be set

[1] With an interpolated scene showing the murder to keep the audience from wondering who did it.

upon the stage, since Tennyson would not write a drama on the theme. Wills came forward instead; when commissioned to write *King Arthur* he had faithfully delivered the MS. and been paid £800, several years before this; in 1891 he died. His work had to be altered; it was sent to Comyns Carr, who preferred to write Arthurian blank verse of his own and had his way. What the Lyceum staged on 12 January, 1895, was a triumph for both painter and actor. Shaw spoke of " the eternal beauty of the woodland spring "—also of " a great bit of acting " when King Arthur learns that his wife loves Lancelot.

Mystical feeling we are too afraid of—we prefer the trivial explanation of hard fact to belief in the ebb of fortune so well known in all ages that it has many a name besides Nemesis. On climbing his stairs at Grafton Street, after the revival of *Richard III* on 19 December, 1896, Irving slipped and injured his knee. For two months he was unable to act and the effect on the box-office was such that the season ended in a loss of nearly £10,000. By the time he had made a financial recovery, the store of scenery for all his productions except *The Bells* and *The Merchant of Venice* was destroyed by fire. *Peter The Great*, by Laurence Irving, in which he played the Tsar at the Lyceum in the January of 1898, failed. His next choice was worse. That he was out of his reckoning in the harsh new century was made clear in May by *The Medicine Man* (H. O. Traill and Robert Hichens), a melodrama with little to be said for it.

That summer his tour opened badly. In the autumn he had a serious illness. From misfortunes a man may recover, especially a man with many powerful friends. Irving's behaved queerly. Some did nothing. Others persuaded him ill-advisedly. Gordon Craig has put it plainly. Business men turned the Lyceum into a limited liability company when they could have turned it into the National Theatre, " so obvious and so easy, one would have thought, considering how many men of power and wealth had for twenty-seven years been Irving's guests at this same Lyceum."

As his own power through illness and misadventure declined, he saw how many there were to inherit it. Tree's busy emulation until now had been a joke, and the public also had laughed when Jones's Tempter tried to steal the fires of Goëthe's Mephisto. But when *Trilby*, Paul Potter's version of George du Maurier's novel, was staged at the Haymarket in 1895, the rivalry became real, for Tree could now exploit his sibilant articulation and the embarrassing paleness of his eye: Svengali, enthralling in the book, was horrible in the theatre. Next George Alexander (Faust at the Lyceum) discovered a new world of romance. When Anthony Hope's novel " The Prisoner of Zenda " was dramatized at the St. James's in 1896, the public already knew that Ruritania was a sanctuary for melodrama. Its hero found romance while on holiday; and the millions who worked for fifty weeks each year with the dream of unknown happenings during the remaining fortnight, accepted his idea thankfully. Yet another management championing stage romance sprang from Irving's company. While with him on American tours Martin Harvey and his wife, Nell de Silva, decided to set up in management for themselves; they began with *The Only Way*, a new version of " A Tale of Two Cities " with a plot entirely subordinated to Sydney Carton and the little sempstress, which ran on and off for forty years.

Sardou's *Robespierre* was played at the Lyceum in 1899. Two years later Irving staged the last of his Shakespearean revivals, *Coriolanus*. From that autumn to the spring of 1902 he toured the United States. At the end of April he began his last season at the Lyceum; it ended at a Saturday matinée of *The Merchant Of Venice* on 19 July, 1902. The theatre remained closed. On 23 April, 1903, it was put up for auction. No acceptable offer was made. There was a meeting of shareholders on 30 September. They were unmoved by a message from Irving, who was willing to " pay any share or proportion—say, for two or three years—of any sum which might be required to meet the expenses of debenture interest, sinking fund, and other necessary matters ". They decided to turn his theatre into a twice-nightly music-hall. Irving was now rehearsing at Drury Lane, where at the end of April he appeared in *Dante*, especially written for him by Sardou; it had a moderate run in London and a short one on Broadway. But with *The Merchant Of Venice*, *The Bells*, *The Lyons Mail* and *Louis XI* he made a final triumphal progress to the United States and Canada, for the magic of his name had not dimmed. His last appearances in the chief cities of Wales, Scotland and England began in the autumn of 1904.

" Farewell tour " meant impressive occasions which gave dignity to the dowdiest Theatre Royal. For the actor it meant one provincial hotel after another, varied only by week-end travel. " Beetles in the beds ", Ellen Terry's diary had recorded on one tour. Even with a chance to sleep, the ordeal was more than most men would face gladly. Young players in " theatrical lodgings ", even hardy mummers under a canvas flap, would not feel as desolate as the star in grim hotels. Neither the countryside nor the great cities had anything in common with the industrial centres, where everything was sacrificed to the making of money—usually for spending elsewhere. Gloom made the actor's work, nerve-wracking in its demands on failing health, a joyous relief from the torment of boredom.

" Farewell tour "—municipal welcomes at an hour when rest ought to have been imperative, leisure in bleak bedrooms that would make the most unsentimental mind sick for home, distractions when he needed quiet, loneliness when he was ready to relax, harassing worries of management throughout the evening when concentration was needed, and then the return to a building upon which night descended like black death. A glass of wine, a cigar and some friends, were all he asked of private life. On tour he was denied even these. For twelve weeks in the autumn of 1904 he fulfilled engagements, some for three nights, that kept the soot of railways continually in his lungs. In January the ordeal began again. After a month of wintry weather his health broke down. Yet after a farewell season at Drury Lane, he planned an autumn tour.

It began at Sheffield. The second week was at Bradford. The usual luncheon had to be attended, and at that he said the sands of his life were running fast. He played Shylock, Louis XI and then, on the Thursday, Mathias. Ellen Terry said that every time he heard the sound of the bells, the throbbing of his heart must have nearly killed him. " He used always to turn quite white—there was no trick about it. It was imagination acting physically on the body." His death as Mathias—the death of a strong, robust man—was different from all his other stage deaths. " He did really almost die—he imagined death with such horrible intensity. His eyes would disappear upwards, his face grow grey, his limbs cold." He had agreed that he would play the part no more. The next night he was Becket, suffering and dazed but unflinching. The courteous little speech to the audience, the signing of a drawing for a small boy at the stage-door—" all that he had done for years, he did faithfully for the last time ". He was tired and asked one of his staff to drive with him to the hotel. Before this he had through fatigue stumbled and fallen on the way to his room. What oppressed him now was heavier.

Feeling the shadow of death upon him he went into the hotel lobby and sat down on a chair. In his last breath, at that unforeseen moment in that out-of-the-way spot, there was an historic sense of the final. It was not simply the end of a man, of a great man, but the close of an age. The curtain had rung down at last on the performance of centuries. He had stood against the gale. There is nothing in all the wrack it blew away, for our respect, save his tall, gaunt, imposing figure. He alone compels some regret for the cloud-cap't towers that are gone. He raises a hand in warning that while we are avid for the truth it would be as well, since we can never know the whole truth, to believe in something more.

22 High Life at Drury Lane

The Derby Winner

SOCIETY was faced with an urgent necessity to choose between the old and the new, between the ancient pretence that there was virtue in wealth and station and the modern insistence that virtue was a costly business, demanding millions for slum clearance, education and old age pensions, among many other unexciting things. Which should it be, romance or realism? Cavaliers were again at war, though mainly in words, with Roundheads, but the public as a whole were steadfastly resolved on unheroic compromise. That period is too recent to be seen in clear perspective. To some it is gay, festive, full-blooded, a revival of the Regency spirit with a milder dash of raffishness. To others it is the last sordid fling of " privilege " when imitation aristocrats were making what profits they could out of sweated labour in order to squander it lavishly before the new " deluge ". To a great many more these years were the " naughty 'nineties ", full of an incredible childishness which expressed itself as much in the imbecile fads of the New as in the self-conscious worldliness of the Old. That " charming, wicked creature " Lord Darlington in Wilde's *Lady Windermere's Fan*, at the St. James's in 1892, is nothing if not naughty. " Nowadays ", he says, " so many conceited people go about Society pretending to be good, that I think it shows rather a sweet and modest disposition to pretend to be bad." Lots of people say he has never really done anything wrong in the whole course of his life. " Of course they only say it behind my back." No pastiche written to-day could copy that even as caricature.

While the general tone of *fin de siècle* society cannot yet be described confidently, evidence from the theatre is certain. Three of its manifestations are beyond all dispute. The evocative spirit of Irving was held in awe by the many; the prophetic utterance of Shaw was respected by the few; the exponents of compromise, no matter how glib or hollow, were the idols of the day. The period mainly expressed itself, after that third fashion, in plays which are melodramas disguised as advanced thought. " Problem play " was their current label.

Though accepted as "New" they were drawing-room dramas with no other difference than that the chief character was a female sinner instead of a male sinner; and the old notion that sins had sex still prevailed. When opinions on this point changed, the "problem play" was dismissed as rubbish, but when inspected as a photograph of late Victorian life it has a value not to be despised. Everybody in the group is, of course, carefully posed and wearing Sunday best. Deportment is shown as it ought to have been, not as it was. There was a vast difference between the two, though this was most determinedly ignored. What was not spoken of did not exist. Adultery was unspeakable. Therefore it existed only when the Divorce Court caused it to be made known in the public prints. All social offences were judged by this double standard. Any exalted personage who kept up appearances in the public eye might be as blatant as he pleased out of its focus. Any popular players, with no matter what skeletons in their cupboards, could scold "the modern girl" for not observing the proprieties. Any notorious swindler with cunning to keep the right side of the law would be able to preach righteousness and claim that a voice from heaven inspired him. The effect on the stage was an unwavering devotion to rigid moral principles such as the world had not seen since the reign of Louis XVI and Marie Antoinette. This has to be understood before anyone looks into fashion's shop-window as arranged by playwrights who were knighted for their services to the stage.

Take away the respectability from Pinero's plays and what is left? "So engagingly modern", Walkley said of them even while pointing out the "wobbling" of their endings. He admired *The Notorious Mrs. Ebbsmith* at the Garrick in 1895, which was a warning against "irregular unions" in the manner of one who looked upon George Eliot as feeble-minded. The subject had been discussed ever since Olive Schreiner's "Story of an African Farm" appeared in 1883.[1] In the year of Mrs. Ebbsmith, Grant Allen, self-proclaimed atheist, brought out "The Woman Who Did", which told how an ardent young feminist became an unmarried mother rather than turn traitor to her sex by becoming a wife. There was so widespread a desire to be shocked that the novel became a best-seller. At the same time outraged feelings were glad to be soothed by Pinero, whose emancipated heroine was brought to repentance by a clergyman. In another exhibit of the importance of being respectable Pinero's heroine was guiltless. *The Benefit Of The Doubt*, at the Comedy in 1895, is about a wife who leaves the Divorce Court with her reputation not destroyed but seriously

[1] Dramatized at the New Theatre, 1938.

damaged. One play is *Jane Shore* up to date. The other is *East Lynne* in Mayfair. They are merely two of the many bedridden dramas.

If a fashionable atmosphere turned melodrama into something rich and strange, then the autumn dramas of Drury Lane had as good a claim to such promotion as any. One of the last achievements of Harris was to snap the rusty link between lowliness and virtue. If villains were entitled to a good education, so were heroines. The time might even come for upstarts to seduce women of good family, because that was now preferable to any domestic drama which deprived leading ladies of the utmost resources of the dressmaker's art, so robbing them alike of the sympathy of the stalls and the envy of the gallery. In future lasses that loved sailors would be minor parts at Drury Lane where all the abundance of the play panoramic would henceforth be bestowed upon drawing-room drama with its creed, voiced by Captain Swift in his heart-felt cry of, " That's the essential thing to happiness—respectability ". This, the last thought of the gentlemanly bushranger when bound for what he called the Never Never Land, explains why society refused to change its lip-service to Virtue Triumphant, although it was a creed long discredited. Melodrama had become a term of abuse even by those who enjoyed it, and its purpose was mocked as " the painting of vice and virtue in bright colours "; nobody believed that virtue paid, everybody knew that respectability did, but the one idea could not be openly derided without upsetting the other. While religion and science were becoming reconciled, society came to terms with the stage. The world of fashion flocked to the theatres (their own particular theatres) as never before, and in return for its half-guineas was held up to the admiration of the rest of the world as not only well-dressed and well-mannered but well-moralled, which it, quite openly, was not. Yet a little of the truth would out.

Drury Lane had championed the cause of respectability even in the time of Harris. Rather than present any more common-or-garden heroes, he retired from the stage and transferred his place in the limelight to gentlemen. As poverty was not respectable, the lowly of heart henceforth consisted of well-bred people afflicted with gaming debts or dressmakers' bills, and owning nothing except racing-stables occupied by the Winner of the next classic event. Villainy came in the shape of creditors who argued that because of the large sums owing to them they were legally entitled to the horse. Such iniquity brought down upon them social ostracism instead of, or as well as, capital punishment. Sometimes there was no horse. Even then, without sport as an excuse, the new spirit insisted that Norman blood was more than simple faith where female virtue was concerned.

Pleasure (Drury Lane, 1887)

Melodrama took this shape as early as 1887 in *Pleasure* by Meritt and Harris. Jessie is well-born, which excuses her for being pregnant—a novelty for spinster-heroines in melodrama at Drury Lane—because of Jack, the hero, who intends to marry her. But there is a villain, Major Randolph, and it is worth noting that majors have taken the place formerly occupied by baronets; since he hopes to inherit Jack's fortune, he has no wish to see the child born in wedlock and, therefore, heir to the estates. By unscrupulous slander he makes it appear that

A Life of Pleasure (Drury Lane, 1893)

Jack is "not the only one" and prevails upon him to take a trip abroad, where they witness a Battle of Flowers with brightly dressed people throwing bouquets at still more brightly dressed people in real carriages drawn by real horses. Jessie has followed them only to be repulsed at the Carnival Ball; she calls on heaven to punish her faithless lover and heaven replies with an earthquake. Jack marries her and Major Randolph, for some other sins, is apprehended by the police.

Respect for good breeding in human beings as well as horseflesh went further in the Autumn Drama [1] of 1892, for then the heroine, again betrayed, was glad to be made an honest woman of by the villain. *The Prodigal Daughter*, by Pettitt and Harris, was very sporting—country mansion with horses and hounds, Paris Grand Hotel with carriages and gorgeous evening dresses, Aintree with poison for the favourite, the Grand National with a dozen thoroughbreds as well as water-jump,

[1] So called because melodramas at Drury Lane usually ran from the beginning of September, when the London season opened, to the time when the theatre was needed for Christmas pantomime.

yelling crowds, touts, bookies, jockeys and welchers. There was a return to the old manner in 1893 with *A Life Of Pleasure* by Sir Augustus Harris—it was a City, not a stage, knighthood—and Pettitt. The plot began in Boucicault's Ireland and went by way of the Empire promenade, where Arthur Dacre had champagne flung in his face by Mrs. Bernard Beere, to a chasm in Burma where Henry Neville fetched reinforcements with quick-firing guns.

In 1894 Old Drury engaged two new authors. *The Derby Winner* was by Sir Augustus Harris, Cecil Raleigh and Henry Hamilton—Pettitt and Meritt were dead and the Grecian style was no more. "Drawing-room drama " became an understatement when applied to Harris's ancestral halls, where duchesses provided comic relief. Both Raleigh and Hamilton were the sons of soldiers, both had been actors before they wrote for the stage, both had their place in a new kind of community which came under the peculiar heading of " sporting and dramatic ". What had the Turf in common with the stage? " Backing a show ", of course, made money circulate even faster than backing horses and to make money circulate was a good thing. Then again the new kind of chorus girl, as glamorous off the stage as on, did add grace and even loveliness to four-in-hands, pride of the ever-increasing jam of traffic on Epsom roads. Sport and drama brought together by Boucicault in *The Flying Squad* had stayed together. " Real horses ", as long as they were racehorses, saved Drury Lane from being frowsty. The " Grand National Theatre " had to choose not between comedy and tragedy but between flat-racing and steeple-chasing. Henceforward the struggle between right and wrong was usually over a horse, although there were still sins in society—very good sins in very good society.

The Derby Winner even went to the length of using titles borne by real people. Major Mostyn's efforts to cause an estrangement between Lord and Lady X. are, in such elegant surroundings where even servants behave like real servants without a line of exposition or soliloquy between them, somewhat in the nature of flattery carried to the extreme where it becomes offensive. But the trend of the plot excites an uneasy feeling that the devil in Mostyn takes less thought for her ladyship than for the form shown by Clipstone. All his sexual activities are binocular. By first seducing the trainer's daughter and then blaming Lord X. he uses the poor girl's lapse from virtue as an argument to persuade both her father and the jockey not to let Clipstone win the Derby. His most dangerous ally is Vivien, dark lady of old days in Rawalpindi. She comes as a guest. When asked to leave she cries, " Should you ever hear that another wretched woman has sought that one refuge of the desperate—death, remember that it was *you* who shut the door of repentance in her face." But instead of dying she appears at the Regimental Ball, where Lady X. asks the Colonel to have her carriage called : " When I accepted your invitation, and that of the officers of the 43rd Hussars, I did not expect to be insulted by the presence of my husband's mistress ". Scenes in a sanatorium bring Lord and Lady X. together again over the sick-bed of their child, and when Mostyn drugs the jockey, his own jockey changes his colours to ride for Lord and Lady X. and win.

Military glory came back in 1895, but though the Matabele War was the subject of *Cheer, Boys, Cheer* by Harris, Raleigh and Hamilton, scenes at polo, Rotten Row, Lady Hilyard's drawing-room, a Johannesburg hotel, and the grand staircase at Chepstow House were " remarkable for their beauty and extraordinary wealth of accessories ". After Harris's death, Arthur Collins, his stage-manager, took control. Respectability was upheld. In *The White Heather* by Raleigh and Hamilton, the heroine was low-born because her father was nothing better than a prosperous stockbroker. Lord Angus—played by Neville, who was now, at sixty years of age, too handsome to be a hero —weds her at sea, then repudiates her and her child. The sole record of the marriage is in the log-book of his yacht, the " White Heather ", now gone to the bottom. While he is searching for it in diver's outfit, the poor ne'er-do-well, Dick, arrives on the spot, also as a diver, and they clutch each other's wind-pipes in a fight so deadly that the mere poster of it drew full audiences with faces as white and drawn as the disapproving open mouths of the deep-sea fish.

23 The Manx Shakespeare

The Bondman

IN EVERY drama of a sport that excited the thrill of uncertainty the result of the race was—barring mishaps—certain from the start. The Turf that was shown on the stage was nothing more than a toy, and yet it filled the public's heart with pleasure and pride. The racehorse was the emblem of the age. The number of his appearances at Drury Lane, the number of authors who told the same story about him, and the number of different plays so presented to the public without any special protest against the blatant monotony of it all, amount to as much. Diversions such as the problem play may have been tolerated for the sake of variety, but the mainstay of " sporting and dramatic " was the Favourite or the Dark Horse.

History makes this so clear that it may seem hard to " place " Hall Caine. Yet he is as essential to the panorama of those times as the Derby on the stage and off. He fulfilled his destiny as the Manx Shakespeare, with some fellow-feeling for Iceland and Sicily as well, by dramatizing and re-dramatizing his novels until half-a-dozen of them were more to the forefront of affairs than *Hamlet*. He had the appeal in Edward VII's worldly London of an evangelist. People who were rather vain of what they believed to be their artificiality, admired him for his " sincerity ". When he returned in 1897 to the manner of sex-and-salvation the notion might have seemed belated. His novel, " The Christian ", could have shown Ibsen how to make *Brand* pay. Instead of a preacher with a wife and child, here was a saintly parson who was calling sinners to repentance and falling in love with a pretty girl. Here also was an author who coped with the Man, the Woman and the Universe. Here was unblushing belief in the existence of dividend-paying innocence which Thomas Hardy had destroyed.

No one living in that world could be unaware of the peculiarity of Edwardian taste. The public which no longer wanted feuilletons by Thomas Hardy in their illustrated weeklies, knew that he was a great novelist. The same public which had no illusions about the powerful novels of Caine, yet read them avidly whether brand-new at 7s. 6d. (he

LXXXVI Drury Lane, 1907: Lady Marion Beaumont (Constance Collier) escapes having drugged Morris, the pawnbroker (Oscar Adye) and rescued the incriminating box

THE SINS OF SOCIETY

LXXXVII As the troopship " Beachy Head " founders the soldiers salute

LXXXVIII   Drury Lane, 1911 : The earthquake

THE HOPE

LXXXIX   Brenda Carlyon (Evelyn D'Alroy) leads in the Derby winner

claimed to have led the revolt against the three-volume novel at 31s. 6d.) or in paper backs at sixpence. What was this stuff that people ate out of his hand? Life in it was up to date and almost every-day, and in this persuasive form it insisted more strongly than ever before on that dearest of all human illusions—the mystic and supernatural power of sexual love which provides for every human being one completely satisfying mate, and one only. In theory it was conducive to the stability of Holy Matrimony. In practice it kept the Divorce Courts busy, since not even the oldest idyll in the land maintained that the true love and the spouse were necessarily one and the same thing. In the wildest throes of his Sinaitic solemnity our author might be temporarily inclined to agree with that, but only in the wildest.

Whatever his secret, Hall Caine's success was part of the reign of Edward VII. His play of The Christian had had its first existence in London and New York in 1898, but that was experimental. Caine's climacteric began in 1901 with his novel of "The Eternal City", which was dramatized in London and in New York the next year. This done, he annexed Iceland for the purposes of "The Prodigal Son", published in 1904. Cold-blooded history might assess the number of copies sold and make comparison for better or worse with other best-sellers. But statistics are rule-of-thumb. There is no way to measure what are vulgarly known as heart-throbs. They exceeded all speed limits over this tale of a famous author of the Northland who loves Thora in life too little (preferring her sister who becomes a famous actress) and loves her in death too well. Plays have their history told in criticism which describes their impact on the public. Novels leave no other record of this than their sales. The mood of their readers, a passing event like acting and applause, is soon completely forgotten. But here perhaps is an exception, and even if young and impressionable minds did not recall how that book was talked about there is still the drawing-room ballad of " Speak, speak, speak to me, Thora "—a cry from the Icelander who regards her grave as his only landmark when men have forgotten his name—to perpetuate the excitement. The Prodigal Son was the Autumn Drama at Drury Lane in 1905 and it was a success no matter how the peculiar thrill of the novel was missed.

To score again on the same boards Hall Caine turned his novel of 1890 into Drury Lane's Autumn Drama of The Bondman in 1906. This time it is a girl who loves two half-brothers, one a Manxman in Sicily and the other a Sicilian in Man. Jason's mother was not married. Greeba,[1] the heroine, asks whether she had been wronged by his father,

---

[1] The impact of this heroine on real life has yet to be measured. Not only was Caine's Manx castle named after her but many a hotel and boarding house as well.

upon which Jason, in a rage, answers, "Yes, God curse him! He was a low-born man and she was the daughter of the Governor." The relentless march of progress has left the bad baronet and the village Queen of the May a long way behind.

The hold of this author over his public is shown in the number of new plays he now made with old material. Bear in mind that it was a time when the fortunes of all other playwrights were made or marred by "first nights": the verdict at the opening performance was final, for no plays had a second chance—save those written by Hall Caine. *The Christian*, re-written, had a long run at the Lyceum in 1907, when intellectual dramatists were being admired. In a volume which bears on its cover the words, "Lyceum Edition. The Christian Play", the author says, "I have reluctantly consented to the publication of the drama on condition that it shall be sold at the lowest price at which it can be produced". His introduction also declares that he has suffered for *The Christian*, "perhaps justly, certainly severely". Copies of this were distributed to the audience at the 175th performance of the revival, marking "the 3,221st performance in England".

After the preface comes "Author's Note", dealing in resounding prose with "the gravest problem that is on the forehead of the time to come". This thing of the future is "the physical relation of woman to man". The style keeps going in this strain until any audience ought to be trembling with anticipatory excitement, but it seems to have no effect on the play. John Storm, the saintly parson, and Glory Quayle, the pretty girl, leave Man for London, he to rescue fallen women and she to star in musical comedy. In Act IV John shouts wildly, "God sent me to kill you, Glory", then he kisses her instead, and the Watchman outside calls, "All's well".

Why *Mrs. Warren's Profession* should have been banned while Caine's "sensation" on the same subject was permitted, can be explained by the prevailing opinion that sentimental treatment justified anything—adultery, for example, was warmly recommended in many a charming ballad sung by prim young women in suburban drawing-rooms, under the name of love. Shaw did not invoke the sacred word, but Caine did. Matheson Lang, who endowed John Storm with good looks of a most taking boyishness, describes the result in his autobiography, "Mr. Wu Looks Back". The play that had been regarded as a stop-gap went like wildfire. "Hours before the doors were opened, on a bright, warm, summer evening, a seething mass of thousands of people was milling around the theatre, clamouring for admittance to see the first performance of a revival of this old play." That was in the August of 1907. In the October Matheson Lang left the Lyceum for a while in order to play Dick Dudgeon at the Savoy in *The Devil's Disciple*, the play Shaw labels " a melodrama " because while it takes Ibsen's view of virtue as a precious thing to be dearly paid for, there is a last-minute reprieve for its falsely-convicted, self-sacrificing hero.

In Greeba Castle, Isle of Man, the wealthiest author of his day went on making fresh fortunes out of old plays and receiving offers as large as kings' ransoms for new novels.   In 1909, chapters of " The White Prophet " in a monthly magazine caused a stir because they were thought likely to cause trouble in Egypt.   His day was passing, though " The Woman Thou Gavest Me " stuck as staunchly as ever to the formula of salvation and sex.   Still his swan song must be *The Eternal Question* (new version of *The Eternal City*), played at the Garrick in 1910 and printed for private circulation with an author's note.   His first statement is that *The Eternal Question* owes nothing to *The Eternal City* " except the material which that play owed to the novel of the same name "—he is using the same story, with the same scenes and the same characters, to present two problems of life.   He will " indicate the recent trend of the socialist movement, the forces it has had to meet, and the risks it has to run ".   He will also deal with the Woman Question in its " most intimate aspect—the aspect which concerns the sexual relations of man and woman ".   In the play, Roma, Baron Bonelli's mistress, is to snare Rossi, the socialist, but they fall in love; and when Bonelli is accidentally killed they gladly decide to face execution together after they have discussed the question of her past. Since this ran for less than a month, the author's proud record of being the greatest re-dramatizer known to history was rather tarnished that summer of 1910.   In a fit of what looks uncommonly like bravado he dug up the ancient *Ben-My-Chree*, turned it into *The Bishop's Son*, tried it on holiday-makers at the Grand Theatre, Douglas, and then brought it to replace *The Eternal Question* at the Garrick.   It ran a week.

The real racehorse won.   After *The Bondman* Drury Lane made some attempt at the powerful style with *The Sins Of Society* and *The Marriages Of Mayfair*.   Whatever their success these could not compete with *The Whip* by Cecil Raleigh and Henry Hamilton, the autumn drama of 1909 which became (Christmas pantomime intervening) the spring drama of 1910.   " All third-class passengers ", said the villainess as she plotted a train smash in order to destroy the dark horse, and such devilry concealed the awkward fact that morality had become more muddled than ever before.   The hero pleaded that he had taken to a life of gambling because he had " never known a mother's love "; when the heroine brought him back to innocence he proved his

M

sincerity by backing the dark horse for more than he was worth. Its victory, after surviving the train smash, represented virtue triumphant as understood by the twentieth century at its opulent dawn.

Sporting life was again the subject at Drury Lane in the September of 1911 when Raleigh and Hamilton named *The Hope* after the horse they cast as Derby Winner. As late as 1923 the tradition was maintained at Drury Lane in *Good Luck* by Seymour Hicks and Ian Hay. Eleventh Hour was the horse whose owner became a convict, escaped from prison during a fire, and rescued the heroine from the villain's yacht; this gave rise to a report of his death which would have prevented Eleventh Hour from running had not his owner reached the course and proved both his existence and his innocence in time. The real horse gave place to the real camel in *The Garden Of Allah* with a sand-storm so real that the electric fans of the desert coated playgoers in the front row with bran.

By this time Hall Caine had become a somewhat wistful wraith when he haunted the West End, even though he had been created a Knight of the Order of the British Empire in 1918. He continued to write, almost up to his death in 1931, and occasionally, though rarely, admiring references are still made to his books.

XC *Between Two Women* (Terriss, Rotherhithe, 1902) : " I'll make a bargain—my son's life for yours "

MELVILLIAN MELODRAMA

XCI *The Soldier's Wedding* (Terriss, Rotherhithe, 1906) : " After twelve years ! "

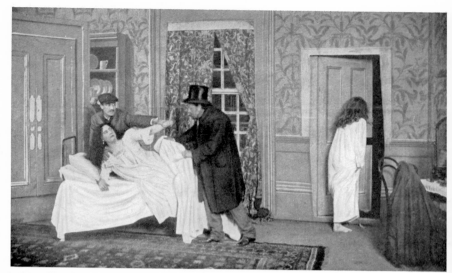

XCII   Aldwych, 1909 : Bess (Violet Englefield), the bad girl, allows herself to be abducted by the villain in place of Gladys (Maud Linden) who beats a hasty retreat

THE BAD GIRL OF THE FAMILY

XCIII   Bess charged at Bow Street : " Then I hope Heaven *will punish you* by making me *your wife* "

24 Melvillian Melodrama

The Worst Woman In London

" THERE is only one Shakespeare and there is only one Melville "—
the words of Walter, eldest of three brothers—was once a very familiar
battle-cry. That " once " was not long ago, but what happened then
now seems remote. Outward changes are not the chief cause of this.
What makes life look, taste, feel and smell so different is the disturbance
within. The public is in an altogether new frame of mind. In the
heyday of the Melvilles moral horror of the theatre still existed—part
of the dread of existence in general. There were thousands of things
that " people didn't talk about "—aspects of life, real or imaginary,
which had to be shunned. Anybody who did take as much as a peep
at them was almost sure to fall over decency's brink into a yawning
moral abyss. Millions believed in the existence of such a pit, though
no one knew precisely what it was.

Fantastic though the myth may seem now, it was fearful enough to
be dramatized. That was the Melvilles' great discovery. They had
the courage to talk about the things people did not talk about. They
could write about that moral abyss as familiarly and intimately as
Dante wrote about the domestic economy of the Inferno. With the
power of righteousness behind them, for virtue triumphant was ever
their theme, they boldly exhibited life's seamy side on the stage.
Their popularity, which was enormous, largely sprang from the
public's readiness to be shocked.

Hoardings advertised that the Melvilles' dramas would be daring.
They brought colour to our cheeks as well as to our streets. There was
never anything improper about them, but they alarmed those who disapproved of " the sensational ". The titles were alarming in themselves even without the more than life-size figures that illustrated them.
There were never such posters before or since. Usually an accusing
finger created a centre of interest in a colour-scheme of yellow and
red surrounding one or two arresting female figures. What an age the
Edwardian was for femininity ! Scores of music-hall songs praised
" the girls ". Musical comedies usually had " girl " in the title.
Melodrama exploited the contrast between good girls and bad.

Champions of this kind of drama should be given their due. Compliments were paid the Melvilles from time to time and their plays usually had an enthusiastic, though occasionally patronizing, Press. But the brothers were far too modest to covet any such compliment. Their plays were never printed and the typescripts were only taken out of the stair-less eyrie under the Lyceum's roof where they were stored, when the possibility of a fresh stage production was being discussed. Frederick Melville was friendly when a critic by his side in a supper-room pew asked (over tankards) for a chance to read them, but firm. He would not admit for a second that they were worth reading. " We are ", he said, " a cheap theatrical family." When corrected with " fine old theatrical family ", he insisted on " cheap "—insisted.

All who are so named on very old playbills must not be brought into the story, for the Lyceum's managers began their stage history with George Melville, a touring actor-manager who lived from 1824 to 1898. Andrew Melville, born in 1853, specialized in melodrama and billed himself with lordly modesty as plain " Em ". All his six children became players as *part* of their theatrical training. Walter (born London, 1875) and Frederick (born Swansea, 1876) began in infancy. When their parents settled down at Birmingham in 1889 at the Grand Theatre and the Queen's, the sons learnt all there was to learn about business management as office-boys. Andrew Melville, the third son, was then five years old. Not until they had acted melodrama, stage-managed melodrama, produced melodrama and made melodrama pay, did any of them write melodrama. They began by re-writing it, for the conditions under which they worked resembled the conditions under which Shakespeare worked. Though " copyright " had become a word with a meaning, there were still bundles of melodramas that had no owners because each represented such a succession of literary thefts that the original author had been lost sight of. *Driven From Home*, played at the Grecian in 1871 as the work of G. H. MacDermott, was quite a short play. Who wrote a four-act drama of a similar title that was already popular before those young Melvilles were big enough to adopt it, has not been recorded. It is worth studying, since it shows what melodrama was like before they brought it into line with the age of feminism.

Laura is driven from home by her father, Old Raybrook, for marrying the man of her choice instead of the plausible Geoffrey. When her husband is killed while poaching, she finds her way to the Thames Embankment, and as she sinks exhausted with her child in the snow, the villain kicks her. Willie, the village idiot she once befriended, helps her to the gates of the Foundling Hospital. Raybrook, arm-in-

THE PEOPLE'S PLAYWRIGHT
OF THE
XVI CENTURY

"THERE IS ONLY ONE SHAKESPEARE
AND THERE IS ONLY ONE MELVILLE."
VIDE THE PRESS

THE PEOPLE'S PLAYWRIGHT
OF THE
XX CENTURY   WALTER MELVILLE

Ignoring Frederick Melville

arm with Geoffrey, passes her by and gets into a hansom just before she
dies. In Act II there is " business " with a real pudding—as necessary
to the comic scenes in those days as real cabs were to the dramatic.
The actress who has died as Laura now appears as her son, little Walter.
Muttering, " Only a life—that boy's life between me and my uncle's
fortune ", Geoffrey decides on murder and hires an accomplice at a
saw-mill. There the child is stunned, placed on the slide that carries
logs to the circular-saw (in the manner of Augustin Daly's drama) and
is about to be cut up when the half-wit saves him. In the graveyard of
Chingford Old Church by night (" green limes ") Laura's repentant
father comes to hear the organ music, the impatient villain comes to do
him in, and Walter, with the half-wit, comes to the rescue. " Enter
Everybody " to see justice done.

There was an eager hunt for novel last-minute rescues. One hero
was fastened at the bottom of a Thames lock while water trickled
through the gates that had been left ajar. Another was placed, bound
hand and foot, on the anvil of a Nasmyth hammer while the villain
started the machinery amid cries from the Surrey's gallery of " Dirty
dog " and oaths unprintable. You can guess what " Great Steam-Roller
Sensation " in the programmes of *Is Life Worth Living?* meant.
These were crime plays. There came a time when the public thought
crime too tame. It felt the attraction of repulsion for the moral abyss.
It wanted vice.

When their father, who was more inclined to stage crime, died in
1896, the Melvilles gave the public what it wanted in *Dangerous*

Women, by F. A. Scudamore, first played at the Brixton in 1898. This went the whole hog with abduction and white-slave traffic in a plot elaborate enough for a three-volume novel. There is a casino run by a vampire who lures innocent girls into a strong-room where they are starved into surrender. The juvenile (as the heroine must be called when Melvillian drama is discussed) holds out until rescued by the comedian who takes her place and indulges in some horseplay at the expense of the semi-comic villain. After many other adventures she is recaptured and drugged by the dangerous women, who carry her into a crypt, dress her in the robes of a corpse and shut her in the coffin alive. She is released by a mad scientist, intent on restoring the dead to life, only to find herself in his private asylum. Meanwhile her rich father, paralysed through grief, is securely under the dangerous women's thumbs, so that the author has to make a violent effort to effect a happy ending. Scudamore originated a species with this play. Shakespeare went in for dangerous men, the Melvilles for dangerous women. In the staging of nerve-racking spectacles the brothers always thought in terms of a leading lady, sometimes good-looking but always of powerful physique.

While Andrew made the Theatre Royal, Brighton, his headquarters, Walter and Frederick operated at the Terriss in Rotherhithe and the Standard in Hoxton. It was at the Standard in 1899 that Walter Melville brought out his first melodrama, the most remarkable piece of its kind. He chose the challenging title of *The Worst Woman In London*, and instead of undergoing a nervous collapse at the thought of trying to live up to it, constructed character and story which justified it up to the hilt and down to the dregs.

Coincidences are masterfully handled. Years ago Jack Felton was driven to murder by Francis[1] Vere, siren of the title, in Paris. Now he is engaged to his employer's daughter, Ruth Milford, whose French governess is Francis Vere herself. Consequently he is easily blackmailed into confessing to the burglary actually committed by her accomplice, Lyle. That spares him nothing, for Ruth is told of the murder while the lights go down and the spotlights dwindle to " pin focus " on Francis's face, distorted with laughter. The scene changes to a full set of Hyde Park, with crowds, attendants, police, soldiers, a nursemaid and a pram. Old Milford, victim to the Worst Woman's allure, arrives with her in a real " Victoria carriage, horse and coachman ". They surprise Ruth and Jack together, and call the police to arrest him for the murder of one, Philip Armstrong, who suddenly appears in very good health and they drive away.

[1] Spelt thus in original MS.

Walter Melville keeps
his eye on the power
of woman—muscular

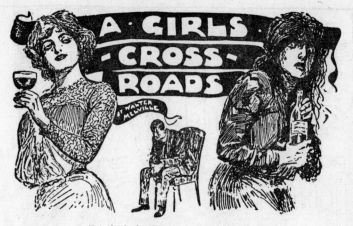

(Standard, also Terriss, Rotherhithe, 1903)

To match this drama of the real carriage, the next scene provides comic relief with the real steak-pudding. Old Milford quarrels with Francis. She shoots him in bed, and when Armstrong rushes in with intent to strangle her, he is arrested for the murder. But Ruth stands between her and the Milford millions. The tenement where the lovers, now performing in a circus, have begun their married life, is secretly visited, drenched with oil and fired. Francis, though disguised as a man-about-town, is seized by Ruth, who cries, " We shall die together ". One fires a revolver; the other draws a knife until her hand is bitten to force her to drop it. Plates are thrown.

Together the two women roll over and over, and each, as she comes uppermost, bangs the other's head repeatedly on the floor. When they regain their feet, Francis raises a chair to strike but is pushed back against the table, which goes over, lamp and all. Ruth falls: she is dragged by the hair (or rather by a concealed rope connected with a leather band round her waist) right across the room and flung into the corner while the Worst Woman escapes to the roofs, where firemen arrive too late to reach the tenement. But Ruth escapes by performing her tight-rope act on the telegraph wires. The mob catches Francis. To save herself she takes off her wig and pulls down her hair over her shirt-front. " What—a woman? " people shout. " Yes," Jack replies, " The Worst Woman in London."

With the ending of the nineteenth century, the days of melodrama were numbered, no doubt, but there was plenty of life in the old dog yet. The stalls might scoff but the gallery, drawn from the old transpontine audiences of " the Surrey side ", still applauded every moral

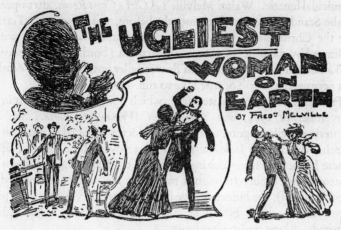

(Terriss, Rotherhithe, 1904)

sentiment and hissed the villain in all sincerity. *The Worst Woman In London* encountered this divided opinion when revived at the Adelphi in 1903. Much to the annoyance of pit and gallery, the stalls sauntered in late—parties of them, finely dressed, intent on mockery—just to see old Milford's last moments when he burnt the Will in Francis's favour before going to sleep.

Far from resenting laughter or wishing to prevent it by altering his play, Walter Melville provided for it in the prompt-copy with these stage directions: " The laugh comes when he first appears, when he turns over the sheets, and when he gets into bed. He is in his night-shirt and has bare feet." Olga Audré (formerly Audrey) entered as the murderess, in her nightdress, but she was not mocked. The Worst Woman in London was then a fine upstanding well-built girl in her twenties and her bearing—unlike anything today when the young stay young—was adult and imperious. You feared for her victims and were glad when they escaped on the stage. She was an altogether different person in real life, a young, tender-hearted mother, and she liked a family holiday by the sea. In this simple-hearted manner she was spending a summer when her child was caught by the tide. Olga Audré died in a desperate attempt to rescue her.

The Terriss, Rotherhithe, was where several Melville dramas first saw the limelight. Here Frederick Melville, his brother's only rival, brought out *Between Two Women* in the autumn of 1902. Its peculiar-ity is a vampire with a strong streak of virtue in her—love for her long-lost blind boy : when he is restored to her, she helps the hero to rescue the heroine from the haunted tower where she is imprisoned with a homicidal lunatic. Walter Melville's *A Girl's Cross Roads*, after opening at the Standard two or three months before, was brought to Terriss's for the Christmas of 1903. This is the drama of a drunken wife— lightened by the antics of a comic character in a bottle-smashing scene— and a faithful juvenile who turns flower-seller until death after death at last permits the course of true love to run smooth.

Frederick Melville's masterpiece, which opened at the Terriss in the November of 1904, was *The Ugliest Woman On Earth*. She is a mysterious veiled figure, assistant of a doctor engaged in perilous research, who attracts Jack Merriman on a voyage home from Naples, where he escaped from a charge of murder. Knowing that illness has destroyed her beauty (though it may, says the doctor, be restored by another illness), she hides her love for him until the villains of the piece throw lime in his eyes and he is blind. They marry. His sight is restored. Illness restores her beauty.

Melodrama-according-to-the-Melvilles was in demand all over the country. Bert Hammond, who managed the Lyceum, directed their extensive touring enterprises. Rehearsals were held in the Standard. In various parts of this theatre twenty-five companies would be mastering at the same time twenty-five different plays. Corridors, bars, foyer and auditorium would all be put to this use, while the stage would be partitioned off by canvas walls into a number of separate stages. What the provincial public wanted was either *The Girl Who* . . . (drama) or *The Girl From* . . . (musical comedy), and the lists of what was then on tour, in the theatrical journals, proved that the Melvilles had a bigger following than George Edwardes.

Each of the brothers was now a hardened playwright. Walter brought out *The Girl Who Wrecked His Home* at the Standard in 1907. He knew what kind of title was liked and chose this even though it did not fit the tale of a wife lured from home and luckily forgiven years after by a husband promoted to the peerage. Walter was also the author of *The Beggar Girl's Wedding* at the Elephant and Castle in 1908. In this Jack Cunningham, suddenly realizing he must marry at once or lose a fortune, takes Bess from the Embankment and marries her. Both are kidnapped and caged in the private asylum of a mad doctor : all ends well. Frederick was the author of *The Bad Girl Of The Family*, at the Elephant and Castle in the October of 1909, followed by a Christmas season at the Aldwych. This is a particularly good specimen of their workmanship. Bess, seduced by Harry, her employer's son, goes to " Lord Erskine's " with a dress for Gladys Erskine, who loves a sailor, Dick Marsh. Being on the brink of financial ruin, Lord Erskine is forcing his daughter to marry Harry. The wedding is arranged, but

Feminine drama and
feminine comic relief
(Elephant and Castle,
1908)

by means of a heavy veil Bess takes the bride's place at the altar. On the night of Dick's arrival there is a murder for which he is tried and found guilty. He escapes from Dartmoor in the snow just in time to rescue his wife on Christmas Eve, to see Harry arrested while his own innocence is proved, and to witness the death of his faithful burglar friend while carols are being sung " off ".

The Melvilles' conquest of London was swift. In 1909 they took over the Lyceum and in 1911 they built the Princes, Shaftesbury Avenue, and opened it with a new version of *The Three Musketeers* by themselves. They had now turned from real life to romance. At the Lyceum in 1912 Frederick Melville's *The Monk And The Woman* (ending in an earthquake which kills all except the monk, his aristocrat wife, and other monks who wish him well) was a costume drama. *Ivanhoe*, in 1913, was a costly and gorgeous spectacle with twenty horses and a castle which swung right across the stage to show the attackers' progress from outside to inside. " With that ", said Mr. Hammond, " we did not take our salt." But romance in modern form prospered in 1917, when Walter Howard's *Seven Days' Leave* showed Annie Saker as a heroine, in bathing dress, who sank a German submarine. And when Albert Chevalier, the Coster Laureate of the music-halls, arrived in *My Old Dutch*, the play which he and Arthur Shirley had written around his song :

> We bin together now for forty years
> An' it don' seem a day too much,

there was, at small expense, a run of nearly 200 performances. All this belongs to the history of the Melvilles as managers rather than as dramatists. The Lyceum was their crowning achievement, but the titles they are remembered by belong to their seasons at the Terriss, the Standard, and the Elephant when there were only two or three Melvilles just as there was only one Shakespeare.

Some mention must be made of rivalry in their own field. No single work of theirs equalled the popularity of *A Royal Divorce*, for which W. W. Kelly was responsible. While a manager in America he " discovered " Grace Hawthorne; in London she became sole lessee of the Princess's, which was conducted under his management. The Napoleon drama that made his fortune was originally written in America by C. G. Collingham. Wills began to revise it. After his death " much of the work that he did upon it was discarded, and the original substituted ", according to his brother. Grace Hawthorne finished the task of fitting it for the stage. In 1891 it was played first at Sunderland, then at the New Olympic and then at the Princess's.

On tour its profits enabled Kelly to become proprietor of Kelly's Theatre, Liverpool, and the Theatre Royal, Birkenhead, as well as lessee of the Shakespeare, Liverpool. He kept *A Royal Divorce* on tour almost until he died at the age of seventy-eight in 1933. It was more than a play; it was an institution. "Not to-night, Josephine", the rude heckle from the gallery when Emperor bids Empress the last good-bye, became a catch-phrase for thirty years or more.

Although the Conquests kept the Surrey which became a music-hall for a time, although the Britannia and the Standard eventually changed with the changing times, melodrama was never so prolific as when its days were numbered. Its authors turned them out by the dozen. Mrs. Charlotte Anne Kimberley, who died in 1939, had *Was She To Blame?*, *Her Path To Sorrow* and *Ruined Lives* at the head of her long list. Walter Howard, who died in 1922, wrote *Why Men Love Women* and *Her Love Against The World*, also *The Story Of The Rosary*, which succeeded not only at the Princes in London but at the Manhattan Opera House in 1914. When the tide did turn, yet another bid for fashion's favour was made by Tod Slaughter at the Elephant and Castle before it was pulled down. There, besides Sweeney Todd, William Corder and other legendary villains, he played in *The Face At The Window*, by Brooke Warren, which had started life at Blackburn and Salford in 1897, and proved the most enduring play in its own class. Le Loup leaves iron daggers in the chests of his victims until his name is disclosed by a corpse galvanized into momentary life by electricity.

The seed of another melodrama sprouted in the Lyceum's box-office. Bram Stoker, Irving's manager, was a novelist. Most of his books are forgotten, but the one he published in 1897 gave vampires their most popular form. "Dracula" became, strictly in this sense, a classic. Years passed before it was adapted to the stage and then it outlived even *The Power Of The Cross; or, The Last Of The Vampires*, which was brought from the provinces to the Elephant and Castle in 1907. Bram Stoker's story, dramatized by Hamilton Deane, was still being acted in London as late as 1939—nurses in attendance and hopeful staggerers with strained faces outside the manager's office, putting up some fine performances in fond hopes of emergency brandy.

Miniature melodramas for the music-halls ought to have a history to themselves. *The Fighting Parson* celebrated the victories of a London curate who knocked wife-beating husbands about. *Humanity* won applause year after year on tour because of its furniture-smashing fight —"£200 worth a night", the bills advertised—and its song of "Only a Jew", but still more for its heart-felt cry of, "If this is your Christian charity, thank God I am only a Jew".

25 Gentlemen Cracksmen

Alias Jimmy Valentine

OUT of that chaos of cold print which bears witness of what the public once wanted, oddities could be picked to prove anything. Evidence could thus be found to show how the wishful thinking of mankind moves round and round without progressing—the easiest theory to uphold in all human affairs. Opera is cited. Directly Wagner rendered the old method of setting melodramas to music "obsolete", Puccini made a masterpiece out of *La Tosca*. For other libretti he went to Belasco, call-boy at the Metropolitan, San Francisco, who promoted himself to stage-manager at the age of fourteen and mastered all theatrical trades by as close a familiarity as Irving's with old plays that would not die. On a story by John Luther Long, Belasco based *Madame Butterfly* for the Herald Square Theatre in 1900. It was seen in London at the Duke of York's by Puccini and it returned to New York as his opera in 1906. Belasco's *The Girl Of The Golden West* at the Belasco Theatre, Pittsburg, Pa., became Puccini's opera at the Metropolitan Opera House in 1910 with Caruso and Destinn in the principal rôles and Toscanini conducting.

Belasco with John Luther Long brought out the drama of Old Japan called *The Darling Of The Gods* at the National, Washington, in 1902. It was presented by Tree in London the next year at His Majesty's (where Cardinal Wolsey, Benedick, Shylock and Malvolio mingled on equal terms with Mephistopheles, Fagin, Micawber and Robert Macaire in the grand manner of Shakespearean melodrama). The sole difference between London now and Irving's London, it might have been thought, was the absence of Irving. But playgoers, no matter how sumptuously old customs of hospitality were kept up in the Dome of His Majesty's, knew the difference. Tree shed the afterglow of sunset. What genius he had, lacked significance.

One of Tree's young men, George du Maurier's son, Gerald, had gauged the spirit of the reign more exactly. His manner on the stage, with a walk described as a slink, expressed dislike of the "theatrical" and was hailed as "natural" although it went much further. It made

CIV *Arsène Lupin* (Duke of York's, 1909): The Duc de Chamerace (Gerald Du Maurier) escapes from the detective (Dennis Eadie): " Stand back—hands up !   You know what this is—a bomb ! "

EXPLOSIVE SITUATIONS

CV *Alias Jimmy Valentine* (Comedy, 1910): Jimmy Valentine (Gerald Du Maurier) opens the safe and Kitty Lane, half suffocated, falls out

XCVI *A Royal Divorce*: Josephine (Edith Cole); " Here at thy feet I throw the diadem I may n
wear on sufferance "

INTERNATIONAL TENSIONS

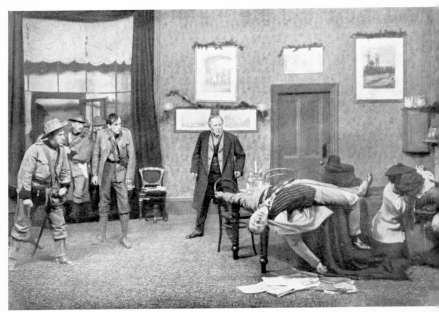

XCVII *An Englishman's Home* (Wyndham's, 1909): Geoffrey Smith the traitor (Lawrence Grossmit
is shot through the heart by the invaders

a cult of the casual, matched in fiction by the well-born burglar of E. W. Hornung's novels, " The Black Mask ", " The Amateur Cracksman ", " Mr. Justice Raffles " and " A Thief in the Night ". When Gerald du Maurier appeared as Raffles at the Comedy in 1906 the true distinction between ancient and modern was manifest. Here was Claude Duval changed in nothing but outward appearance, and even that was not so marked, apart from the now celebrated slink, when du Maurier played the Duc de Charmarace in *Arsène Lupin* (a French Raffles) at the Duke of York's in 1909. Back at the Comedy the next year he presented an American Raffles who first appeared in O. Henry's story, " A Retrieved Reformation ". Jimmy Valentine frustrates all efforts to identify him as the cracksman who opens safes by a kind of Braille system of his own. At last the nobility of his nature forces him to betray himself. He undoes a burglar-proof door solely by means of his sense of touch when a child is suffocating in a strong-room. The feat is witnessed by the detective, who at once relinquishes his investigations. Alexander Woolcot, who made himself historian of this play, told how Paul Armstrong, " a wise old artisan of the theatre ", agreed to dramatize O. Henry's story immediately and then vanished. When the management were frantic he suddenly emerged from the hotel where he had imprisoned himself for a week and drew the four-act play from his pocket. Eleven days later *Alias Jimmy Valentine* was staged at Chicago : it was O. Henry's own story, for he had been in a Texas prison, where he, too, had decided to start life afresh under a different name.

Consequently it is from this reformation in real life that we must derive the epidemic of plays in which no self-respecting protagonist would think of approaching the first act without a neat murder or at least a bank robbery to his credit. It was the vogue of the highwayman over again. *Leah Kleschna*, a Tolstoian study in moral redemption by the author of *The Belle Of New York*, exhibited the female of the species in 1905. It brought Charles Warner back to the limelight four years before he ended his life. Too many revivals of *Drink*, it was widely but not very reasonably believed, dejected his mind.

The last melodrama to be the talk of the fashionable quarter of the town was *An Englishman's Home* by " A Patriot ", otherwise Major Guy du Maurier, at Wyndham's in 1909. " Foreign " forces have invaded England, and an ordinary John Citizen is forced to realize that war is not necessarily something happening abroad. Before the last of its 157 performances quidnuncs' gossip decided against anything so melodramatic. Then and there the belief formed that this particular quality existed solely in fiction and not in fact. As though to substantiate the theory, a " theatrical " Victorian drama was acted in the " natural " Edwardian way, and rejoicing over the very last death of melodrama broke out at Wyndham's in 1913 to acclaim Gerald du Maurier's revival of *Diplomacy* in the new way. His company was off-hand where its forerunners had been tense, and in the big scenes the points were left unmade by the effective process of omitting forceful lines altogether. With all that, it was still the same play. Nothing had been accomplished beyond compromise—the kind of compromise which inspired Barrie's plays. In *The Admirable Crichton* he showed where public opinion wanted to stand. Democratic sentiments went as far as playgoers desired in this pretty little tale of a butler who becomes king when the family is cast away on an island, and then becomes a butler again when they are all shipped back to England. It meant nothing. Neither did the " thriller ", which was first a fad in book form. This became a theatrical fashion when *Within The Law*, at the Haymarket from 1913 to 1914, demonstrated how firearms could be used for personal and private purposes.[1]

The change that did possess meaning affected heroines. " All sensible people " denounced the Suffragette who chained herself to railings and cried " Votes for Women ", but all these sensible people had unconsciously conspired to make Edward's reign ardently feminist. This was the one detail, out of the many that constituted the New Century's much-discussed progress, which signified. Just as a new brand of human nature came into being with monogamy aforetime, so yet another new brand was being invented when the Rights of Women at last began to be vindicated. Not everybody was unaware of the change, for though newspapers could not see big events because of their preoccupation with smaller ones, the theatre was faithfully levelling its camera. Contemporary eyes noted the subject. An article " The New Woman on The Stage " was contributed by A Critic's Wife to the *Lady's Realm* in 1909. From full and sufficient evidence she infers, " The day of the ' woman of no importance ' is over—theatrically; the sinned against and suffering, but always exquisitely gowned and becomingly coiffée heroine is going the way of all the dodos; the problem lady is so out of favour that even the grace and talent of Mrs. Patrick Campbell cannot revive our interest in her. A sense of humour is so much more wholesome than a sense of sin, and as we see from the most successful plays of the moment, may be quite

---

[1] It was based on a novel, the work of Marvin Dana and Esmé Forest who were represented by no other books in the catalogues of our leading lending-libraries. The adaptation was by Arthur Wimperis and Frederick Fenn, musical-comedy librettists. Yet the run of *Within The Law* was among the longest achieved by plays other than farce or vaudeville.

as well dressed." Plays like Somerset Maugham's *Penelope* and Barrie's *What Every Woman Knows* are quoted, not the works of Shaw, though he was now invading fashionable theatreland with *Fanny's First Play* in 1911, *Androcles And The Lion* in 1913, and *Pygmalion* in the spring of 1914. Compared with this intellectual awakening the effect of the war of 1914–1918 on thought was not so great as we thought at the time : it checked, then accelerated the main trend, sometimes very oddly. In 1914 plays dealing with venereal disease, notably *Ghosts* and *Damaged Goods*, were still banned as pre-eminently immoral. A year or two later, when performances of them were subsidized by the authorities, they were pre-eminently moral. And after the war, when " Votes for Women " was no longer a joke for the Widow Twankey, the very thing that had been denounced as harmful for women, destructive to all they held dear, inimical to their best interests, was bestowed upon them as a reward.

Melodrama on the Screen

Ben Hur

FLICKERING shadows on a white sheet, formerly regarded as "last turn" in music-halls or side-shows in booths at fairs, or entertainments for vacant dates between jumble sale and flower show at village halls, at last established their dignity by taking over Drury Lane. With or without prestige "the pictures" had won the favour of the public and were liked wholeheartedly without discrimination. The new medium had a magic of its own. No matter how old the story acted before the camera it became up to date when it became a "movie". What was stale on the stage was fresh on the screen. Consequently the invention that looked like progress put back the clock : twentieth-century means served nineteenth-century ends. "Ostler Joe", deplorable doggerel by G. R. Sims which had been pirated throughout America, provided a story for one of the first films and set a standard of tearfulness for many others. The rich villain, the erring wife, the forgiving husband, could never sin, repent, die and be noble too often.

There were other subjects, and these, by chance, often reproduced effects popular in chap-books 100 years earlier. The persecuted heroine would elope, her foot would slip on a stepping-stone, the hero would help her to the bank and there, half a minute later, he would be planting a simple wooden cross on a little mound. Another story ended with an erring wife setting the soles of her shoes on the sands, whereupon the sea (tinted celluloid being used in honour of tragedy) suffused itself pink to denote expiatory suicide. And in the middle of some stirring story a heroine would be irrelevantly shown weeping by her mother's grave. The vast public who attended the flicks enjoyed no matter what they saw in the very same way that they enjoyed no matter what they heard while playing early gramophone records. The first effect of mechanical progress is usually to paralyse the powers of thought in the same way that the first means of rapid travel are usually employed to carry passengers round in a small circle.

The next development of celluloid melodrama was peril in regular instalments. Every week Pearl White escaped from one danger only

XCVIII *The Perils of Pauline*, shown everywhere, 1914

SILENT MELODRAMA

XCIX *Intolerance*, shown Drury Lane, 1916

C *Ben Hur*, shown Tivoli, 1926

THROUGH NEW EYES

CI *East Lynne* (shown 1930): *L. to R.* Flora Sheffield, David Torrence, Conrad Nagel, Ann Harding, Cecilia Loftus

to be drawn into another, at which point the adventure ended: the next week she escaped from the new danger only to become embroiled in yet more. For this purpose all the old sensation scenes of the stage renewed their mighty youth for the screen. There was a difference. The oncoming express approached considerably faster on the screen than the property train, and the victim was rescued [1] considerably faster, according to the rate at which the film was run, than anybody could be rescued in reality; the heroine lay on the track until the very last moment, when " cutting " (or " montage " as it was later called to show that it did not mean " shortening ") was invented. One glimpse of heroine, one glimpse of express, one more glimpse of heroine, one more glimpse of express—it took the public's eyes ten years to see that two separate sequences were merely being club-sandwiched. *Jane Shore*, made in England, was the first super-film. Tearfulness still meant more than thrills.

How fast spectators would educate themselves was not a very pressing problem. They believed everything the sub-titles told them. Without these the vision of a young woman offering grapes to a recumbent middle-aged gentleman draped in white might suggest kindliness towards the sick uncle. But after the words " Night of wild debauchery in Pagan Rome ", grapes signified things unimaginable and continued to do so; in fact the word " pagan " has never recovered from its link with those emblematical grapes. Public readiness to change sympathy's conventional gift to invalids into sensuality's bribe to the self-indulgent showed how easily the new generation of showmen could conquer the mind by appealing to the eye. According to the unco' guid, that appeal was too strong. It was inflammatory, inciting to passion, to vice, to crime, to bloodshed, to the stealing from orchards of green apples. The play-acting kiss, the make-believe embrace, moved some to amorousness, many more to fury. It was the old fury burning in the same breasts, for minds formed, settled, prejudiced and biased before 1880 still ordered life.

Realizing this power of the old world over the new, the films decided on a policy of piety. Money was spent lavishly on entertainments that justified their existence by claiming to be historical or patriotic, Biblical or religious. David Wark Griffith, a screen-actor in *Ostler Joe*, silenced religious hate by appealing to national pride in the film he made in 1914 of the American Civil War, *The Birth Of A Nation*. Two years later he attempted still more in *Intolerance*, which

---

[1] What the films could add to an old story was proved in 1928 by the *The Branded Sombrero*, in which Buck Jones, the cowboy, when placed senseless on the railway line, was saved by Silver Buck, his horse.

was shown at Drury Lane. This bold and singular experiment was an attack on the enemies of the human race. It told more than one story concurrently. In one an ancient people obeyed a Christ-like ruler: in another modern law unjustly condemned falsely-accused innocence. Hordes of barbarians advanced on the fair city; officers of the law pursued the fugitive. The camera returned to the hordes, then to the American heroine's efforts to save her man; next the siege of Nineveh was contrasted with the trial in the police-court, and though virtue B.C. was overthrown, justice in 1916 was done. It was exciting. It was laughed at. It was remembered with respect until critics who saw a private view of it in 1946 praised it above the films of 1946.

The easier way was Wilson Barrett's way. *Quo Vadis?* was always a popular subject, with the grapes of sensuality, on the screen. Old actors trained in the school of sex and salvation now came into their own. Fred Niblo was one. He proved his powers with *The Three Musketeers* and then set a landmark in the history of films with *Ben Hur*. This made plain what the screen could do and what the stage should never again attempt to do. In 1902 and again in 1912 Drury Lane had presented W. Young's dramatized version of Lew Wallace's novel. On this vast stage the lower deck of a trireme had exposed itself as a vast empty space, decorated on either side by supers, sparsely ranged at varying levels, with bars of wood in their hands. Make-believe had to exert itself to assume that these stumps represented oars, that each slave had the inconceivable strength needed to move such oars by holding the tips, that a vessel as large as the one represented could be moved by whatever influence their exertions had upon the water. "Noises off" on a darkened stage would have put much less strain upon imagination, but as long as the old awe of realism remained, the spectacular drama might be counted upon to use something tangible for the representation of any impossibility.

By the time Lew Wallace's novel came to be read in Hollywood all that was changed, including the financial problem. A theatre had to pay its players every week and stars' salaries were mounting rapidly; there were bill-posters, scene-shifters, railway companies and fodder for the chariot-teams to think of, as well as insurance premiums, and losses when a star fell ill. When a complete entertainment could be put into a can and sent by post, the whole question of expense began and ended with what an old trouper would regard as rehearsals. Consequently reckless expenditure was no longer reckless. Super-spendthrifts would change that opinion in time, but in 1925 Niblo had *carte blanche* to rebuild the Circus Maximus, exact in every detail as far as modern scholarship was able to decide, for real chariots to race at the greatest possible speed with the greatest possible accidents. There were thousands of willing slaves to row real galleys upon real sea into which real ships could really sink.

That spectacle was unrivalled. Yet attempts to emulate it kept alive the name of de Mille. First came Henry C. de Mille, dramatist. One of his sons, Cecil, was educated at the H. C. de Mille Memorial School and lived at 2000 De Mille Drive, Los Angeles, California. He was first an actor, then a playwright. Deep religious feeling made him a power in Hollywood. After filming the Old Testament as *The Ten Commandments*, he made the New Testament the subject of *The King of Kings*. The colossal was his foot-rule. Anything smaller put his reckoning out. *The Godless Girl* may be remembered chiefly for the word upon a foreground dustbin, " Trash ". His grand opportunity came, after talking-films had been invented, with *The Sign Of The Cross*. At this period of the world's history real lions were more easily obtained than real Christians, but though real asses supplied real milk for Poppea's real bath, the super-film could not cause hysteria of the intensity excited by the old play. The grapes reappeared and Charles Laughton as Nero with a considerably false nose sighed, "Delicious debauchery", as though he had feasted on them. His remark was the most memorable thing in the whole performance. Neither sex nor salvation made itself felt upon audiences that Hollywood labelled " sophisticated ".

When first the camera recorded acting, the cry went up that at last the actor's art would not prove ephemeral. After the lapse of a very few years playgoers looked again at a film of Sarah Bernhardt and wished that it would. Films were mechanism, a mechanism that changed and was improved, which meant that performances before the camera were subjected to a decay more deadly than moth or rust. What exists in celluloid is often mere gesture and grimace to make the sceptical laugh and the judicious grieve. Memory unaided is more to be trusted, and memory recalls how the screen had its great actor before he was overwhelmed by the melodramatic formula. Jannings was borrowed from the German theatre to make the German film industry respected through the world. He did so in *The Last Laugh*, the sorrow of an old man at losing the uniform which had made him a magnificent presence outside the Grand Hotel. But why we remember Jannings chiefly is because he gave his age its Devil.

In the German film of *Faust* he was distinct from any seen in any other *Faust*. The tempter in his old shape had no power over the new world, but who could resist this new Mephisto of the screen? Lewd of eye, round of face and royally paunched, Jannings was the confidence man or three-card trickster of the racecourse mounted into the

firmament. First he visited the town with plague; then offered the aged
Faust curative powers in exchange for a day's loan of his soul. After
performing his miracles Faust was stoned. He poured out a bowl of
poison only to see in its shining blackness the image of his own youth.
There were still several hours to run and he might just as well receive
the full interest on his loan. So Mephisto jovially argues and Faust,
convinced, mounts himself to scale Olympus' top, over mountains,
forest and torrent to Parma, bright with bridal lamps. Faust comes to
earth as an Eastern prince, borne on dazzling white elephants, served by
polished black slaves; and as the bride yields to him Mephisto exacts
the full price of damnation through eternity. But in the end melodrama triumphs. When Marguerite is at the stake Faust staggers into
the flames, once more an aged man, though still young and handsome
in her eyes. Together their spirits soar into the skies while a Guardian
Angel answers the Devil's claim to his bond by saying, " Faust is saved
by one word. That word is—LOVE."

No truth is more definite than the truth of fiction. While you may
question the facts in a biography you cannot doubt Dicken's word
concerning Oliver Twist. About the lives of the heroes of history
there is very often an air of inaccuracy, since neither their contemporaries nor they themselves could always be quite certain what they
were up to. But in a novel there is one mind to make itself up for all
the rest, so that what is written is written. Even should the why, the
when and the hour of the deed be in dispute, the deed itself is not to
be denied. Directors of films changed all that as in *Faust*. For a time
French pictures dealt honourably by their authors—*Les Misérables* was
almost meticulously exact—but faithful films were dull and the policy
ended. The stamp of melodrama was over all.

When playgoers saw John Barrymore play Hamlet on the stage they
respected him as a conscientious actor. But when they saw his shadow
acting Don Juan on the screen they could but ask why. If a familiar
name were wanted for a hero who goes through fire and water to win
a blooming bride (his own bride), Crusoe, Columbus or Charlie Peace
would be more suitable. But at climbing to fair ones' balconies; at
duelling, upstairs, downstairs and in my lady's chamber; at escaping
from a condemned cell; at rescuing beauty from the torture chamber;
at leaping with his lovely prize from the tower's top; at carrying her
off with a squadron in pursuit; at bowling all the troopers from their
saddles like ninepins; at making love or waging war, John Barrymore's exploits were excelled solely by Douglas Fairbanks, ever youthful though his son's appearance on the screen caused him to be labelled
" senior ". As a pirate who was all and more that the Red Rover was

meant to be, he would descend from crow's nest to deck by sticking his knife into a sail and letting his weight draw the blade down the canvas. Neither melodrama nor Penny Dreadful ever thought of that. Barrymore's *Manon Lescaut* was not worth considering because it was mainly acrobatics and swordplay. The German version aggravated the problem. How much of Prévost's " exemple terrible de la force des passions " can be illustrated? No one could then expect to see on the rigorously censored pictures his charmingly provoking idea that Manon is a sort of sugar-stick, bound if left lying about to be tasted by somebody or other. But in order to enjoy that German film you had to grant to the camera absolute liberty to alter as fancy pleases. Manon became a melodramatic heroine, very much sinned against and never sinning.

However preposterous it may sound, Hollywood's change of heart, in the days before talkies, was due to the influence of Tolstoy. *Resurrection* was exceptionally intelligent, although it caught the silent film at a disadvantage. Nightingales trilling while the moon rises over the barn, the crackling of sorrel stalks as a colt gallops from the scented meadow, the sound of the villagers' arguments borne along the river— these give life in the book to Tolstoy's arguments that no man has a right to own land. Similarly the convicting of Maslova through the impatience of judge and stupidity of jury, expresses what he thought of legal justice. Much was altered by Hollywood, with Count Ilya Tolstoy as literary adviser, but altered so intelligently that something of Russia's prophet survived.

And then when films were progressing, mechanical progress again paralysed thought. *The Singing Fool*, the first film with " sound ", made Al Jolson the world's favourite. Later, in a prison melodrama on the screen, he sang to his brother convicts a sentimental ballad with a moral about living in harmony :

> Little birds can do it
> Why can't you ?

which clashed in Great Britain with a music-hall comedian's song about the hen's ability to lay an egg :

> Can Lloyd George do it ?
> Can Baldwin do it ?
> Can Winston do it ?
> Why no !

After following fashion after fashion in a manner which almost parallelled those of nineteenth-century melodrama with a Gothic series, a spell of horrors, and an admirable revival of *East Lynne*, the talkies reached the standard of the movies and then passed it. The film *All Quiet On The Western Front* deserved to make history as a civilizing influence, though it succeeded in preaching peace only to the converted.

27 Marriages and Murders

Maugham to Wallace

CONSEQUENCES had to be faced. Destroy moral fabric and what follows? The question, silenced by the first world war, was again asked when the uproar of peace subsided. There was little response : the public had given its mind to the mechanical marvels of films and talking-films. But the problem pressed. Virtue did not pay, virtue instead had to be paid for; if the price were so high that we would rather go without, what was there instead? In *Our Betters* at the Hudson, New York, Somerset Maugham had shown as early as 1917 how people with the means would solve the difficulty. *The Vortex*, with which Noel Coward went from London to New York in 1925, drew a picture of hedonism carried still further. These were, in the way of playwrights, about people fairly well up in the social scale. In life the pursuit of pleasure affected all classes. Brainless amusements devised for wartime played to packed galleries and pits as well as stalls and boxes during years of peace, testifying, in a harmless way, to that same irresponsibility which flaunted itself more expensively, more excitingly, more exotically among sybarites of more leisure and more means. One playwright tried idealism. Monckton Hoffe's *The Faithful Heart*, with its skipper who would rather go back to sea than settle down with a rich wife because he must do " the thing you can't explain because you know it's right ", belonged to the period of demobilization. Not until Leon M. Lion read it by chance in 1921 was it staged—an act of faith at a time when Barrie with all his whimsy could not avoid the prevailing cynicism in *Mary Rose*, the dearly-loved daughter whose return is an unmitigated nuisance until she yields to musical appeals from a chorus of unseen fairies.

" Butterflies on a skull ", which became a catch-phrase for describing the whimsies of Barrie, might serve as a crest for the 1920s. Starving men marched from the workless north to London, where sympathizers, in the shining black jam of limousines between theatres and restaurants during the hour before midnight, decided ardently to leave things to the Labour Government. When new factories were built, good-will was

shown by elegant debutantes who attended the opening in evening dress
and drank champagne to the night-shift's health.   It was well meant.

The public, no matter how vaguely aware of lost principles, made a
moral code of whatever came to hand.   Sport became sacred.   Tennis
no one dared play slackly; from Wimbledon's Centre Court to six-
penny courts in public parks all upheld its rules like ritual, while newspapers reported international contests with Homer's gravity.   Each
swimmer and golfer set his heart on efficiency.   Character, said the
preacher, will out.   People found something they could believe however unlike it might be to anything the New Thought had expected
them to believe.   True, the intellectual drama came to blossom now;
it was amazing—particularly when, at the height of Shaw's apotheosis,
the old idea of the clerical matinée was employed upon *Saint Joan* so
that dog-collars swarmed to the theatre as they had not done since *The
Sign Of The Cross.*

To fill imagination's vacuum there was the " semi-scientific " story-
telling of Poe, available, though neglected, all these many years.
Murder mysteries flooded the stage.   Mary Roberts Rinehart, expert
in detective stories, collaborated with Avery Hopwood, the playwright.
The Bat, by them, nerve-wracked New York in 1920 and London in
1922 with its " Who done it? " murders.   *The Cat And The Canary*,
seen by New Yorkers and Londoners in 1922, was by an American
actor, John Willard.   Critical opinion hailed the now popular technique—the withholding of essential information from the audience until
the last moment—as a brand-new twentieth-century novelty.   None
suspected that the novelty lay solely in the mood of the public, now
willing at last to be stirred to no moral (or immoral) end.

There was immediately a new fashion in heroines.   The young
woman who lived in their atmosphere of horror was never born of
author's fancy; she simply grew out of the public's desire to be thrilled.
In all performances where lights were switched off suddenly while
crooked fingers clutched at curtains, she conformed to the same model.
She suffered.   Whether there were reason for it or not she went on
suffering.   Once the author omitted to provide a reason: though
without any cause for complaint whatsoever she appeared in the usual
dire distress until she fainted and was carried " off " to bed without a
word of explanation for the state she was in.   Sometimes, of course, she
had justification enough.   In one play she was roasted, in another she
came very near to the electric chair, in another she was locked in a
cabinet on the understanding that it would fill with acid fumes to
corrode the skin off her face.   Her virtue was not endangered or even
mentioned.   Such fears troubled her slightly compared with " the

cops ". What she signified was a general awareness, first that the village maiden who feared the flattery of the young squire was extinct, and next that the damsel whose distress had kept legend-making alive for centuries was so essential to a plot that playwrights could not do without her.

Work which set itself a slightly higher standard was beset by the selfsame problem and solved it by employing the dissatisfied wife. Here again the tendency was to pay less and less attention to cause and then to omit it altogether. Sometimes a happy ending would be contrived by making the husband promise in future to pay less attention to his work and more to keeping his wife amused. In passing, it may be recollected that the 1920s witnessed a boom in night-clubs and made a cult of eccentric parties. But the happy ending was dull. The hero was usually the co-respondent. In him the young squire might be recognized, still amorous but no longer villainous because of a doubt in the audience's mind whether sex were immoral or not.

For the truth about the heroine of uneasy virtue, examine plays by Somerset Maugham. When *Our Betters* reached London in 1923 the public was in the right mood to delight in being shocked. Maugham had already declared himself no upholder of conventions; in *The Circle* the dissatisfied wife wished (in brief) to run away with the tea-planter after a game of tennis, and did. In the spring of 1927 the author carried feminism further. The heroine of *The Constant Wife*, who had a faithless husband, went into business, attracted a lover and declared that fidelity was merely a matter of finance; having become independent she would assert the goose's right to serve herself with all the sauce of the gander. Other comedies besides Maugham's recalled in these years the spirit of the Restoration. There was no moralizing and more than a little wit.

Virtue now in any shape or form was a dull subject. Even as an unobtrusive flavouring it rapidly vanished after a final flare up in *Lightnin'*, which broke New York records with a run of three years from 1918. It took its title from the elderly husband of a hotel land-lady; two lawyers, unable to gain his consent to their purchase of the property, advise his wife to get a divorce; in court evidence discloses the swindlers' motive, and virtue triumphs in old age. All parts of the world acclaimed it before the London season in 1925 at the Shaftesbury, where it had a normally good run. One of the authors was Frank Bacon, who played the title part until he died in 1922. The other, Winchell Smith, once the telegraph operator in *Secret Service*, became the wealthiest of playwrights with a fortune of over £300,000. He had " cashed in " on the old order only just in time.

" Moderns " were not alone in breaking with taboo. The change was real. The old order had gone. Play after play championed the " free soul "—the 1925 label for what Dumas *fils* had called *L'homme-femme* and what in plain terms meant a wife with one or more lovers. She claimed public sympathy in Galsworthy's dramatized inquest, *The Show*, at the St. Martin's in 1925, where she suffered because her private life was discussed at the enquiry into her husband's death. Farce, comedy and dismal realism by American, French or English authors based elaborate superstructures on faith in woman's infidelity. In one the co-respondent was a dipsomaniac whose reform had been resolved upon by a heroine old enough to have known that if the amorous instinct and drink fight for possession of a man's soul, the latter nearly always wins. This play failed.[1] From now on most plays of the type did likewise. The public that had not for many years been moved by a heroine's distress when threatened by marriage or worse against her will, became equally indifferent to a heroine's distress caused simply by the need of such excitement. Yet the dissatisfied woman was still the mainspring of plays. A character called the Sheikh was invented as the answer to her prayer. He appeared not only in flicks and novelettes but also in a French adaptation of 1926 called *Prince Fazil*. The heroine, rescued from his harem, still desired her master and in the end they died together.

In 1927 an era ended and by chance it coincided with the revival at the Lyric, Hammersmith, of *George Barnwell*, first played at Drury Lane in 1731, to show how a man who takes to bad ways comes to a bad end. In the autumn of 1927 two plays by Noel Coward about uneasy virtue provoked excessive anger: in October *Home Chat* at the Duke of York's raised the stage co-respondent to his apotheosis, and in November *Sirocco* at Daly's demanded sympathy for an unfaithful bride. The gallery, restive at the first, treated the second with an unprecedented display of ill-humour, and the leading lady, returning thanks with " This is the happiest moment of my life ", succumbed at once to a loud " Boo ". Pinero, well past three score years and ten, tried to change with the changing times, too late. His last play, *A Cold June* at the Duchess in 1932, was about a girl with three fathers and an impenitent mother. The moralist who had once declared himself in favour of an unblemished life for the male now favoured a blemished life for the female. He had unreformed with the loose 1920s, which were now as dead as the strait-laced 1880s.

" Modern " morals ceased to be modern. The experiment had

[1] But will long be remembered for the lie with which the villain shattered the poor heroine's nerves : " They are saying that he is your mistress."

failed. Would the old beliefs return? Their place was empty but
they did not. Instead civilized humanity, in the decade that gained the
name of " the over-optimistic 'thirties ", acted in the belief that
decency (virtue's new name) would prevail not in spectacular triumph
but in kindliness. *Sheppey*, Somerset Maugham's play of 1933, em-
bodies this in a barber who wins a sweepstake, then resolves to lead a
Christian life, gives all he has to feed the poor and keeps a few of them
at home (for his wife to wait upon). It was a warning, a parable of
civilization, but though the public had turned against vice it showed no
interest in virtue either. It showed very little interest in anything of
vital importance.

" Escapist " fashions ruled now. Whereas audiences had formerly
experienced real emotion while watching unreal spectacles, they now
indulged unreal emotions while watching faithful representations of
ordinary policemen tracking down ordinary criminals. " Melodrama " was misapplied to such plays. They ranged from detective-
stories and murder-mysteries to thrillers and straightforward studies of
criminological verisimilitude. Such entertainment varied extensively.
One strain can be traced first to Cutliffe Hyne's Captain Kettle, who
appeared on the stage of the Adelphi in 1902, and then to Sapper's
Bull-Dog Drummond, who appeared at Wyndham's in 1921, when
Gerald du Maurier described the genre as " thick-ear plays ". Another
strain showed in the thrillers of Edgar Wallace, beginning with *The
Ringer* at Wyndham's in 1926, and *The Squeaker* at the Apollo in 1928,
early in the murder-mystery craze. The desire to feel horror at fictitious dangers now existed without any righteous thirst for disgust at
villainy. Wallace belonged to the imagination of his day; prodigious
sales in nearly every country of the world testified less to his imagination than to his power to evoke the sensational out of the ordinary.
He wrote what everybody was ready for—what was already in every
mind. Imaginations exercised upon newspapers found themselves at
home in his universe of police-courts and racecourses.

Victories of right over wrong had nothing whatever to do with it.
The Lyceum of the Melvilles acknowledged the new rule. In 1937,
for one of its last plays, *Wanted For Murder* was chosen—it had police,
criminal and corpse instead of villain, heroine and baby. It was
meticulously photographic, so much so that when Mr. Hammond
suggested some raising of the voice as the customary signal for " The
Act ", it could not be done—not by an actor skilled in the modern
way. This was eloquent of the end. The old world took pride, on
the stage and off, in raising the voice. Righteous indignation required
it. Tumult and shouting died when new ways of thinking wiped out

righteous indignation. You no longer felt that way about the things you disapproved of. Villains belonged to the realms of witches and ogres. Psychology had changed all that—psychology made itself heard everywhere. "Psycho-analysis" proclaimed itself, spreading peace with its magic word, "complex", which signified that evil-doing was not a man's fault but his misfortune. The four-ale bar knew all about it, and fighting stopped because everybody understood. The theatre lagged behind the four-ale bar in intelligence, but a beginning was made. *The Lash*, by Cyril Campion, demonstrated at the Royalty in 1926 how a man's character might be determined by a forgotten scare in childhood. Dr. Freud was unopposed; there was no protest, not a vestige of the old religious wrath which had raised violent pro-tests in 1912 against a chemist's proposal to find a formula for life and so bring discredit upon the Book of Genesis. All that zeal had gone. Freud's arguments had set men's minds in motion. Magnify as you please the effects of the century's mechanical inventions, but the real marvel of the new world lay here. In the stillness of a world at peace you could almost hear the gentle whir of humanity's brains ticking over as though to fulfil Shaw's prophecy of " a whirlpool in pure intelligence ". Meanwhile democracy in its ever-multiplying cinemas was laughing at its discovery of two loud-mouthed, over-acted villains who did, while ranting into microphones over the heads of thousands massed beneath their balconies, raise their voices prophesying war.

II *The Vortex* (Everyman, Hampstead, 1924): Nicky Lancaster (Noël Coward) condemns his mother (Lilian Braithwaite)

DOPE AND DISGUISE

III *The Ringer* (Wyndham's, 1926): *L. to R.* Gordon Harker, Henry Forbes, Dorothy Dickson, Franklin Dyall, Leslie Faber

TEARS, LOVE AND LAUGHTER

CIV *Young England* (Victoria Palace, 1934): (*Top*) Scoutmaster Ravenscroft has an argument wi[th] Jabez Hawk, Junior, a true son of his father, and also a scout. (*Middle*) The Grand Finale. (*Botto[m]* Walter Reynolds, author of the play, in his box

28 Grand Finale

Young England in 1934 and 1939

IN THE dim light of rehearsal the tall bespectacled figure against the orchestra-rail dominated the whole theatre. Something in his voice and bearing stirred a memory of the Virgil who once conducted Irving at Drury Lane through Sardou's Inferno. It was Walter Reynolds, an actor forgotten in retirement these twenty years though in his time he had not only played many parts but written several plays, including *The Sin Of A Life* for Charles Warner at the Princess's in 1901. The piece he now directed was his own—a message, he had declared, for the heedless London of 1934. The leading lady listened to her instructions. She had had about enough when the old author began telling her how to wear her hair. When her offer to wear any wig to suit his fancy prompted a lecture against modern neglect of woman's crowning glory, praised by poets in countless ages, she objected. The author answered that the character she represented was a great part, and told her she would never play a greater. She was countering this with the times and places where she had played Portia, Cleopatra, Ophelia, Lady Macbeth . . . when he interrupted. " I did not say a larger," he chided, " I said a greater."

On 10 September 1934, his play, *Young England*, opened at the Victoria Palace before unsuspecting playgoers. That Boy Scouts and Girl Guides had been engaged in large numbers they knew : nothing much besides of an untoward nature. Some preliminary scenes of heroism and villainy during a Zeppelin raid had passed before they guessed that Walter Reynolds' work was unusual in any other way. Some remark that a female character had been " as innocent as a babe before she left the Girl Guides " caused a titter; and the next few minutes decided that *Young England*, far from being a very bad play, was the play of a lifetime. Row upon row of mouths opened for laughter before the end of every line. No droll or wit ever faced an audience readier for mirth. " Old-fashioned " misrepresents because it implies that something like it had been seen before. Nothing of the sort had. The plot was about blue-prints in a competition over plans for a new town hall. That was new. Both the hero and the villain were Scoutmasters, and the heroine was a Guidemistress. All this was new. There was a harking back to Boucicault when the crime was photographed by an untended camera (as in *The Octoroon*), but as the record was not just one negative but a reel of film to be shown later on the screen, enough of this was new. The finale was altogether new, for three walls fell like the walls of Jericho to reveal ranks of Scouts, Guides and policemen, flanking a girl dressed as Britannia, while above them " Young England " shone in letters of electric light.

There never had been anything like that play. Probably there never will be. It takes its place as the queerest jest in stage history. It cannot be surpassed as unconscious humour, since it lasted not for moments but for months. As a craze it outlasted any other that fashion or intellect ever affected. What enhanced its peculiarities was the arrival at the Garrick of *Love On The Dole*, a masterly study of industrial unemployment which clearly showed that the drama of democracy had divorced itself completely from unquestioning belief in virtue triumphant. Elsewhere players " guyed Victorians " by acting melodramas absurdly. *Young England* eclipsed all these it if could be classed with them; it should not be. It gave expression to simple faith in the old doctrine that the good would be profanely rewarded and the bad punished. Numbers of people had that faith. Some of them told the manager, night by night, how much they liked the play and how much they disliked the behaviour of the audience, winding up regularly with the words, " I have never been so disgusted in all my life ". The behaviour of the audience was peculiar : more so than the play. Not every antic of stalls, pit and gallery could be ascribed to the enjoyment of a joke. Heckling prompted by laughter lost its good-nature.

At first there was a general desire simply to join in. Groups who came regularly liked to anticipate events by shouting, " Give him half-a-crown ", when the war widow was about to do so. Not wit but high spirits inspired nearly all such interjections. Should a woman of the streets fear suicide because of " something after death ", stalls, pit and gallery heavily sighed " A-a-a-ah! " (while upper circle sensed blasphemy). Any hint of a love-scene provoked comment and any touch of humour a vast guffaw. Such humour was nothing if not forced, for many plays would lend themselves more readily to such treatment. Pennies were thrown on the stage when a female begged to be excused for a few minutes. When the bad Scoutmaster gazed at the brass handle of the safe he had robbed and took out his pocket-handkerchief, he prolonged the agony while voices cried, " Wipe it ". Shouts of " the duchess " greeted Lord Headingly's references to his mother.

The author had been too long an actor to provide any worse opportunities for hecklers' zeal than these.

As a regular spectator in a prominent box he, in all sincerity, showed a better way. There was an accident in the Scouts' camp. " Who will fetch a doctor? " asked the hero. " I will," said a Guide, wheeling forward her bicycle. Here Reynolds himself led and prolonged the applause. Apparently he was always there to mark approval with undiminished vigour when the boys defied the police to arrest their falsely-accused Scoutmaster and when the landlord who wished to eject a poor widow came beneath an upturned pail of water. Reynolds knew his play was good. Nobody disputed its ability to draw the public even though lessees of empty theatres would not accept a transfer when it had to leave the Victoria Palace. When a full house welcomed it to the Kingsway, it was still a concerted effort between cast and audience. At the curtain the author rebuked the busy mockers. If they did not agree with his ideas there were others who did. He read a list of well-known people who had seen *Young England* ten, twenty, some nearly thirty times, and he argued from such great names as these—including a future King of England—that the elect found merit where the common herd did not. It was a fighting speech and he retired, without bowing, amid cheers which rang true—upon which stage policemen at P. and O.P. reached across the orchestra towards playgoers in corner front-row stalls. Hands were linked for the singing of " Auld Lang Syne ". No one quite knew why but it fitted.

Night after night the frenzy grew. So far the drama had been speeded on its way. Now it was interrupted. Self-appointed conductors rose in the stalls, back to the stage, in order to urge the parterre to more noise over the chorus of " Boy Scouts, Boy Scouts ". The part that custom had hallowed for voices in front was departed from. Anybody shouted anything that came into his head. No words at times emerged from the uproar. What it expressed seemed to be not humour but rage. The play moved on to the Piccadilly Theatre, where the pandemonium grew until the Lord Chamberlain gave warning and the Riot Act, figuratively speaking, was read. All self-control had gone. The licence of *Young England* was withdrawn. The hecklers were like wild urchins who have rebelled against their schoolmaster and got the upper hand. The joke had gone. Even mischief could not be sensed. There was the anger of the disillusioned, of old gods falling. These disturbers of the peace were plainly annoyed because the play was, in the sense used by Pinero's profligate, *good*.

Other events interested the public. Melodrama suddenly decided all the world must be its stage. " But—but," cried young players

O

who believed that nothing was so dead and buried as " ham " (by which term the melodramatic had become known), " but it's such bad theatre ". They took this short cut to express what astonished all the millions of spectators in cinemas, who had looked on one menace as a clown and the other as a tout—and yet both menaces were real. War had become an accepted part of existence when *Young England*, to supply gaiety to a hard-pressed nation, was revived at the Holborn Empire. The preliminary scene of the Zeppelin-raid reached the point where the audience used to say, " Give him half-a-crown ". Somebody in the stalls said it without much urgency. The great moment with the girl's bicycle absented itself because the good Scoutmaster casually told his signallers to transmit an S.O.S. for a medical man on their " walkie-talkie " now they were up-to-date. But the most significant change occurred when the villain, a shirker, was confronted by a woman of the streets who told him what other men from Canada, New Zealand, Australia and Africa were doing. Such an attitude, of course, had originated the whole series of auditorium versicles and responses in the past. There was not so much as a smile now. Virtue, like the heraldic lion who sentimentalizes over its own tail, stood passant regardant.

Postscript

The Trial adapted from Kafka

IT WAS in the cinema that the public first showed a distaste for melodrama. For a time after the second world war, subjects that kept to the vice-*versus*-virtue rule or followed any such familiar pattern were shunned by talking-films as a whole even though " Westerns " never went out of fashion. Neither did Ancient Rome : though accustomed to the plain fact that the latest thing in entertainments is usually the most old-fashioned, elderly playgoers felt slightly dazed in 1952 to see *Quo Vadis?* exhibited as the glossiest novelty in super-films. In the same period (the 1950s) the melodramatic creed was effectively answered by French films. In one Manon Lescaut appeared in modern dress as an illegal immigrant into mandated Palestine; it was more faithful in spirit to its original than any version in costume. In another, *Le Diable Au Corps*, a tale of love was told without consideration for our moral feelings : the boy and girl did not forfeit sympathy although the husband was in the trenches, and the betrayal, almost a monopoly of melodrama for over a century apart from Guineveres and Mélisandes in fancy dress, happened without relation either to virtue or to villainy. As a medium of thought the cinema had won more respect than the stage (more particularly now that playwrights had discovered how to be melodramatic and intellectual at one and the same time), or perhaps I ought to say that it would have done so if mechanized marvels had ceased to be invented. Some early examples of television-drama were bad enough but new inventions in the cinema were worse. Let me quote from an account by Miss Dilys Powell in the *Sunday Times* of a three-dimensional film called *Sangaree* at the Plaza in 1953 ... " the enemies are piracy, bubonic plague and an asinine story. It is, however, a story which admits a good deal of throwing : knife-throwing, chair-throwing, barrel-throwing, even, in a fight, the throwing of human bodies. During these exercises we are conscious as we shelter behind the head in front. ...." When melodrama can thus make you feel you are going to be hit by a body in full flight, we have obviously progressed so far that we are back to where our great-grandparents were when they hailed the miracles of the " sensation drama " with which this history began.

One night in Paris I saw a play—Gide's stage version of *Le Procés* by Kafka—that made me think the existence of melodrama had ended. Barrault presented himself to all of us as ourselves. Each scene was a glimpse of the human mind where we watched our introspective faculties at work. I saw myself arrested, tried, mobbed, and executed by my own self-accusations, which kept a large number of actors very busy.

Here, in the one performance I have witnessed which could be accepted as peculiar to the middle of the twentieth century, the sense of guilt was exhibited according to the spirit of the age. Now, I thought, I may write CURTAIN to my drama of humanity's obsession with virtue rewarded and villainy punished. But from that day to this I have been watching a revival, both on the stage and in private life, of renewed belief in all the odd delusions that made melodrama grow. The plays and novels which please us now are often based on fictions which have flourished for the past 200 years; and that strictly modern play, enjoyed by thousands of ordinary pleasure-seekers in Paris, came to London, as *The Trial* at the Winter Garden, only to be damned out-of-hand.

Nevertheless, in my own time I have seen melodrama grow old and then die. I have written its history accordingly. Those who are industriously presiding over its rebirth may learn something from studying the course of its previous existence. And as this is being written, one of our intellectual haunts is showing *Senza Pieta*, a film of post-war Italy with a plot that recalls *George Barnwell*, the oldest melodrama in any language.

INDEX TO PERSONS AND PLACES

(Roman numerals in capitals refer to halftone illustrations)

INDEX TO PLAYS

(Roman numerals in capitals refer to halftone illustrations)

INDEX TO FILMS

(Roman numerals in capitals refer to halftone illustrations)

INDEX TO THEATRES

(Roman numerals in capitals refer to halftone illustrations. Theatres are in London unless otherwise stated)

Bodies roped to railway lines, heroes in cellars where tide-water is rising, circular saws or steam-hammers threatening the lives of helpless victims, early Christians about to be thrown to the lions, sinking ships, cars over precipices, earthquakes, volcanoes, tempest, fire and flood—spectacles such as these are expected by audiences that await the rising of the curtain in melodrama.

But it still functions when deprived of scenic excitement, says the author. In an entertaining account of the stories and background of the principal melodramas Willson Disher shows the more common ingredient was virtue triumphant or crime exultant, from which one might argue that the characters must be either black or white, or how could right do battle with wrong? That, he concludes, is reckoning without the sense of guilt. This, says Willson Disher, is the heart of the matter. It is the sense of guilt which contains the struggle within one breast.

So we follow the theme, from *Jane Shore* down to *The Vortex* and later. For melodrama took on a new lease of life, started a fresh existence in films, talking-films, radio, television and now in 3-D.

"Such lively survivals of the spirit which is my study, means that this book cannot be regarded in a purely antiquarian light"—indeed it cannot, for the Postcript brings us to Barrault in *The Trial* of Kafka.

Over 130 illustrations and colour frontispiece

Date Due

MAY 1 7			